HOLY TERROR

Armageddon in Tokyo

by D.W. Brackett

New York • WEATHERHILL• Tokyo

HOLY TERROR

Armageddon in Tokyo

First edition, 1996

Published by Weatherhill, Inc., 568 Broadway, Suite 705, New York, New York 10012

Library of Congress Cataloging-in-Publication Data:

Brackett, D.W.
Holy Terror: armageddon in Tokyo / by D. W. Brackett.
p. cm.
ISBN 0-8348-0353-4
1. Oumu Shinrikyo (Religious organization) 2. Terrorism—Religious aspects—Oumu Shinrikyo (Religious organization) 3. Terrorism—Japan. I. Title.
BP605.O88B73 1996
365.1'523'0952—dc20   96-427
                                                                        CIP

Contents

Foreword

The Aum sect's nerve-gas attack on Tokyo's subways came as a shock but did not surprise the small group of government and academic analysts of terrorism. The possibility that terrorist groups, organized crime, or fanatical cults might acquire and use chemical, biological, radiological, or improvised nuclear weapons is not a new concern. In 1985, *TVI Report*, a specialist journal that focuses on terrorism, conducted a poll of its readers asking them what they thought terrorists might do before the year 2000. Sixty-nine percent of the respondents, mainly government officials and academic experts devoted to the topic of terrorism, thought it "likely" or "very likely" that terrorists would employ chemical weapons by the end of the century.

The attacks in Matsumoto and Tokyo demonstrated that their concern was not unwarranted, and understandably have increased worries that what occurred in Japan represents the crossing of a threshold, the breaking of a taboo, the creation of a headline that will provide inspiration to others, increasing the likelihood that further incidents involving chemical weapons will occur. Where does the Tokyo attack fit in the trajectory of contemporary terrorism? And what does it mean for the future?

Prior to the Tokyo attack, there were numerous reports and threats involving the criminal use or suspected use of deadly chemicals. Deranged individuals, criminal extortionists, and, in fewer cases, political extremists plotted or threatened to use chemical or biological weapons. A smaller number of attacks were actually attempted. Very few resulted in fatalities.

The most ambitious schemes were the products of madmen. Most frequent were the threats made by criminal extortionists who threatened reservoirs, food, or bottled beverages. The poisons they mentioned or employed were readily available substances like cyanide or strychnine. Incidents involving the large-scale use of chemical or biological substances were rare: the 1978 Jonestown murder-suicide in which nine hundred eleven members of the Jim Jones cult died (how many were murdered—certainly the children—and how many committed suicide is not clear); the 1984 plot by members of the Rajneesh cult in Oregon to contaminate the food of local townspeople in order to make them ill and thereby unable to vote in a local referendum; the 1993 World Trade Center bombing, which contained cyanide; and the incidents in Japan. It is significant that religious fanaticism inspired all these episodes, and all but one involved cults whose members had isolated themselves from society.

This suggested even before Tokyo that the perpetrators of the chemical attacks might not have come from the ranks of typical terrorists with political goals. In a very speculative essay written in 1975, I suggested that the members of a group contemplating the use of any weapons of mass destruction would have to place themselves above the constraints of conventional morality. "They might claim divine inspiration (or at least tacit approval by God)."[1] This thought was echoed in a 1980 report made by the Rand Corporation. The subject of the report was the possible motives for nuclear terrorism, but the same idea would apply to the use of nerve or any other scenario of mass destruction:

> Terrorist groups with more millennial aims, as opposed to those operating on behalf of concrete political programs, may be less contained in their actions and hence more willing to cause or risk mass casualties. These more fanatical and extreme terrorist groups tend to hold apocalyptic views, devoid of specific political content, and seek the creation of new and continuing disasters as the precondition for the emergence of a new heavenly order on earth.[2]

The most dangerous combination would be a group whose charismatic leader asserts divine inspiration that his obedient devotees accept, an apocalyptic vision, a fascination with violence, and a shared paranoia. Add to this lethal mind set ample financial resources, scientific know-how, and a remote redoubt for experimentation, and you have Aum Shinri Kyo.

Terrorism, is imitative behavior. A spectacular event invites repetition. The Tokyo attack has already had an inspirational effect as reflected in new threats and reports indicating that some terrorists may now at least be thinking about chemical weapons. The probability of a second event exceeds the probability of the first, but we have no gift of prophesy to state what that probability may be. Nor, despite increased attention of the possibility of chemical attack, can we be certain that authorities would be able to identify and thwart any new attack. It could come from a group resembling the Aum Shinri Kyo cult; it could come from an entirely new direction.

This, in turn, poses a dilemma for all democratic societies. We impose constraints on domestic intelligence gathering. We do not want the authorities investigating every political group or every religious cult. At the same time, we want to reduce the risks of future Tokyos, wherever they may occur. The authorities' ability to promptly apprehend the perpetrators must be the goal, but how? Indeed, how democratic societies can deal with the threat of future Tokyos, and remain democratic societies, has become the topic of intense debate.

The story told by D.W. Brackett is not just the story of a grotesquely comical scam that turned into a diabolically deadly scheme. It also raises the issue of evil. A court in Tokyo will decide how Shoko Ashara and his lieutenants will be judged as criminals. Where history should ultimately place them in the pantheon of villains, real and fictional, the reader of this riveting account will decide.

NOTES

1. Brian Jenkins, *Will Terrorists Go Nuclear?* (Los Angeles: Crescent Publications, 1975), 22.

2. Gail Bass et al., *Motivations and Possible Actions of Potential Criminal Adversaries of U.S. Nuclear Programs* (Santa Monica, CA: The Rand Corporation, 1980).

Preface

Tracking down the story of Aum Shinri Kyo has been like living for ten months in a cross-cultural kaleidoscope. Changing constantly before my eyes were facts, non-facts, truths, half-truths, lies, distortions, and omissions. Only at the end did I appreciate how innocent I was at the beginning.

After only a couple of months of digging into the voluminous research I had gathered on Aum Shinri Kyo, I began to toy with the idea of dedicating this book to Herman Melville's obsessive hunter, Captain Ahab. In searching for solid details, I seemed to be chasing a modern Japanese incarnation of Ahab's great white whale. Too often I found that the facts would all hold together for only a few hopeful weeks, then disappear beneath a new layer of watery reporting, much of it different from the version that had just appeared. Absorbed, I watched as firmly sourced news reports about Aum appeared one day only to be contradicted by different firmly sourced reports a few days later; eye-witness accounts were refuted by other eye-witnesses; attributions such as "police sources" and "investigators told newsmen" became stop signs rather than the usual caution markers of credibility. As the story shifted uncertainly back and forth, I quickly relearned the lesson of Basic Reporting 101—even the most obvious facts require double checking. But often that was like trying to hug a cloud.

Direct interviews with senior Aum officials were out of the question; most were in jail, where only the police and lawyers could speak to them. Interviews with lay members, as the Japanese media demonstrated too often, added little that was new to the story. Reading their continued adulation for Asahara and Aum often became the print equivalent of going down in warm molasses for the third time. I discovered that sometimes the truth was not to be had, leaving me to make a best guess about where it possibly lay.

Even the dead would not be still. For months the press said twelve people died in the subway gas attack. Then, later in the year, officials announced that doctors could not confirm that one of the dead had died as a direct result of the gas attack. It may have been an unrelated illness that caused the death, they said. Considering the millions who daily travel on the Tokyo subways, that was not implausible and I accepted it. But then there was a problem about the number of injured. At the end of the year, the commonly used figure of five thousand five hundred injured was suddenly dropped downward by government prosecutors to slightly more than three thousand seven hundred. The new figures, they said, were based on a more accurate count than the earlier police estimates. However, in the absence of more convincing proof, I, along with most of the news media, continued to accept the five thousand five hundred figure as more accurate.

And there were other problems. For example, the details of the murder of the Sakamoto family present discrepancies that have yet to be fully explained. In the fall of 1995, two of Japan's largest newspapers were replete with police details, first-person confessions, and other statements about the killings. The Sakamotos had been killed or incapacitated by potassium chloride injected by an Aum doctor named Nakagawa, they said. The baby died first, because he cried; the wife was next to die from an injection and fought for her life; Sakamoto the lawyer, was also injected, the poison failed to work, and he was finally strangled; afterward Nakagawa was seen to be depressed by sect leader Shoko Asahara.

Yet at Nakagawa's trial in March, it all came out differently. According to prosecution statements, the baby died last, smothered in his parents' bedding despite his mother's pathetic plea that he be spared. But he cried out, and they suffocated him. Or so that version of the story goes. The first version is from police sources who did the initial interrogation of Nakagawa, the second from the prosecution. Where the truth lies between the two, and why it became so scrambled, only the murderers know. In the book I give both versions of this tragic tale because it will probably be years before history finally settles on a comprehensive, acceptable set of facts about the murderous activities of Aum Shinri Kyo. Even then there will be small pockets of unsolved mystery to keep imaginative writers busy.

Holy Terror—idea, book concept, and title—is the brainchild of Jeffrey Hunter, the president of Weatherhill, Inc., whose doctoral degree in Buddhist Studies gave him more than a passing interest in the emergence of a deadly religious-terrorist sect in Japan, where he lived and worked for many years. I am most grateful he thought of me when putting together this project. In trying to decipher the truth about Aum, I must thank a number of people whose contributions, scholarship, advice, and assistance made my task easier. First and foremost is my clever daughter, Beverley Brackett, who took precious time from her law studies to attend Senate hearings on Aum and spend many hours in the Library of Congress and in university library stacks tracking down news reports and odd bits of information. Without her tireless research and intelligent advice this book would not have been written. The editing of Jeffrey Hunter and Elmer Luke added tremendously to the telling of the story and saved me from any number of errors. Reiko Tomii was very helpful in reading dozens of Japanese sources and making them available to me. I also thank my informed friends in Japan and America who contributed to this book in numerous valuable ways.

Beside the lake in South Carolina, where most of the writing was done, I was fortunate to have the wonderful friendship and protection of two great neighbors—Gladys and Lamar Ezelle. Not only did they vigorously fend off strangers while I tried to write, but they often nourished me with some of the finest Southern cooking to be found outside my mother's kitchen. Equally supportive were Dr. David Price and his charming wife Ginger— without their friendship my wife and I would never have known the placid beauty of Walker Point.

Special mention must go to the Democratic staff of the Senate Permanent Subcommittee on Investigations for their outstanding report on Aum Shinri Kyo. Like Senator Sam Nunn, theirs is a lonely voice in the wilderness trying to educate the American public—and the Western democracies— about the grave new danger they now face. Professor Richard Young of Meiji Gakuin University, one of the first Western scholars to write on Aum, was kind enough to read a draft and offer many useful suggestions. His articles on the subject added immeasurably to my understanding of the impact of

Aum Shinri Kyo on young Japanese. Professor Susumu Shimazono of Tokyo University deserves special praise for his seminal work in English exploring the faith universe of Aum Shinri Kyo. His remarkable exposition is a rare English document about Aum Shinri Kyo's faith history, and the only one I have seen which lucidly discusses the important implications of societal pressure on the sect. His work, like Professor Young's, should be studied by those who want to know how a religious group like Aum Shinri Kyo evolves into ultraterrorism.

Finally, but by no means least, in Chapter 2 I relied in part on an article that appeared in *Tokyo Journal* in 1995. "Death in the Air" by Andrew Marshall puts a bright young writer working at his sensitive best on a very dark topic. The opening sentence of his story on the Matsumoto sarin attack and the tragedy of Yoshiyuki Kono, the man wrongly accused of perpetrating it, is a modern journalistic classic: "It was a pretty normal evening until the dogs died."

Prologue:
March 20, 1995

The first calls for help start coming into Tokyo's emergency assistance telephone switchboards shortly before 8:20 A.M. on Monday, March 20, 1995. These early calls from subway attendants and passengers complain about the "strange smells" and "powerful odors" encountered in the Kamiyacho Station on the Hibiya Line, odors that make some passengers vomit and cause others to collapse on the platform.

Within minutes, the calls increase in frequency and urgency, each new caller repeating the earlier complaints of foul, strong, "chemical" smells in the subway and people being sickened by them. Worse, the operators note that more subway stations are being hit by the mystery fumes.

At 8:33 A.M., a caller to the fire-department emergency squad reports that six passengers have collapsed on the Nakano Sakaue Station platform and numerous others are ill. They need help immediately, the man says. The Nakano Sakaue Station is on the Marunouchi Line. Both the Marunouchi Line and the Hibiya Line are major subway arteries that criss-cross the heart of downtown Tokyo carrying hundreds of thousands of passengers each day. The unidentified affliction is not only spreading from subway station to

I

subway station, it is also moving from one subway line to another—and at a chilling pace.

A rescue squad team speeds out of the Nakano Fire Station to the nearby subway stop. There they pick up several passengers and station employees and rush them to a nearby hospital.

By 8:44 A.M., senior police supervisors monitoring the emergency calls at the Japan National Police Agency in the center of Tokyo have heard enough to convince them that something frightening is under way in the capital's subway system. They immediately order the establishment of an emergency unit to coordinate and direct the city's police, fire, rescue, and medical-response systems.

By 8:50 the police suspect that a powerful chemical agent of some type has leaked into the subway system and they ask the Japanese Army to send two chemical warfare experts to the emergency unit. Shortly afterward they set up a joint police investigative unit to begin probing the mysterious subway fumes.

At nearby Kasumigaseki Station, a major subway intersection serving government offices and the headquarters of the National Police Agency, a number of police investigators descend into the depths of the station, where they encounter the gas fumes and become suddenly ill. This report flashes to police headquarters, and the police agency orders all police and emergency workers entering subway stations to wear gas masks.

At about this same time the word comes in that a third major subway line, the Chiyoda Line and many of its central Tokyo stations are stricken by the gas. Passengers and subway attendants on the Chiyoda Line, which cuts across the center of Tokyo like the Marunouchi and Hibiya Lines, are reporting noxious gas fumes, ailing riders, and people so sick they are unable to walk or talk. Pleas for emergency medical help, ambulances, and rescue teams are flooding in from everywhere.

Central Tokyo is ringing with a cacophony of sirens as police cars, ambulances, and fire trucks rush to the beleaguered subway stations. The workday has just begun, and employees at the Tokyo Kyodo Bank near Kamiyacho Station rush to the windows and peer out at the chaos in the street below. What they do not see is what is unfolding in the station below the streets.

Some thirty passengers have detrained in a crush, handkerchiefs pressed to their eyes and mouths as they flee toward the station exits. Screams of "Help!" and "I can't see!" echo from the platforms and down the warm corridors of the station where dazed passengers sink to their knees in agony and fear, unable to understand what is happening to them and why their bodies do not function properly.

The first stricken passengers to climb out of the station depths to street level are now making their appearance outside the Kamiyacho Station entrance. But the fresh winter air filling their lungs brings no relief, and those most heavily exposed to the fumes take only a few steps before collapsing in a heap on the sidewalk. Others are bent double in agony; everyone who had been below is pale. Many are vomiting and several people are frothing at the mouth, their eyes open but unseeing, as they are carried away on stretchers. Others lie prostrate on the concrete streets, some receiving heart massages from passers-by who mistake them for heart-attack victims.

"I was in the car when suddenly there was a smell like paint thinner," a twenty-eight-year-old company worker from Meguro Ward in Tokyo later said. "The next moment my eyes ceased to focus and I lost my vision. What happened?"

Away from the scene, the Japanese public is glued to their television screens. The first reports are being broadcast, just in time for the 9:00 news. The anchors are talking about gas and terrorism. The vagueness of the reports only makes them more frightening. But the first reaction of many is incredulity. Terrorism in Japan?

At Kayabacho Station, scrambling rescue workers cry out, "Make room! Make room!" as they haul one victim after another out of the station that services Tokyo's busy stock-market district. Some of the victims being carried out wear oxygen masks; their faces are twisted in agony. On the sidewalk outside the station, several young female office workers in identical company uniforms lie prone on a blue plastic sheet as medical attendants hover over them, offering emergency medical treatment.

The effect of the gas seems to follow no single pattern. Some passengers are quickly injured by it, while others seem unharmed or only mildly nauseated.

"I saw a woman collapse in Kodenmacho Station on the Hibiya Line," an uninjured thirty-one-year-old company employee from Saitama told reporters. "I was riding in the third car from the front of the train and I saw something like a rolled-up newspaper on the floor. . . . One of the police found the rolled-up newspaper that the gas came from and brought it out of the subway car."

The hospitals nearest the gassed subway stations are the first to be overwhelmed by patients. Victims begin flooding into Saint Luke's Hospital near Tsukiji Station at 8:40 A.M. Within an hour, their numbers exceed one hundred fifty. The hospital halts all other admittance to concentrate on the subway patients who are laid out on long benches in the hallways and in the chapel.

Typical of many patients is twenty-six-year-old Miyuki Kume, a company worker who was trying to get to her office when the gas struck her down. "I was in the third car from the front on the Hibiya Line," she said, calmly sitting on a sofa with an intravenous drip running into her arm. "When we arrived at Ningyocho Station, I heard the sound of another passenger in the car hitting the floor, then a woman screamed. Someone nearby yelled 'Open the windows!' We had stopped at Ningyocho, so I went out on the platform to transfer to another train, when I smelled a sharp smell and suddenly everything went black. My eyes are still flashing and are clouded over."

At 9:12 A.M. the British Reuters news agency is the first to tell the world outside Japan that something unusual is happening in Tokyo's subways. Their brief news report states that an unidentified noxious gas has appeared at eight subway stations in Tokyo and more than two hundred commuters are harmed. But by then the aggressive national media in Japan is already broadly hinting that a poison gas attack has taken place in the subway.

At 9:45 a request goes out from the National Police Agency to the Self-Defense Forces to send six military doctors to the police hospital in Iidabashi. At about the same time, Shizuka Kamei, head of the Ministry of Transport and Transportation, sets up an emergency desk and orders the highest level of security on all transporation systems throughout Japan.

As he leaves his residence, Defense Minister Hirozo Igarashi speaks to reporters. His comments are of course broadcast nationwide. "This is an indiscriminate attack against a large number of ordinary citizens. We will investigate it thoroughly and get to the bottom of it," he says.

At 9:52, the Associated Press files an urgent report stating that Tokyo's subway system has been attacked with poison gas.

At 10:30 the National Police Agency reports that three hundred and fourteen have been hospitalized. Prime Minister Tomiichi Murayama orders the Defense Minister to make the rescue of victims the nation's top priority.

At 11 A.M. the National Police Agency announces that five people are dead from the gas in the subway and the fire department reports that more than five hundred are hospitalized with serious injuries. Shortly afterward, the Criminal Investigation Division of the National Police Agency tells a news conference there is a strong possibility that the gas in the subway is a nerve agent called "sarin," and they are investigating the incident as a murder case. An hour later, the police raise the death toll to six and the hospital cases to more than six hundred.

By early afternoon, the dead and dying, a total of eleven persons, are taken away, and the injured, now more than five thousand, are receiving medical care in hospitals and clinics throughout the city. The world's first ultraterrorist attack on the capital city of a major industrialized power is, for all intents and purposes, over.

The news story of the nerve-gas attack in the crowded subway bounces around the world for a few weeks, drawing predictable expressions of shock from government spokesmen and the usual editorials and commentaries about the need to stop terrorism and violence. Thereafter, its longevity on the front page and in television news shows is extended by fresh reports of police raids on the facilities of Aum Shinri Kyo (Aum Supreme Truth), the small Japanese religious sect that produced the sarin and carried out the gas attack.

But despite all its media coverage, the underlying significance of what took place in Tokyo was barely noticed. With few exceptions, only two groups of people understood that a horrible bell had tolled in the Tokyo subways, one that the world will surely hear again. The first group to realize the enormous implications of the sarin-gas attack was the small handful of counterterrorist experts who daily monitor the activities of the world's known terrorist organizations. They understood immediately that the Tokyo gassing crossed an unprecedented threshold of terrorist violence. Weapons of mass destruction, specifically chemical and biological agents, had been produced by a small group of religious terrorists with the will to use them. The counterterrorists also knew that the odds were good that other terrorist groups would try to copy the new form of terrorism pioneered by Aum Shinri Kyo.

The second group to instantly recognize the underlying importance of the Tokyo attack was the international terrorist groups themselves, those who pursue political and religious goals at the expense of human life and suffering. They, too, realized that a new chapter in terrorist violence was opened on that March morning in Tokyo. Terrorists do not follow "rules of engagement" in their operations, but they do absorb the lessons to be learned from "successful" acts of violence. A successful terrorist operation is one that receives broad publicity for the death, injury, and destruction it causes. By that standard, the Tokyo gassing was a huge success. With that precedent-setting example before them, many terrorist groups will now feel free to use chemical or biological weapons, if they can acquire them. With those weapons they can conduct terrorism on a scale so horrific that all the bombings, assassinations, and skyjackings that have gone before will pale into insignificance.

What did the terrorists of Aum Shinri Kyo accomplish in the Tokyo gassing? Not their stated objectives. A major priority was to paralyze parts of the government, especially the headquarters of the National Police Agency, by killing and injuring thousands of people. Although more than five thousand were injured, the death rate—eleven people—was surprisingly low for a nerve-gas attack. That was due in large part to the relative weakness of the sarin—estimated by chemists to have been only thirty-percent pure—and the crude method used to disperse it. Had the gas been stronger—say, seventy- or eighty-percent pure—and its method of dispersal more effective, the death and injury toll could easily have soared into the tens of thousands. But though the two essential factors in the attack, the sarin and its dispersal method, were not exactly right, the resulting deaths and injuries demonstrate a grim truth: even when poorly produced and disseminated, chemical weapons are devastatingly effective.

Tokyo's sprawling subway system—a network that transports more than six million people daily—was paralyzed, but only for a matter of hours. By late afternoon on the day of the attack subway officials had the system up and running again. Passenger volume dipped slightly but soon returned to normal after the system went back on line, transport officials said.

With a death count of eleven people and a police estimate of more than five thousand five hundred persons injured by the gas (other government agencies revised that figure downward to three thousand seven hundred by the end of the year, but the press and this author continue to accept the five thousand five hundred figure as the most accurate), Aum Shinri Kyo's attack represents a world record for a single terrorist operation. It also frightened the citizens of Japan, and especially those living in Tokyo, in ways they had not experienced since the darkest days of World War II.

Perhaps one of the toughest blows to absorb in the aftermath of the gassing attack was that it was committed by Japanese against Japanese. Aum Shinri Kyo, the small religious sect that carried out the attack, was a product of Japanese culture and socialization. Not only that, but the sect's top leadership included a large number of young men and women who, in many respects, were among Japan's "best and brightest." They graduated from Japan's top schools and came from solid middle-class families. The gassing made Japanese society a lot less certain about the way it raises its children.

Finally, Japan's image as one of the safest countries in the world took a terrific beating in the news media—and none worse than in its own. But the Japanese are nothing if they are not resilient. They are often said to have a "typhoon mentality," which is the ability to weather the storm, sustain the damage, and then move forward without looking back. To make sure that a terrorist threat like Aum Shinri Kyo does not recur at some future point, the Japanese government is making changes in everything from the laws that regulate religious corporations to stiffer controls over ownership of certain chemicals. As they make these adjustments, they must also address the question why the world's first ultraterrorists evolved from an obscure group of Japanese religious fanatics. As they are now learning, the answer to that question is both complex and difficult.

Beware Beginnings:
Murdering a Dangerous Man

ecause the baby cried out when the men first entered the bedroom, they murdered him first. The killing began shortly after three o'clock in the morning, only a few minutes after the Aum Shinri Kyo "action squad" quietly opened the unlocked door of a small apartment in a middle-class Yokohama neighborhood and let themselves in. The six men were tired and nervous, but they had the presence of mind to wait for a few moments to let their eyes adjust to the darkness before easing their way into the bedroom where their three victims lay sleeping.

Clad in cotton pajamas, fourteen-month-old Tatsuhiko Sakamoto was in bed between his parents when the men crept into the apartment. Several of them would later sheepishly confess to police that he was the first to awake and when he saw them, suddenly began crying. After the infant's first cry, one of the men leaned over and snatched him from the bed, smothered his mouth with a cloth, then delivered him into the waiting hands of his killer, a thirty-two-year-old medical doctor named Tomomasa Nakagawa. His hypodermic needle ready, Dr. Nakagawa quickly jerked down the baby's pajama pants and injected his buttock with a large dose of potassium chloride, a powerful poison. Nakagawa then watched the child with coldly clinical eyes, waiting patiently for the deadly poison to make its way through his small body. The infant's cries gradually snuffled out, then ceased altogether when a series of limb-shaking spasms swept over him as the poison first seized then fatally stopped his young heart. It was like putting an unwanted puppy to sleep.

The baby's frightened cry and the shuffling commotion in the bedroom awakened the child's parents, Satoko Sakamoto, his twenty-nine-year-old mother, and Tsutsumi Sakamoto, thirty-three, the boy's father. The scene confronting the groggy Sakamotos was straight out of a nightmare. Their small bedroom was filled with strange men, one of whom held their struggling son in his arms. Alarmed and badly scared, both parents tried to rescue their son but were no match for the overwhelming force of their attackers. Seeing her baby in the hands of a stranger with a hypodermic needle, Satoko Sakamoto desperately fought back against her assailants, but within a few minutes they overpowered her and she was given a lethal injection by Nakagawa. Within minutes he confirmed that she, too, was dead.

Tsutsumi Sakamoto was the last to die, but unlike his son and wife he did not die quickly. Battling furiously for his life, he managed during the fray to bite one of his attackers on the arm, hard enough to draw blood. But the odds against Sakamoto were now five to one, and within a few minutes he, too, was finally subdued. While several of the men held him tightly in position, Dr. Nakagawa jabbed a hypodermic needle filled with potassium chloride into his buttock. This time the drug did not work as expected, however, and after several minutes of painful writhing Sakamoto remained very much alive. Members of the squad told police that in order to finish him off, it was necessary for the team leader, Kiyohide Hayakawa, to hold down his legs while Tomomitsu Niimi straddled his chest and strangled him with his bare hands.

The above account of the murder of the Sakamoto family was printed in the Japanese press in the fall of 1995. Six months later, in mid-March 1996, a different version of the Sakamoto murders surfaced during Nakagawa's trial for his part in the killings. According to a report filed by Tokyo correspondent Nicholas D. Kristof of *The New York Times*, prosecutors told the Tokyo district court that Sakamoto and his wife were strangled and that the baby was suffocated. There was no mention of the lethal injections that earlier reports persistently stated were administered by Nakagawa.

But like the previous news reports—all of which were based on police statements made to the Japanese news media in the fall of 1995—the prosecution statements quoted by the *Times* described an equally harrowing death scene. They said the first to die was Sakamoto, who was strangled by one member of the group, while another kicked his wife, Satoko, in the abdomen. "Please spare the child, at least," she is said to have screamed before she, too, was strangled. The report said the baby then began to cry, and the sect members suffocated him with the bedding.

The trial also shed new light on possible motives for the murders, raising questions about the actions of Tokyo Broadcasting System, a major television station. The prosecution alleged that the decision to kill Sakamoto was made after the station informed sect officials in advance about a television interview in which Sakamoto strongly criticized Aum Shinri Kyo. TBS canceled the program after the Sakamotos vanished, but later aired excerpts from it. The *Times* said TBS admitted that Aum officials visited the station to protest the proposed program, but denied sect members were shown the video. However, Japanese press reports said unidentified Aum officials told police they had seen the video at TBS offices. In late April 1996, Hirozo Isozaki, the president of TBS, who resigned to take responsability for the affair, told a news conference that TBS had shown the video to sect officials. Sect protests caused TBS not to run the interview, Isozaki said.

Whatever the reason for the differences between the earlier police and prosecution version of the killings, murdering the Sakamoto family took between fifteen and twenty minutes, and at the end Aum's action squad had three dead bodies on their hands. Their plan was not simply to kill the Sakamotos, but to make them disappear without a trace. The next critical step was to remove the three bodies from the apartment to the getaway vehicles outside without being seen. Here luck and timing worked for them. Because it was the morning after a major national holiday, there was no one about in the winter darkness as they hauled the bodies outside, placing them in the car and station wagon they'd rented for the operation. By 4 A.M. they were on their way back to the sect's compound in Kamikuishiki, on the north slope of Mount Fuji.

With one exception, the members of the death squad that killed the Sakamotos were all senior disciples and close confidants of sect leader Shoko Asahara, the man who ordered the murders. The exception was a young man named Satoru Hashimoto who joined the team at the least minute on the strength of his recent victory in an Aum Shinri Kyo martial-arts tournament. Asahara had not wanted to include Hashimoto because he was a junior member of the sect, but the others had pressed the guru, arguing that his muscle might come in handy during the mission. Faced with a consensus, Asahara finally relented. More than anything he wanted the dangerous threat posed by the troublesome Tsutsumi Sakamoto behind him. If achieving that success might hinge on young Hashimoto's martial arts skills, then let him go along.

The seeds of the death of the Sakamoto family were planted in the early spring of 1989, when a group of distraught parents whose children were members of Aum Shinri Kyo walked into the Yokohama law office of Tsutsumi Sakamoto. Sakamoto had already developed a reputation as a tough, iconoclastic, and fearless lawyer with a penchant for taking on the unusual cases that other Japanese lawyers shunned. In 1982 he had graduated from the Law Department of Tokyo University, the most prestigious in the country, and by 1987 he received his certification as an attorney and was working for the Yokohama Law Office in Naka-ku, Yokohama. Sakamoto despised injustice and had a strong, natural sympathy for the underdog. He was deeply involved in legal efforts to protect the rights of Japanese National Railway workers when the government-owned corporation was privatized and large numbers of its employees were forcibly reassigned or laid off. As an advocate for children's rights, he had some experience in confronting new religious groups like Aum Shinri Kyo; in the past he had assisted parents in efforts to free their children from the ranks of the Unification Church.

The parents gathered in Sakamoto's office in Yokohama to discuss Aum Shinri Kyo came as supplicants; all the other lawyers they spoke to had politely but firmly turned them away. What they were looking for, indeed, what they needed to be successful against Aum, was a bright and energetic lawyer with the tenacity of a bulldog—someone who would sink his teeth into the evasive religious sect and not let go until justice was done.

As Sakamoto listened carefully to the complaints of the distraught parents, he noted that in each case the story was much the same: The new religious sect Aum Shinri Kyo had taken their children from them by means of some kind of mind control. First their children had attended meetings of the sect, one of the many *shinko shukyo*—literally "newly risen religions," or more commonly, "new religions." Then the children abruptly left home, explaining to their startled parents that they were going to live in an Aum commune, where they would become monastics. Upon arrival at the commune the inductees were required to relinquish to Aum all their financial assets, everything from partially used telephone cards to bank accounts, and were forbidden to have further contact with their parents and friends.

And there were more disturbing rumors as well. The worried parents told Sakamoto they had heard dark stories about Aum's supernatural and occult practices involving mind control, drugs, and the drinking of human blood. The police were powerless to help, since most of their children were adults and free to do as they pleased. The sect vigorously denied the presence of any underage followers, though some of the parents disputed this. Further, perhaps most importantly, Aum Shinri Kyo was an official religion protected from government interference by Japan's rigidly observed freedom of religion laws.

The Japanese police, like the governmental bureaucracy, exercised extreme caution in handling complaints made against official religious groups. Partly as a reaction to the harsh oppression of religious freedom by Japan's prewar military government, the postwar constitution and police policy nationwide called for scrupulously avoiding even the appearance of religious persecution. For the aggrieved parents who believed that Aum had taken their children from them, civil law and a tenacious lawyer who would press their cases to the fullest in civil court were the only recourses. But like the police, most Japanese lawyers avoided becoming involved in civil cases with the new religions, and most especially with Aum Shinri Kyo, which had a nasty reputation among Japan's legal community as a sect which filed countersuits that were both time consuming and terribly expensive. At first, Sakamoto's reaction was no different from those of the other lawyers, and though what he had heard was interesting, he told the group he was inclined not to take their case. As a libertarian, he firmly supported freedom of religion. But the group continued to press for his help, and as they did he began to listen more closely to the frustrated, angry voices. The details of their stories, in particular the charges that Aum followers were forced to pay exorbitant fees for religious training and gimmicks of highly dubious value, appealed to Sakamoto's sense of justice. After hearing the families out, he suspected that Aum Shinri Kyo was using its religious status to prey on its gullible members, young and old, for financial gain. On the surface, it sounded like his kind of case, and finally he agreed to represent the families.

One of his first steps as counsel to the parent group—"The Association of Victims of Aum Shinri Kyo," as they had dubbed themselves—was to dig into the background of the sect. In his first few weeks of prying into the sect's history Sakamoto became convinced that it was deliberately victimizing its members. Wasting no time in coming to grips with his new adversaries, Sakamoto served official notice on the sect that he represented a mother who was demanding a face-to-face meeting with her daughter, a young Aum member.

The first sect official to meet Sakamoto was Yoshinobu Aoyama, who at age twenty-nine was Aum Shinri Kyo's talented chief lawyer and the architect of its successful defense strategy of expensive countersuits and legal intimidation. At the meeting, Sakamoto firmly insisted that his client be allowed to speak with her daughter or he would seek a court order forcing Aum to show cause why the young woman could not be made available to meet her mother. After some legal dickering back and forth, Aoyama finally agreed to set a date for a meeting between the mother and daughter at the sect's general headquarters in Fujinomiya, Shizuoka Prefecture, some ninety minutes by car from Tokyo. The meeting between mother and daughter was attended by Sakamoto, Aoyama, and two of the sect's senior leaders: Kiyohide Hayakawa and Tomomitsu Niimi. Sakamoto could not know it at the time, but as he entered the meeting and exchanged the ritual Japanese introductory bows with the Aum leaders, he had politely greeted two of the men who would murder him and his family less than four months later.

Yoshinobu Aoyama was the son of a wealthy Osaka family that owned a large clothing firm. Bright, articulate, and savvy, he was a graduate of Kyoto University Law School, and while there distinguished himself by becoming the youngest person in his class to pass the tough national bar exam. He joined Aum in 1988 and became its chief legal counsel two years later. Aoyama prided himself on being a shrewd judge of character. He had very carefully sized up Sakamoto on their first meeting, and what he saw in the young lawyer's determined face and steely demeanor was extremely disturbing. Sakamoto, he concluded, was a very dangerous man because he was intelligent, tenacious, and well prepared, not the sort of lawyer who could be scared away by Aum's usual bluster and threats. For that reason, Aoyama decided to take a softer approach and agreed to schedule the meeting between the mother and daughter in the hope it might dampen Sakamoto's interest in pursuing Aum. However, he badly underestimated the young lawyer from Yokohama. In Sakamoto, the parent's group found the legal bulldog they were looking for. Now that his teeth were sinking into Aum Shinri Kyo's flank he had no intention of letting go.

Sakamoto recognized the meeting between the mother and daughter as a sop offered by Aoyama. He viewed it not as a major concession, but as the opening gambit in a series of actions he planned to bring against the sect. In addition to a number of other cases involving parents and missing children in the sect, Sakamoto was now representing a former Aum member who claimed the sect had cheated him. It was this case that raised the conflict between the two lawyers to a new level.

In the late 1980s, Aum Shinri Kyo's religious practices had taken a rather sudden entrepreneurial turn toward the supernatural and the occult. As part of this new twist the sect began to peddle several "powerful" spiritual tonics made from the hair, bath water, and the blood of its guru Shoko Asahara. For ten thousand dollars,* Aum offered "select" new members a special cult initiation rite in which they could drink the blood of Asahara, which was supposed to vastly improve the effectiveness of their spiritual training. Drink Asahara's blood, the new members were told, and you will be on the inside track to *saishu gedatsu*, or "final liberation." Further down the line in spiritual effectiveness was a special tea brewed from Asahara's hair clippings, and toward the bottom was a two-hundred-cubic-centimeter bottle of his bath water (or "miracle pond," as it was touted by Aum). All these tonics from the body of the guru came at a stiff cost, and it was here that Sakamoto hoped to score a telling victory over the sect for practicing fraud and extortion.

His client had paid the standard ten-thousand-dollar fee for the blood-drinking "initiation," but it failed to deliver; the pricey libation brought him no closer to liberation. Sakamoto pressed his client's claim for a refund based on non-performance. In response, Aum attempted to boost the credibility of the ritual by claiming that research conducted by the Kyoto University Medical School proved there was a "secret power" in Shoko Asahara's blood. In a letter to Sakamoto, Aoyama said the tests demonstrated that "when the blood of the Worthy Master (Sonshi in Japanese) is taken into the body, the *kundalini* spirit is stirred and higher consciousnesses that had until then been only potential manifest themselves." Sakamoto called

* All U.S. dollar equivalents are based on a rate of one hundred yen to the dollar.

this bluff by contacting the school and asking for the test results. In its September 20, 1989, reply to Sakamoto's inquiry, the medical school stated unequivocally that it had never conducted any tests on the guru's blood. When confronted with this statement Aoyama began to backpedal vigorously. In a memo dated October 13, Sakamoto recorded a telephone conversation with Aoyama that began with an apology from the sect lawyer for failing to explain the DNA test clearly. Aoyama asked Sakamoto to believe that the test was done by a Kyoto University student of genetic engineering working toward his doctorate. The test was carried out at Aum facilities, with equipment that Aum "had purchased at great expense." But the good news, Aoyama said, was that the test "was notarized."

Unfazed, Sakamoto asked to see the test data. The next day Aoyama called and informed him that the student who performed the test would not be available for ten days to two weeks because he was participating in "underwater meditation"—a practice during which advanced meditators demonstrated their ability to slow or even stop their breathing by entering a sealed box that was then submerged in water.

Sakamoto said he understood and would be glad to wait for the data.

At that point, Aum Shinri Kyo's legal team realized that Sakamoto was not a man who was going away.

Events in October underscored chief attorney Aoyama's darkest assessment that the upstart lawyer from Yokohama was determined to expose them as religious frauds once and for all. On October 11, Sakamoto called a general meeting for victims of the deceptive practices of Aum. The meeting, which was well attended, produced more damaging data for further suits against the sect. According to the *Yomiuri Shimbun,* in a radio interview conducted by telephone five days later, Sakamoto strongly condemned the sect's fraudulent and unethical practices. He charged Aum with persuading minors to leave their families and take up residence in sect communes and accused Asahara of demanding large cash donations from his followers for which they received little if anything in return. This interview with Sakamoto was perhaps the most critical public attack ever made against the sect on radio and it created a storm of anger among the Aum hierarchy.

The sect's response to the charges was immediate and typical. Shortly after the program was broadcast, handbills bitterly attacking Sakamoto were distributed in his residential Yokohama neighborhood and he began to receive telephone threats at his home and office. In the same month,

Sakamoto was interviewed for a television documentary on Aum produced by TBS, a major television station. In the interview he again delivered a scathing attack on Aum's fraudulent practices. Asahara learned of the program's contents and on Halloween, October 31, sent Aoyama, senior disciple Hayakawa, and a charismatic sect spokesman named Fumihiro Joyu to Sakamoto's office in Yokohama for a showdown. Full details of this discussion have not been made public, but the Aum leaders confirmed that they had the data on the magical efficacy of Asahara's blood. Though they did not give the data to Sakamoto, he made notes on their explanation: Several members had drunk Asahara's blood and their religious practice had improved. Sakamoto learned that there had been no genetic or any other analysis of the blood, no control group for any test made on it. What that meant was that by any reasonable standard of scientific measurement, Aum in fact had no proof that their guru's blood contained a "secret power." The sect leaders also demanded that Sakamoto retract his TBS interview statements and issue an apology to Aum. Sakamoto refused.

At that point the meeting quickly disintegrated into a screaming match that filled the air with personal insults. According to one witness, Aoyama angrily declared that Aum could do as it pleased with its members and their money because the sect was an official religious corporation under Japanese law and therefore protected by the government against interference from outsiders. Though outnumbered three to one, Sakamoto didn't flinch. He told the threesome that Aum did not have a right to cause personal harm and suffering to others. Before ordering the Aum delegation to get out of his office, he informed them he was filing a suit that would challenge their official status as a religion and that he'd soon see them all again in court.

It was a defining moment for both sides. All the cards were now face up on the table. What happened next sealed the fate of the Sakamoto family.

The next day, in a meeting with the sect's hierarchy, Aoyama reported the failure of the talks with Sakamoto to Aum Shinri Kyo leader, Shoko Asahara. The bad news, he told the guru, was that he was unable to persuade Sakamoto not to file a suit. But worse was that Sakamoto now knew too much about how the sect operated; the young lawyer had done his homework entirely too well. If he went ahead with his suit, it would present a grave risk to Aum's official status as a legal religion. This was no small threat. Everyone present at the meeting knew that religious incorporation in Japan had a one-year probationary period, and Aum had only received its papers as of August 25. If the sect was found guilty of committing any illegal acts during that period, its official status could easily be revoked by the government. Those present also knew that if that happened the sect would be severely harmed, maybe even finished for good.

There now seemed no doubt that Sakamoto was leading a movement to destroy Aum, Aoyama said, and his threatened suit was only the opening shot in the fusillade that was sure to follow. But there was more at stake than the sect's official status. Another top aide at the meeting told Asahara that the sect's ambitious political campaign to win seats in the lower house of the Diet (Japan's national assembly) in the upcoming 1990 elections would fall flat on its face if Sakamoto could make any of his charges stick in court. This young lawyer in Yokohama was a very dangerous man and he must be removed before he could act, the aide advised. The Aum leaders were right. On the very same day they were meeting, Sakamoto was making a presentation to his colleagues, arguing persuasively that Aum could be successfully prosecuted for duping consumers with false advertising.

Asahara understood all too well that the small religious empire of wealth and privilege he had built for himself over the past five years now faced a mortal threat. He acknowledged that loss of Aum's governmentally sanctioned religious status would be disastrous, both for the sect as a new religion and for his long-planned election campaign for the Diet. The Diet election was the culmination of one of his oldest personal ambitions. Asahara himself was running on the sect's ticket and was convinced that both he and Aum's slate of candidates would be swept into office by the voters. A sect victory at the ballot box would give him the two things he had long yearned for, national recognition and political power. The source of the threat was clear: Standing squarely in his path was this troublesome lawyer from Yokohama, a man of conscience who would not be reasonable and go away quietly. Asahara's choice for resolving the threat was no less clear: If Aum was to survive and achieve the political clout he believed it deserved in Japan, then the sect would have to permanently remove the threat presented by Sakamoto.

His mind made up, Asahara dismissed his legal and political counselors, then immediately summoned five of his most trusted senior disciples to an urgent meeting the next day, November 2, at the sect's headquarters in Fujinomiya. As Asahara pondered his options, he realized that timing was everything. Externally, the timing of the Sakamoto crisis could not be worse—if Sakamoto got before a court and the public with his complaints,

Aum's future was jeopardized, a pressure point not lost on the clever Sakamoto. But internally, within the convoluted dynamics of the cult's most senior leadership—that echelon of leaders who ranked directly under Asahara—the timing for action was also right. For several months a high-level power struggle had been under way in Aum for the number-two position in the cult. The man selected for the coveted position would sit at the right hand of Asahara. Jockeying for the job was intense and it is a mark of Asahara's manipulative brilliance that he chose the top three contenders for the position to attend the urgent meeting he called to plan the murder of Sakamoto.

Openly competing for the number-two spot were Kiyohide Hayakawa, forty-six; Hideo Murai, thirty-six; and Kazuaki Okazaki, thirty-four. All were senior members of the sect. Okazaki had been with Asahara since the very earliest days and was a founding member of Aum Shinri Kyo. Leading up to the Sakamoto kidnapping, he was considered first among equals in the leadership directly under the guru. There is no doubt that his status was higher than that of Hayakawa and Murai. But for reasons not clearly understood at this time, Asahara appointed Hayakawa leader of the Sakamoto action squad while Okazaki was relegated to the rather lowly position of driver. There is speculation that by this time Okazaki had dropped out of contention for the number-two slot, possibly because of "his weak personality," one police investigator said. In any event, Okazaki was near the end of his stint as a member of Aum Shinri Kyo. Just before the February 1990 Diet elections, he left the sect after being accused of trying to steal three million dollars from its coffers. Badly frightened that Asahara might seek to silence him by ordering his murder or abduction, Okazaki assumed a false name and went into hiding in his native Yamaguchi Prefecture. He was arrested in 1995 and charged with conspiracy to commit murder, a charge that stemmed from the strangulation of a young Aum member, Shuji Taguchi, in February 1989. Police believe this killing, ordered by Asahara, was Aum's first murder.

Hayakawa was the man who eventually captured the number-two position. In 1975, Hayakawa received a master's degree in environmental planning from the architecture department of Osaka University. He worked in various architecture-related enterprises until 1986, when he joined the precursor of Aum Shinri Kyo, a group called Aum Shinsen no Kai, and became a monastic the following year. Hayakawa was quickly recognized for his leadership abilities, distinguishing himself as director of the Osaka division of the sect. He later became Construction Minister when Aum adopted the same organizational functions as the Japanese national government, an idea which Hayakawa proposed to Asahara. After his promotion to second in command, Hayakawa began spending a lot of time in Russia developing contacts there for the sect's militarization program. There were also rumors that after the Sakamoto murders, Hayakawa deliberately seemed to be distancing himself from involvement in Aum's lethal criminal activities.

Hideo Murai, although a relative newcomer who entered an Aum commune in mid-1989, had a meteoric ascent through the sect's ranks due to his scientific background and brazen ambition. After graduating from the physics department at Osaka University, he entered graduate school, where he majored in astrophysics. In 1987, while working for the research and development department of Kobe Steel, where he conducted studies on aircraft, he happened to read one of Asahara's books. The next day he entered an Aum commune with his wife, enrolling in a six-day Aum training course at the compound at Kamikuishiki. After completing the training he told his parents that he felt as if he had become a "Jonathan Livingston Seagull," the existential bird in Richard Bach's best-selling novel of the same name. Murai would later become Aum's Minister of Science and Technology.

In selecting Hayakawa, Okazaki, and Murai for the death squad Asahara knew he had a loyal core whom he could trust to carry out his orders. The other two men present were not high ranking, but their dedication to Asahara was unquestioned. One of them, Tomomitsu Niimi, thirty-one, would later be elevated to Home Affairs Minister. The fifth person present at the meeting was Tomomasa Nakagawa, a doctor who joined Aum while a medical student at Kyoto Prefectural College of Medicine in February 1988. After passing the national medical exam in April 1988 and practicing medicine for a little over a year, he took up residence in the Aum commune at Kamikuishiki in August 1989. Asahara chose him for the Sakamoto death squad because he had medical expertise that would be used in the murders. Nakagawa would later become head of the Household Agency, where one of his primary duties was to act as Asahara's personal doctor and provide medical care for the guru's family.

There are conflicting versions of exactly what happened at this seminal meeting but most of the senior members present later told police they sat in a circle with Asahara who stated matter-of-factly that the lawyer Sakamoto was trying to destroy Aum Shinri Kyo and must be eliminated in order to save the cult. By most accounts it took the group less than thirty minutes to plan the death of Sakamoto. These initial plans included only the abduction and murder of Sakamoto; there was no mention of harming his wife and young son.

According to one account given to the police, Asahara was quite specific about how he wanted the murder to take place. He ordered the men to "take Sakamoto into a vehicle. Nakagawa has a drug that can kill a man in five minutes." With that, the member recalled, the guru raised his hand and casually snapped his fingers.

The next day, November 3, 1989, the group, now including martial-arts specialist Hashimoto, left the Aum compound in two cars and headed for Yokohama. Excellence in planning was never one of Aum's strengths and this, their first major operation outside the sect, would set the tone for many of the forays that followed. As they motored down the expressway toward Yokohama, the small group had overlooked an important detail in their planning: November 3 was Culture Day, a major national holiday that is also a commemoration of the birthday of Emperor Meiji, whose government transformed Japan into a modern nation. In forgetting that November 3 was a holiday, the planners inadvertently added Sakamoto's wife and son to the list of people they would kill in the coming hours.

The original murder plan as laid out by Asahara called for the Aum action team to wait for Sakamoto at the local train station in Yokohama where he arrived each afternoon on his way home. Hayakawa and Niimi had both met Sakamoto in an earlier legal session and could identify him for the group. As he walked out of the station toward his home, members of the team would snatch him off the street—in broad daylight with crowds of witnesses and perhaps even police nearby—and bundle him quickly into the getaway car. Speeding away from the scene, several team members would hold Sakamoto down while Nakagawa injected him with a lethal dose of potassium chloride. They would then return to the Kamikuishiki compound where they would burn the body and scatter the ashes. The idea was for the troublesome Sakamoto to simply vanish from the face of the earth, never to be heard from again.

But as the group waited impatiently outside the station, pacing back and forth in the brisk winter air, Sakamoto's usual arrival time came and went. When darkness began to descend and he still hadn't appeared, they began to suspect something had gone wrong. It was about this time that it dawned on one of them that it was a national holiday. That led to the realization that the young lawyer had probably not gone to his office but instead had stayed home with his family. Later in the evening, team-leader Hayakawa sent Kazuaki Okazaki to inspect the Sakamoto apartment and determine how the group could gain entrance. In his reconnaissance, Okazaki tried the door of the darkened apartment and discovered to his surprise that it was unlocked. Hurrying back to the group he conveyed the good news.

The Japanese police later learned that a hasty call was made to Asahara, who listened to the problem of the no-show lawyer and then ordered the team to wait until 3 A.M., enter the apartment, kill the entire family, and bring their bodies back to the Aum compound.

When the police investigated the family's disappearance they said the door showed no signs of forcible entry. They speculated that Satoko Sakamoto was happy to have her husband home for the day and simply forgot to lock the door when the family went to bed. Further, residential breaking and entry is very rare in Japan and it is not so uncommon for people to leave their doors unlocked. Whatever the reason, at 3 A.M. the Aum Shinri Kyo death squad opened the apartment door, quietly slipped inside, and then began its brutal work.

When the team arrived back at the Aum compound early on the morning of November 4, they immediately briefed Asahara on the murders. During that meeting the guru noted that Nakagawa, the doctor who administered the poison to the Sakamotos, was pale and shaking. Asahara asked him if he was ill. Years later Nakagawa would confess that although he could not say so at the meeting, deep down inside he was "horrified" by murdering an infant; guilt also haunted him because he was the only member of the team who was personally involved in all three deaths. Concerned by his depressed state, the other members of the team tried to cheer him up by praising his role in the killings to Asahara.

Discussion next turned to getting rid of the bodies. Originally they had planned to cremate Sakamoto, but due to the oversight about the Culture Day holiday, they now had three bodies to burn and the guru was afraid a large fire would attract attention. Within the next few years the cult solved its growing body-disposal problem by purchasing an industrial-size microwave oven that it adapted into an incinerator for the purpose. The bodies of at least a dozen or more Aum members along with a number of victims outside the cult are believed to have been cremated in the device.

After pondering the body problem for a few minutes, Asahara told the group to wrap them in blankets and bury them in different prefectures well away from the Aum compound and as far away from each other as possible. By burying the bodies far apart he hoped to postpone their discovery and identification as long as possible. If by chance they were uncovered, the geographical separation would further delay and confuse any police investigation because each body would be in a different prefectural legal jurisdiction. Thus Sakamoto was buried in Niigata Prefecture; his wife in adjacent Toyama Prefecture; and the baby was interred in nearby Nagano Prefecture. All three prefectures are northeast of the Mount Fuji area and located in cold, snowy regions facing the Japan Sea. With the bodies buried as Asahara instructed, it would be six years before the Japanese police finally recovered them, and only then because they were told where to look by members of the Aum death squad.

On November 9, after the team returned from burying the bodies, Asahara called them to a meeting at which he personally thanked each one for the murders. He spoke to them about the fourteen-month-old child they had killed, justifying the infant's death by saying: "The child ended up not being raised by Sakamoto, who was trying to repeat bad deeds from a previous life." He assured the killers that the baby would be "born again in a higher-level world."

On November 15, the people of Japan first heard the news that a Yokohama lawyer named Sakamoto had disappeared along with his wife and son. Relatives and coworkers, of course, noticed the absence—and the silence—earlier. Sakamoto's mother had telephoned the small apartment repeatedly from November 4 through November 7, and grew more worried as each day passed without an answer. Both Sakamotos kept in frequent touch with their relatives, especially their parents. On November 2, Satoko phoned both her parents and her in-laws to tell them that a vacation to the southern island of Shikoku had been canceled because her husband was coming down with a cold and had decided to rest over the long holiday weekend. At seven o'clock in the evening on November 3, Satoko called another relative, thanking her for a gift of apples that had arrived. Then silence fell.

Sakamoto's work schedule after November 4 included several important appointments related to his Japan Railway cases. He told his colleagues he would be staying overnight at the office on November 6 to complete some important paperwork. When he failed to show up at work or return calls, his coworkers became concerned; Sakamoto was the reliable type.

On November 7, Sakamoto's deeply worried mother and an office associate went to the apartment together. They were extremely disturbed by what they found.

The door and all the windows of the apartment were locked, and the lights were out. After making their way in, they found a perplexing scene. Sakamoto's suit and company badge were in the closet, as were the rest of their clothes; the wallets of husband and wife were both there, Sakamoto's containing several ten-thousand-yen notes. His glasses were on the desk. The rice cooker was on, and dirty dishes lay in the sink. The baby's diaper, his stroller, car seat, and carrying sling were all there. Oddly, their futon bedding was missing as were their pajamas. A dresser was marred with a smear of blood and on the threshold of the open closet was a badge from what was identified in press accounts for several days as "a certain new religion": Aum Shinri Kyo. Nakagawa had dropped it.

Alarmed by what they had seen in the apartment, Sakamoto's mother called the police, who began an investigation that continued for a week before the disappearance was made public on November 15.

While the public grew more intrigued by the mysterious disappearance of the Sakamoto family, Shoko Asahara was busy tying up loose ends. The English-language *Mainichi Daily News* reported that shortly after the murders Asahara called all the members of the death squad in to have them hear a reading of the Japanese Penal Code as it relates to punishment for murder. Held in the guru's personal quarters at the Kamikuishiki compound, all six members attended, along with Aum Finance Minister Hisako Ishii. At the meeting, the *Mainichi* report stated, Asahara asked Ishii what the maximum penalty was for murder and she read aloud the provisions of the penal code dealing with murder. During the meeting there was never any specific mention of the Sakamotos. Okazaki, who confessed to his part in the kidnapping, said he believes the purpose of the meeting was to make it clear to those present that they had committed a crime that carried the death penalty. The *Mainichi* said police theorize that Asahara wanted to ensure unity among the action-squad members and to tacitly indicate that if one of them went to the police, all would face the death penalty.

With the public announcement of the family's disappearance, a strange dance of the Japanese media, police, Aum, and Sakamoto's coworkers and relatives began. On November 16, the day after the announcement of Sakamoto's disappearance, his law office held a news conference. Suspicions of

Aum's involvement in the incident ran high among Sakamoto's associates, but before they had a chance to speak they got a phone call from Aoyama denying any connection to the disappearance and threatening serious legal action if Aum Shinri Kyo's name was mentioned. The law office bowed to this demand.

What followed was even more mystifying. On November 18, Aum called the Tokyo Press Club to announce its own press conference, to be held in an apartment in Yokohama. They would answer questions about the Sakamoto incident on the condition, dictated by Aoyama at the outset, that neither personal names nor Aum Shinri Kyo would be mentioned in any reporting. The Japanese press agreed, resulting in news reports that began, "A certain new religion announced today that it had no involvement in the disappearance of the attorney Sakamoto."

However clumsily, Aum was busy covering its tracks on other fronts as well. When it became known that an Aum lapel badge, called a *purusha*, had been left at the Sakamoto apartment, Asahara ordered a speedy mass production of the trinkets. It was then left to Aum spokesman Fumihiro Joyu to perform a deft public flip-flop. Aum spokesmen and literature had stated on several occasions that *purusha* were only awarded to serious members of the faith who had achieved a certain level of spiritual attainment. But at his press conference Joyu explained the presence of the badge by saying that they were produced in great quantities and were commonly available to all sorts of people, not only members of Aum. In fact, he said, Aum had received requests from people outside the sect for the badges. He then went on to suggest that the Soka Gakkai, another new religion for which Asahara exhibited a special hatred, left the badge at the apartment to purposely implicate Aum in the disappearance. Joyu concluded by saying that while Aum would not cooperate with attorneys investigating the matter, they would cooperate with police.

The police were quick to accept the offer, but not quite quick enough. The next day, November 19, they formally requested Aum's cooperation with the investigation. Unfortunately, Asahara and other high-ranking members, including Hayakawa, suddenly decided to embark on hastily scheduled "overseas propagation activities." They left Japan on November 21, effectively removing themselves from questioning. The police did not learn of their departure until after they were gone, and only then by witnesses at the airport who phoned Sakamoto's law office to report the exodus of the Aum retinue.

Despite posters, exhaustive media coverage, and the offer of a reward, no trace of the Sakamoto family was to be found. Sakamoto's mother, who had found the empty apartment, continued to knit clothes for her grandson, each year increasing the sizes to fit a growing child. In the end, it was an act of faith and hope that went unrewarded. The Sakamoto family bodies were recovered in 1995.

2

Matsumoto's Miasma: A Nocturnal Prelude

They probably started late to begin with and then never got back on schedule. It had been a busy day for the small group of Aum Shinri Kyo terrorists anxiously speeding down the expressway toward the mountain city of Matsumoto. Somewhere in the rush they had lost track of time, and when they rolled into the outskirts of the scenic city it was late in the afternoon of June 27, 1994. They had come to Matsumoto to conduct a field test on the effectiveness of a new batch of sarin nerve gas that the sect's chemists had recently produced in their lab near the slopes of Mount Fuji. The plan of attack, tossed together in a last-minute frenzy of discussion, was as bold as it was dumb. Not only was the sarin gas new and untried, but so was the method of its dissemination—a refrigerator truck the cult had specially adapted to spray the gas. Their confidence in both the gas and the new spray system ran high, and all that remained was the field test in Matsumoto to prove that both components worked.

They planned to park the truck directly outside the district courthouse located in the heart of downtown Matsumoto—only a short distance from a major police headquarters—and then spray the sarin through the front doors of the multistoried building to the rooms inside. They intended to do this in

27

broad daylight as large numbers of innocent people walked along the side-walk, entering and leaving the busy courthouse and other buildings nearby.

Predictably, it was a legal matter that brought Aum's nerve-gas team to the doors of the courthouse. The targets selected for the sarin attack by Shoko Asahara were three district court judges who were deciding a tangled real-estate case involving Aum's purchase of a piece of land near Matsumoto in 1991. The man who sold the sect the property had filed a civil suit charging the religious group with buying the land through a front company to purposely keep its identity hidden. The property owner and other residents were distressed because Aum was opening a Matsumoto branch office—which meant their young people might become targets of recruitment by the controversial sect—and by Aum's plans to construct a religious training facility on the land. The unspoken core of their concern was the cult's unsa-vory reputation and the many ugly rumors circulating about its antisocial behavior and strange practices. Most residents didn't care whether the rumors were true; their mere existence was quite enough to stir opposition. They wanted Aum Shinri Kyo off the land and out of Matsumoto, and it now looked as if they were about to get their wish. The case had been in litigation for many months, and the three judges were expected to hand down their decision in mid-July. According to many legal observers, the sect's prospects of winning the suit were not favorable.

One key lawyer who did not like the way things were shaping up in the trial was Yoshinobu Aoyama, head legal counsel to sect leader Asahara and, later, Aum Shinri Kyo's Justice Minister. In early June, Aoyama met with the guru and advised him of the strong possibility that the judges would rule against them. But now Asahara had a new and extremely deadly weapon at his disposal, one with which he could strike back at his tormentors in a hor-rifying way. According to police confessions made later by senior Aum offi-cials who were present at the meeting, the angry guru promptly ordered his top aides to launch a sarin attack on the judges. If they were killed, he told the group, then they could not return a decision against the sect. For Aum's scientific and technical staff the order presented an excellent opportunity to test not only their latest technology for producing sarin, but also the truck they had modified to disperse the toxic gas. As they had recently learned from experience, producing sarin was relatively easy compared to dissemi-nating it.

The sect's first abortive attempt to test their new gas weapon against human targets occurred in the early spring of 1994. Senior members told police that Shoko Asahara personally ordered a sarin attack against Daisaku Ikeda, the leader of the large Buddhist organization Soka Gakkai. Dressed in protective clothing, the Aum action squad conducting the operation parked their specially converted truck outside the building in Tokyo where Ikeda was speaking and activated the sarin-spraying mechanism. But instead of ejecting the deadly gas into the building as planned, the dispersal system malfunctioned and caught fire, leaking gas fumes and acrid smoke inside the truck. The group managed to escape unnoticed, but one member of the team was overcome by the nerve gas and had to be taken to an Aum-operated hospital for treatment.

Military chemical-warfare specialists familiar with sarin speculate that the failure of Aum's first spray system was probably due to a fault in the mechanism that turns the liquid sarin into a sprayable gas. In its normal state at room temperature or lower, sarin is a liquid. Spraying it into the air as a gas—the most effective dispersal method—requires raising its temperature, a process that is not only time consuming but extremely dangerous. Developing a foolproof dispersal system had plagued Aum's Science and Technology Ministry for months, but gradually they learned from their past mistakes. In the weeks following the abortive attack on Soka Gakkai, Aum's scientists went back to their drawing boards and developed a new computer-controlled spraying system that contained three tanks to hold the liquid sarin, a heater to generate the right temperatures to produce the deadly vapor, and a fan to disperse the atomized agent. They built the device at their compound located next to the farming village of Kamikuishiki near Mount Fuji. When it was completed, Aum's technicians installed the system in a two-ton, white refrigerator truck that was modified to conceal the new apparatus. All that remained was a target for a field test, and with the mercurial Asahara at the group's helm, that was not long in coming.

On the afternoon of Monday, June 27, the new sarin truck, accompanied by a rented black station wagon which served as a lookout car, pulled out of the Aum compound at Kamikuishiki and headed directly for Matsumoto, some sixty miles away. In the tanks on board the truck was the group's latest batch of sarin, manufactured only ten days before in Aum's nerve-gas processing lab at Satyam Number 7 in the main compound next to

Kamikuishiki. The nerve gas was made by Masami Tsuchiya, chief of Aum's chemical team and a subordinate of Hideo Murai, the sect's ambitious Minister of Science and Technology. Asahara liked the bold and confidant Murai and had personally selected him to lead the attack in Matsumsoto.

En route to their target city the group was delayed when they stopped to alter the numbers on the vehicle's license tags with spray paint, and then again when they purchased several workmen's uniforms that they planned to use as disguises. It was those two stops that made them late for their afternoon attack on the district courthouse. Both stops undoubtedly saved the many innocent people who happened to be in or near the large building that afternoon. But one of fate's fickle trade-offs resulted in the deaths of seven equally innocent victims and the injury of hundreds of others in a quiet neighborhood not far away.

Matsumoto, "the city of mountains," sits beside the banks of the Takase River in Nagano Prefecture on Japan's main island of Honshu. Flanked by the soaring peaks of the Japanese Alps, its two hundred thousand residents quietly live their lives in the best of both worlds, a scenic rural setting that is also blessed with most of the creature comforts of a big city. But despite its breath-taking beauty and the fact that it's only three hours by train from Tokyo, Matsumoto somehow remains off the beaten track for most international tourists. The city's dominant feature and main tourist attraction is a sixteenth-century feudal fortress known locally as the "Crow's Castle" because of its black stone walls. Declared a national treasure by the government, the four-hundred-year-old castle is bathed in light at night, a starkly beautiful reminder of Matsumoto's ancient samurai past.

Like many regional Japanese cities during the "bubble economy" of the late 1980s, Matsumoto was eager to expand its cultural attractions and tourism income, so the city fathers embarked on a discreet promotional campaign to modernize the city's appeal. The first important step in their drive to promote the city came in 1990, when famed conductor Seiji Ozawa agreed to organize an annual classical-music festival in Matsumoto, allowing the city to lay claim to being the Tanglewood of Japan. Another big break came when it was decided that the 1998 Winter Olympics would be held on the snow-capped mountains nearby, an event that promises Matsumoto greater prominence on the international tourist map. With Ozawa appearing annually and the Olympics in the offing, things were looking up for Matsumoto in late June, 1994. But the month was not over—not by a long shot.

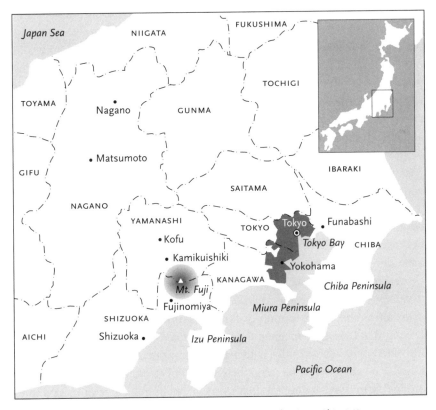

Map of Central Honshu, the region of greatest activity by Aum Shinri Kyo.

Any lingering hopes for the success of the Aum team's plan to spray sarin through the front doors of the district courthouse vanished when the tardy group arrived on the scene well after 5 P.M. By then the judges had already left for their lodgings in a government apartment house located a quarter-mile away. At that point a more experienced and professional terrorist group would have called it a day and gone home to critique their timing problems and await a more favorable opportunity. But the Aum team was not composed of professionals. At best, they were a group of lucky amateurs led by a man who was singularly determined to prove the effectiveness of his ministry's science and technology. That leader, Hideo Murai, meant to carry out the orders of his guru, and no small detail like being a few minutes late was going to stop him. In that regard, he had the solid support of his team, a group that like Murai had been carefully selected.

As he did with most of the sect's terrorist operations, Shoko Asahara, in consultation with his senior ministers, personally chose each member of the group making the field test in Matsumoto. His selection criteria called for men with skills in martial arts, driving ability, and total loyalty to the sect. As events that night would prove, Asahara's most important decision was to appoint Murai as the attack team leader. Murai was considered by some to be the sect's nominal number-two leader under Asahara, even though that post was officially held by Kiyohide Hayakawa. Widely recognized and feared within Aum, Murai had a reputation as a determined and aggressive leader who liked to stir up trouble for other people. No one doubted that he had devoted his life to carrying out Asahara's orders, although later some members would describe Murai to the police as Aum's "biggest war criminal." In appointing him to head the Matsumoto team, the guru was certain he had chosen someone who would not falter in the face of adversity.

Three days before the attack, Murai went to Matsumoto to case the courthouse and its surroundings for sites from which to launch the sarin. During that time he happened to learn the location of the apartment building where the judges lived. That small bit of information became crucial on Monday evening, when he faced the prospect of either failing in his mission or quickly improvising a new attack plan. Dreading the idea of returning to the Aum compound and telling Asahara they had failed, he decided to release the sarin at the judges' apartment building.

Gathering his six-man team together in the parking lot of a supermarket near the judges' quarters, Murai briefed them on the new plan as the men changed into the work uniforms they'd bought and made ready for the final phase. A quick check of the truck's dispersal system showed that everything was ready to go. But there was one element they still had to consider, and it was a vitally important one—the weather.

Unlike many other weapons, nerve gas does not have an "all-weather" capability. Conditions must be exactly right to successfully carry out a gas attack in the open air, and nothing is more critical than the wind direction. As the long summer evening faded into night, Murai anxiously scanned the soggy, gray skies hanging low over the city, patiently waiting for just the right conditions. He sniffed the air; the outward signs were not good. The wind had been moving gently, but in the wrong direction. Then shortly after

10:30 P.M. it all came together. The soft northwesterly current slowed ever so slightly, shifted steadily to the west, and stayed there.

"It was not even a breeze," a city meteorologist would later note in dismay. But it was enough to convince Hideo Murai that the right moment had arrived.

Before that Monday evening, none of the residents of Matsumoto and very few of the citizens of greater Japan had ever heard the word "sarin." Among the truly innocent in Matsumoto was an industrial-machinery salesman named Yoshiyuki Kono. But like everyone else in Matsumoto and Japan, Kono was poised on the edge of a cruelly steep learning curve, and before the night was over his life would be changed forever.

The new attack site selected by Murai was a small public parking area in the quiet, middle-class neighborhood of Kita Fukashi. First the small group inside the spray truck changed into protective suits and gloves, but before buttoning up they injected themselves with a precautionary sarin antidote. Next they put special plastic breathing bags over their heads connected to small, portable pumps that injected fresh air into the bags through tubes at the bottom. But like so much else about the operation, the air bags were another of the great unknowns facing the team. No one really knew how well the headgear would perform if the sarin leaked inside the truck. Finally, covered from head to toe and looking something like astronauts, they were ready to begin. All business in his leadership role, Murai wasted no time in activating the heater to transform the liquid sarin into a gas. Once that was accomplished he switched on the computer system that began spraying the toxic fumes from the atomizer nozzle into the warm night air outside.

With that move, Hideo Murai became the man who launched the world's first ultraterrorist attack.

The gas left the truck's nozzle and moved on its path toward the judges' apartments, some thirty feet away. Or so Murai thought. But shortly before Murai turned on the spray nozzle, the wind again changed direction. Initially moving slowly west from the launch site, it suddenly shifted to a northerly course, sending the sarin spraying from the truck swirling off in the wrong direction. That was just the beginning of the disaster that would follow.

Satoru Hashimoto, Aum martial-arts specialist and a veteran of the Sakamoto murders, was driver of the sarin truck and in the best position to see everything during the attack. He would later confess to police that the team spent nearly twenty minutes on the edge of the parking lot spraying sarin from the dispersal system's three heated containers, all but a small portion of it drifting off in the wrong direction. Tomomasa Nakagawa, Aum's Household Agency chief and another member of the Sakamoto death squad, was also present during the attack. He told police that the sarin used at Matsumoto had a cobalt blue color because too much isopropyl alcohol was added to the mixture, creating hydrogen fluoride. When the hydrogen fluoride evaporated in the warm air outside it instantly created a huge cloud of white vapor that surrounded the truck before it floated off. The large white cloud enveloping the truck also attracted the attention of residents in the neighborhood. Later they told police they had seen a "big white mist" and two people clad in "space suits" near the parking lot on the night of the attack.

The appearance of the white mist was undoubtedly the point at which panic took a firm hold on the action squad. Frightened by the mist itself, alarmed at the probability of being spotted by neighborhood residents, and above all, terrified that they were about to become engulfed in the nerve gas they had just released, the group departed the neighborhood at high speed. As he sped from the parking lot, the agitated driver of the lookout vehicle ran into a concrete pillar on the side of the street, slightly damaging the rental car. But it was left to team-leader Murai's group in the truck to make an even worse mistake. In their haste to get away, they forgot to replace the cap on the nozzle of the sarin spray device. As they sped through the narrow, dimly lit public streets near the launch site, deadly nerve gas poured out of the nozzle and into the night air. Fortunately, only a small amount was left in the sarin tanks, but even that small amount was enough to sicken a number of residents along the group's exit route.

The terrorist team left the city immediately, heading back to the Kamikuishiki compound. En route they called Asahara and used a prearranged code to inform him of the successful attack. Behind them a horrifying nightmare was slowly descending upon the residents of the neighborhood they had just attacked.

In the first few minutes after the team departed, the sarin achieved its primary mission. Though the wind had shifted just as the gas began to spray, sending it slightly north of the judges' apartment house, enough of the powerful fumes drifted into the building to sicken all three of them, one quite seriously. There is little doubt that the change in wind direction spared the lives of the judges and the other residents in their building. Others were not so fortunate.

A fifteen-year-old student named Kayoko Meguro recounted the gassing in her school newspaper, which was reprinted by the mass-circulation daily newspaper *Yomiuri Shimbun*. At the time of the attack, Meguro was living with her family on the second floor of an apartment house owned by the Meiji Life Insurance Company. The Meiji building is located next to the judges' apartment house. The young student's first symptom was a bout of severe coughing.

"After a coughing fit in the living room at 11 P.M., I went into the bathroom to gargle," she wrote. "All of a sudden the lights were half as bright as they usually were. I dropped some eye drops into my eyes but they did not heal."

She went to bed shortly after that and recalls hearing the loud wail of an ambulance siren outside. Then at 11:30, as she was about to fall asleep, she heard a voice speaking on a megaphone outside her building.

"There is a gas leak," the voice announced urgently, "those of you who are feeling unwell should notify the ambulance officer nearest you."

Aware that something unusual was happening, Meguro left her bed, dressed, and went to other apartments in the building to wake the residents there.

"The only resident who did not wake," she continued, "was one living on the third floor. We opened the door with a master key . . . and I entered the apartment with my father. [Mr.] 'E' was not moving in the bathtub, which was in the bathroom on the north side [of the building]."

A medical technician checked the man's pulse and pronounced him dead. The "Mr. E" in Meguro's account was forty-five-year-old Tetsuji Enokida, a Meiji Life Insurance Company employee. The small windows in his bathroom were open. Meguro's vision problems, a classic symptom of sarin poisoning, worsened later that evening and she was hospitalized for more than week.

Sixteen-year-old Shingo Fukazawa left his home at 11 P.M. to buy a container of juice at a nearby convenience store. When he went outside, he noticed that the air seemed smoggy.

"After walking a little while," he said, "I started feeling dizzy. My eyes stung and I felt like throwing up." Later he became extremely ill and was hospitalized.

The best-known victim of the Matsumoto gassing is Yoshiyuki Kono. As he remembers it, the evening of Monday, June 27, started out like any other in his life. He had put in a long day at the office, returning home from work at 8 P.M. to eat a light dinner of rice pilaf with his wife. Then he settled down with a cold beer to read the newspaper until 10 P.M., when the couple decided to watch a television program, a cabaret on the government-sponsored network NHK. The Kono children, a son and two daughters, all teenagers, were upstairs in their rooms studying.

Quiet, reflective, and like many salesmen, keenly attentive to the accuracy of details, Kono's personal life reads like a laundry list of what makes a responsible member of Japanese society. Solidly middle class, devoted to his wife, a caring father of three well-behaved children, hard working, unflinchingly loyal to his company, relatives, and friends, he fills all of Japan's important societal squares. Indeed, there was nothing in Kono's life to distinguish him from millions of other law-abiding Japanese men and women until the sarin swept into his home on June 27.

The Kono family residence is large by Japanese standards, a rambling, two-story, traditional wooden house set on the edge of a spacious, treed lot. It is surrounded by boxlike multistoried apartment houses and company dormitories on one side, and on the other by a number of smaller, nondescript residential homes. Though not luxurious, the Kono residence easily occupies pride of place in its neighborhood. The roof of the house, covered in dark ceramic tiles, is the dominant feature. In a bow to the region's rich samurai past, the Japanese character for the Kono family name is molded in bas relief on the end of the tiles extending over the eaves. In front of the house is a large, manicured garden that sits placidly amid tall, leafy trees. The garden is interspersed with decorative rocks placed in traditional Japanese fashion and includes a small pond near the boundary of the Kono property. The back edge of the Kono property, near the pond, is hemmed in by a waist-high wire fence. On the other side of the fence is a cul-de-sac that ends in a public parking area easily approached by car from the adjoining streets.

Approximately thirty feet from the parking area is the government apartment house where the three district court judges lived. The easy accessibility of the public parking area on the edge of Kono's property and the close proximity of the judicial apartment house made it an ideal gas-spraying site for Hideo Murai and his team. They had no trouble finding parking space for their vehicles.

The NHK cabaret program ended at eleven and the couple were preparing to go to bed when Kono heard a strange, scratching noise in the garden.

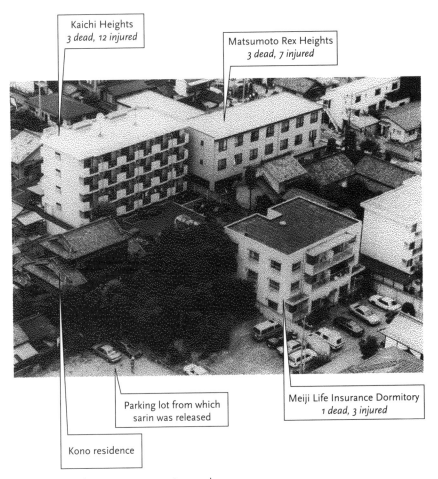

Kaichi Heights
3 dead, 12 injured

Matsumoto Rex Heights
3 dead, 7 injured

Parking lot from which
sarin was released

Meiji Life Insurance Dormitory
1 dead, 3 injured

Kono residence

The scene at the Matsumoto sarin attack.

Stepping outside, he found his setter dog squirming on the ground in agony. Looking closer in the dim light, he saw that white foam specked with blood was oozing from her mouth. Alarmed, Kono spoke softly to the stricken dog: "Hold on, girl."

Hurrying back inside the house, he got some water and returned to find the dog dead, along with her puppy, whose body lay nearby. Extremely upset by the dogs' violent deaths, Kono immediately decided to summon the police.

"Mother!" he yelled back inside to his wife, "I think we should call the police. Mother!" But the interior of the house was ominously silent.

Quickly returning to the living room, he found his wife writhing in pain on the floor, her body twitching violently in muscular convulsions. He tried to assist her by loosening her clothes, but as he worked the spasms became much more violent. Frantically grabbing the phone, Kono called for an ambulance, then yelled upstairs for his children to come down quickly. In the few seconds it took the children to reach the living room, Kono himself was suddenly overwhelmed. He had a severe headache, his nose was running, and his breathing became labored and difficult. Most frightening of all, his eyesight was fragmenting, breaking into kaleidoscopic pieces as the lights in the living room grew darker. Panicking, certain he was dying, he reached for his son's hand.

"Mom and Dad might not make it through this," he told the frightened youth. "You're going to have to take care of things from now on, son."

Kono's call for help was the first in the flood of tortured cries from his neighborhood recorded that night by medics, police, and firemen. The first emergency teams that poured into the area witnessed a scene of mass confusion and terror. Scores of men, women, and children were staggering about drunkenly in the dark streets, while others were fully prostrate on the sidewalks, unable to move or unconscious. Many were wheezing and gasping hard for breath, vomiting, coughing blood, unable to see, crying out in agony for help. The emergency crews initially assumed there was a gas leak somewhere in the neighborhood. But as the number of casualties steadily grew, the doctors noted with increasing alarm that what they were seeing and hearing were not the usual symptoms associated with a gas leak. If not gas, then what? And how were the injured to be treated? Meanwhile, there were the growing numbers of victims, some already dead.

Blood tests quickly taken from the first persons to arrive at the hospital gave the baffled medics their first important clues. The tests revealed the victims had abnormally low levels of cholinesterase, an enzyme that carries electrical signals through the body's nervous system. Some patients' cholinesterase levels were down by twenty-five to fifty percent. Like diminished vision, this is a another prime indication of sarin poisoning, though it would be two weeks before doctors could put a name to the deadly gas. In the meantime they treated the victims for organic phosphorous poisoning. The standard antidote for that is the same as for sarin: injections of atropine.

Before the night was over, the doctors in Matsumoto's hospitals would treat more than five hundred victims and hospitalize fifty-nine of them. But some were already beyond medical help. When the sun came up the next morning there were seven bodies in the Matsumoto morgue, all of them victims of nerve gas. Among the luckiest Japanese survivors of the sarin attack was the one who would become best known, Yoshiyuki Kono.

The batch of sarin produced by Aum's chemists for the Matsumoto test proved to be extremely pure, and as with most nerve agents, the purer the gas the more lethal its effects. In a macabre twist of fate, the stunning lethality of the sarin unleashed in Matsumoto may have inadvertently saved the lives of hundreds, perhaps thousands, of Tokyo subway riders nine months later. The potency of the Matsumoto agent surprised even Hideo Murai. In one of his first critiques of the attack, he forcefully told chief chemist Tsuchiya that the gas was "too dense, too toxic," and ordered him to dilute it in the future. No humanitarian, Murai was undoubtedly thinking of the lives of future Aum dispersal teams when he gave the order to his head chemist. Nonetheless, the people he really saved were the innocent citizens of Tokyo. But how did the deadly gas find its victims once it was dispersed in Matsumoto?

Released on the edge of Kono's property, the odorless and invisible sarin at first remained low on the ground as it crept silently forward on the breeze wafting through the trees in the garden, then into the Kono residence. Swirling round, in, and past the house, it then pushed up against the walls of the dormitories and apartment buildings nearby, where it climbed slowly upward on the warm night air, eventually to disperse, but not before its poisonous fumes entered the upper floors of the concrete buildings. It was there the gas did its most deadly work. The afflicted in the neighborhood, those who died or were seriously injured, had their windows and doors open or their air-conditioners on. People in rooms with the windows closed fared better, becoming only mildly ill if they were affected at all.

Kono was at ground level as the gas spread, moving back and forth to tend his dying dogs. This activity may have saved his life by partially shielding him from full exposure to the gas. Even so, his location and movements were not enough to prevent him from being stricken, though they apparently were enough to avoid the direct exposure that killed or permanently injured others. His wife, inside the house the entire time, was not nearly so lucky.

After being sickened by the gas, Kono remembers events as if he was in a deathlike trance. He recalls wandering out to the street, knocking in slow motion on the window of the ambulance, thinking perhaps of food poisoning, speaking slowly, deliberately, and desperately to the attendants inside: *"I-ate-rice-pilaf-for-dinner."* Inside the ambulance, speeding to the hospital, he vomited uncontrollably. Then he watched in fear as medics pumped his wife's failing heart, keeping her alive, even though later she would slide into a coma from which she is unlikely to ever recover. In the hospital swarming with victims, he heard the terrified voice of a woman on a stretcher screaming, "What's happening to me?!" His own voice seemed to be saying to someone, *"If the police don't need the dogs for evidence, bury them under the lilac tree."* Then the painful muscular spasms that had seized his wife took him in their grasp, whipping through the entire length of his body. He would remain in the hospital for more than thirty days struggling to regain his health. But long before he was released, Yoshiyuki Kono discovered his problems were just beginning. Less than a day after the attack, the Matsumoto police and the news media had targeted him as their prime suspect in the gassing.

The Japanese National Police were quick to respond to the crisis. Eventually more than three hundred investigators fanned out across Matsumoto, interviewing victims, taking chemical samples, talking to residents. They seemed to miss nothing, but in reality they missed practically everything, at least as far as Yoshiyuki Kono was concerned. Sarin gas, by its very nature, is an indiscriminate killer. It kills birds, large and small animals, insects, and plant life with the same relentless efficiency that it kills humans. In Matsumoto, the gas killed pigeons, insects, and even the carp and crayfish in Kono's small garden pond. But it was the dead plants in Kono's garden that intrigued the police investigators and first drew them to his bedside. Plants exposed to sarin quickly wither, then turn brown and die. The deadly gas had carved a small swath of dead, brown foliage across Kono's garden, and that was one thing the police did not miss. Leading from a point a few feet behind the Kono's property line, the trail of dead foliage pointed a powerfully incriminating finger at one of the first victims of the attack.

Despite Kono's impeccably normal life, if the Matsumoto police had to come up with an immediate suspect for the gas attack, they couldn't hope to find a better-qualified candidate. All the leads seemed to point toward him. The gas was released just behind his property, but not on it, as Kono would repeatedly point out to police and journalists. He would tell them time and again that the track of dead, wilted foliage clearly showed that it was released several feet across his property line. But the police and reporters simply nodded when he made his defensive points. And the more the police looked at Kono, the worse it seemed to get for him. The police background check revealed that Kono had previously worked as a salesman for a chemical manufacturing company in Kyoto. Though he had left that job six or seven years before, the police noted ominously that he still had a license to handle hazardous chemicals. Even more incriminating was the cache of chemicals they found on his property.

Because he had been the first to call for help on the night of the attack, and because the gas had been released near his property, the day after the gassing the police took a search warrant to Kono's home and seized what one detective described to the press as a "treasure trove" of chemicals. Among the chemicals was a form of cyanide, one of the ingredients used to make sarin. Kono repeatedly protested his innocence, explaining over and again that the chemicals were for mixing insecticides for his garden and for his hobby of photography. He swore he hadn't touched them in a year or more. But no one seemed to be listening.

As the investigation proceeded in the slow, methodical way of the Japanese police, rumors began to spread in Matsumoto that Kono had somehow accidentally brewed a batch of poisonous gas. Largely stemming from public statements and leaks to the Japanese press by the police, the rumors became so persistent that Yoshiyuki Kono was well on his way to becoming a pariah in his own community.

But in their pursuit of prime suspect Kono, the police and the media had overlooked or ignored several important details. Just over a week after the attack, police chemical analysis of the traces left by the gas revealed something new and alarming. The gas was not some accidental deadly combination of home chemicals, but sarin, a complex nerve agent. To produce it requires a sound knowledge of organic chemistry and a laboratory with rather sophisticated equipment. Any good organic chemist in Japan could have told the police and the media that their accidental insecticide theory contained three robust contradictions.

First, even though sarin is old technology, it is all but impossible for an untrained chemist to accidentally make it. One week after the attack, Kanagawa University Professor Keiichi Tsuneishi, a scientist familiar with the gases used in chemical weapons, bluntly told the press that sarin could not be made accidentally "by mixing chemicals." Science University of Tokyo Professor Shunji Ishikura was even more direct. He said the possibility of accidentally making sarin was about the same as "a monkey writing a sentence that makes sense while playing with a word processor."

Second, the cyanide notwithstanding, it is impossible to make sarin with the "treasure trove" of chemicals seized by police at Kono's home. The necessary ingredients for producing a nerve gas simply weren't there.

Finally, the production of sarin requires the knowledge of a graduate-level organic chemist who has access to a laboratory with special equipment. It is probably safe to say that in the entire city of Matsumoto, the chemicals and equipment needed to make sarin were not available. But it took a long time for the Japanese police and the press to uncover and absorb these facts. In the meantime, traces of the deadly gas surfaced again, once more in a most unlikely place.

In July the residents of Kamikuishiki, a small farming village near the front range of Mount Fuji, complained to police about strange, offensive smells that were coming from the sprawling compound of Aum Shinri Kyo located next door to them. Aum's property abutted the village and the villagers, rural and conservative, had grown to actively dislike the strange and reclusive sect. They wanted them out.

When the police came to investigate the complaint, the villagers pointed out places near the cult property where vegetation had mysteriously died. They thought it might be connected somehow to the strange smells coming from the compound. The police listened politely, made notes, took soil samples, and then left. What the police learned from analysis of the samples taken at Kamikuishiki was that the soil contained trace elements of chemical compounds used in the manufacture of sarin. But it would be five months later, on New Year's Day, 1995, before Japan learned of this important discovery. It was then that the following carefully worded report appeared in the *Yomiuri Shimbun*: "Traces of an organic phosphorous compound that could have resulted from sarin [have been] detected in Kamikuishiki, a small village at the foot of Mount Fuji. . . . Police suspect sarin could have been produced in Kamikuishiki about twelve days after Matsumoto's poisoning incident."

By now it had to be self-evident that if a nerve gas had been unleashed in sleepy Matsumoto and found in the volcanic soil on the slope of sacred Mount Fuji then the deadly gas just might turn up anywhere.

The Japanese police were also realizing that Yoshiyuki Kono was a very slender reed on which to hang the deadly events that occurred in Matsumoto.

Yet they kept Kono on the books as a suspect in the investigation, though they made no move to arrest him. The distinction is a critical one in Japan.

In the eyes of most Japanese, being arrested by the police is tantamount to a verdict of guilty in a court of law. There is solid evidence to support this public conviction. The Japanese police have a ninety-nine-percent arrest-conviction rate, easily the highest in the world. The primary reason for this high rate is that the police refrain from making arrests until they're positive their case will produce a conviction in court. Despite the rumors of his guilt, the police failure to arrest Kono spoke volumes to the perceptive.

Yoshiyuki Kono would have to wait almost a year for complete vindication. When it came, the ugly accusations and rumors about him were finally laid to rest. In the process, Kono received more public apologies from the news media and police than any other Japanese citizen in recent memory. He still lives in his home in the Kita Fukashi district of Matsumoto, and his wife remains in a coma. In the unlikely event she ever recovers, she will be permanently blinded.

The Dawn of
Ultraterrorism

um Shinri Kyo's sudden emergence as the world's only known ultraterrorist group is a phenomenon that most Japanese find hard to understand. "Ultraterrorism" or "ultraterrorist" is defined here to mean any
terrorist group that possesses or uses chemical, biological, or nuclear
weapons—weapons of mass destruction—for political purposes. The idea
that a religious group would unleash weapons of mass destruction on innocent people is both foreign and incomprehensible in a nation that prides
itself on the safety of its streets and its famously low crime rate. Until Aum
came along, most Japanese, if they thought about it at all, probably considered themselves immune to religious terrorism—at least in their own country. Extreme religious fervor is an attitude largely unfamiliar to the Japanese,
most of whom worship privately in the sedate calm of their temples and
shrines. That an individual's or group's religious passion could ignite the
same violent emotions as political ideology is a very strange notion.

This view is common elsewhere besides Japan. Although some extremist and highly politicized religious factions are now getting more attention
in the media, the coverage of this relatively new phenomenon is still not
comparable to the challenge it poses to peace and order in many parts of the
world. But whether in Asia, the Middle East, or elsewhere, religious zealotry

and politics, when blended together, almost always result in a dogmatic brew of emotions that are difficult to contain and control.

Late in the eighteenth century America's founders recognized this problem by including a number of safeguards in the U.S. Constitution to insure the separation of church and state. Other nations were not so fortunate, and the inevitable clash between politicized religious extremists and the state is a growing trend that will extend well into the twenty-first century. To understand the increasingly aggressive role of religious politics in contemporary life, consider the recent impact it has had in the dark arena of terrorist violence.

Thirty years ago, in 1965, there was not a single religious terrorist group anywhere in the world. Fifteen years later, in 1980, only two of the world's sixty-four known terrorist organizations had a religious basis. Since then the number of groups has climbed to more than a dozen, all of them driven by religious rather than political zealotry. Located in such diverse areas as Europe, North America, the South Asian subcontinent, Northeast Asia, and the Middle East, these extremist religious groups include Christian white supremacists, radical Jews, militant Sikhs, and most threatening of all, Islamic fundamentalists.

The dynamic hard core of modern-day religious terrorism is located in the militant Islamic groups operating in and out of the Middle East and North Africa. Fanatically dedicated to imposing Islamic governments that will enforce "God's law" as revealed by their fundamentalist interpretations of the Koran, they are the most pervasive and deadly religion-based terrorist groups operating in the world today. Anti-Western, and in particular anti-American, the Islamic radicals have in recent years pushed well beyond their traditional areas of activity and are now attacking targets in Western Europe and the once "terrorist-free zone" of the United States. It was fundamentalist Muslim terrorists who bombed the World Trade Center in New York and all but paralyzed the city of Paris during a summer campaign of indiscriminate bombing attacks in 1995.

As the limits of their operational ability have expanded steadily outward, they have become decidedly more effective. U.S. State Department counterterrorist experts recently reported that while the overall incidence of terrorism has declined in the past few years, the death and injury rate in individual attacks has increased. The spread of religious terrorism accounts for a large number of these deadly operations. Terrorist attacks conducted by extremists of the Muslim Shiite sect were responsible for more than a quarter of all deaths from terrorism in the past fifteen years.

International terrorism experts and a growing number of academic and diplomatic specialists in Middle Eastern politics believe Muslim radical violence could increase dramatically in the future because the prospects are bleak for reconciling secular law—increasingly bolstered with human rights and other social baggage Muslim extremists find unacceptable—with the rigid and less tolerant interpretations of Islamic law demanded by the fundamentalists. The Middle East, then, is the current cutting edge of religious militancy and a model for the emerging religio-political violence that may be the dominant feature of terrorism in the early twenty-first century.

Further east, in Asia, religious emotions have been a good deal calmer and more predictable, at least in the twentieth century. Despite its rich array of contradictory religious and spiritual beliefs, modern Asia has been largely spared the religion-inspired political violence occurring in the Middle East and elsewhere. The latter half of the twentieth century has produced only a small number of Asian religious-terrorist examples worthy of note. In the mid-1950s, several syncretic and highly politicized religious sects in South Vietnam violently opposed the government before being squashed by the army. Directly across the South China Sea from Vietnam, a centuries-old animosity between Muslim separatists in the southern Philippine islands and the predominantly Christian central government in Manila continues to fester, sparking random terrorist incidents by the Muslims, mainly on the large southern island of Mindanao. Except for isolated incidents such as these, however, terrorism in twentieth-century Asia has been largely motivated by political ideology and nationalism.

Japan, like the rest of Northeast Asia, had no modern history of terrorism or violence by religion-based groups until its spiritual calm was rudely shattered by Aum Shinri Kyo. Japanese domestic terrorism, which reached a peak in the Vietnam War protests of the 1960s, has never posed a serious threat to the stability of the government. Taking its life from politics, Japan's terrorist activities consisted mainly of sporadic incidents conducted by right-wing fanatics, or more commonly, by radicalized left-wing youths. Incidents of domestic terrorism were always treated as criminal matters for police to handle. Japan's police force is considered one of the most efficient in the world at monitoring the activities of its violent political groups.

Japan's most publicized international terrorist group was the Red Army, a bizarre band of highly radicalized young leftists. The Red Army is best remembered for the 1972 Lod Airport massacre in which three of their members indiscriminately slaughtered twenty-six people and wounded seventy-six others, most of whom were a visiting group of Puerto Rican religious pilgrims. Two members of the Red Army team, which had been recruited for the attack by the People's Liberation Front of Palestine, an extreme anti-Israeli terrorist group, committed suicide in the airport immediately after the attack; a third member was captured and imprisoned by the Israelis. Near the end of its life in Japan, the Red Army subjected itself to a vicious internal purge in which it tortured and killed a number of its own members.

The 1980s saw a resurgence of militant activity by Japan's leftists, still the nation's most persistent violent group. During this period radical groups emerged that fired inaccurate, makeshift rockets and used homemade flame throwers. A land dispute over the construction of Tokyo's Narita Airport, a frequent target of violent radical protest, turned the airport into one of the most heavily guarded in the world. Terrorist violence from the left declined in the 1990s, and groups showed a marked preference for detonating low-order explosive or pyrotechnic smoke devices in public places. The primary motive behind many of these ritualistic acts was to embarrass and intimidate the government rather than to inflict injury on innocent civilians, even though some injuries and deaths did occur.

When television screens suddenly filled with scenes of the dead and injured being hauled out of Tokyo's subways, astute Japanese immediately realized that the nation's assiduously earned reputation as one of the world's safest societies had suffered a terrible blow. The harsh truth was now unavoidable: Aum Shinri Kyo's nerve-gas attack had driven a long nail in the coffin of Japan's uniqueness as a peaceful society. Perhaps never again would the island nation be confident it was immune from the indiscriminate violence plaguing other parts of the world. The question uppermost in the minds of many Japanese was twofold: How could something like this happen in Japan? And where did we go wrong?

Almost as soon as the Tokyo subways started running again, the Japanese public began a nervous and uncertain inward search for the reason for this massive violence. In the months ahead no end of pundits, commentators, politicians, educators, and ordinary citizens stepped forward with answers to those questions. Employing the perfect clarity of hindsight, the Japanese press, police, and government agreed, more or less, that Aum's numerous early warning signs—not the least of which was the shrill alarm sounded by the gas attack in Matsumoto—had been there all along, shining out like beacons for those with the vision to see them. For many critics, that was precisely the problem: There had been no vision, no questioning, no sense of urgency, even after Matsumoto, the one indubitable sign that terrorism of a particularly lethal type was now loose in the country and almost certain to strike again.

Dismayed critics in the press noted that Aum Shinri Kyo's criminal activities had taken place over a five-year period during which a number of serious criminal complaints were made to the police and press about the group. But Aum seemed to enjoy a curious immunity from public complaints. The police investigated each charge made against the sect promptly, yet it never went any farther, and there were never any arrests. But there were solid reasons, at least to the police and the larger government bureaucracy, for their unusual reluctance to become more deeply involved in the affairs of Aum Shinri Kyo, or any other religious group for that matter.

Fearful of being accused of religious persecution, Japanese officials at all levels were often extremely hesitant to aggressively pursue criminal complaints lodged against religious groups. In all fairness, their foot dragging was not a recent problem that the Japanese authorities had created for themselves; its seeds were unwittingly planted more than forty years ago when the American military occupation government drafted Japan's postwar constitution. As one Japanese wag noted, only half in jest, it was the Americans who put the fear of God in modern Japanese government. But Americans today would probably view what happened as a ringing affirmation of an old religious truth: The road to hell is paved with good intentions.

From the first quarter of the nineteenth century through the first half of the twentieth century, Japan experienced a sudden growth of new religious sects from outside the well-established Buddhist, Shinto, and Christian denominations. That growth was not unlike the flowering of new religions which occurred after the Second World War and continues to this day. Although at least one of the prewar sects exhibited some paramilitary features and preached an apocalyptic message similar to that of Aum Shinri Kyo, none of the new groups openly advocated violence or strong opposition to the government.

The Japanese government had strictly controlled religion since the intro-duction of Buddhism in Japan in the seventh century. From about 1600 on, that control was strengthened, as the government basically made Japanese religion part of the apparatus of the state. The modernization policies adopt-ed from about 1870, on the model of European governments, allowed nom-inal recognition of religious freedom, but the government kept all sects, new and old, under careful watch and strict regulation. Shinto, which deified the emperor, was made the state religion, and all Japanese were required to observe Shinto rites, both in public and private.

By the late 1930s, as Japan drifted deeper into armed conflict in Asia, its authoritarian government began to view the independence and rapidly grow-ing memberships of the new sects with suspicion. The matter finally came to a head when Japanese authorities concluded that the new sects' increas-ing numbers and hefty financial resources might pose potential internal security problems for a nation on the brink of a wider war. For a government dominated by a military accustomed to total control of the population, the growth of the independent new religious sects was cause for concern.

Like many of the new religions in Japan today, the prewar sects were highly skilled in marketing their spiritual messages and attracting new con-verts. Using radio and newspaper advertising as well as street-corner prose-lytizing, the groups brought in millions of members and in the process accu-mulated huge amounts of money. Recognizing the serious threat of this new competition, the powerful hierarchy of State Shinto, in concert with the other established religious denominations, urged the government to take action.

The charges leveled against the sects during this period echo much of the public criticism raised against Japan's new religions today. The press, the government, and some segments of the public accused the sects of bilking vulnerable people of their money and assets with promises of spiritual attainment and miracle cures for illnesses. Charismatic sect leaders were portrayed as charlatans preying on the marginal, uneducated elements of society with superstitious nonsense. At the time, rumors of sexual orgies and physical abuse of members, fueled by lurid press accounts, were pervasive.

Undoubtedly, with some of the new sects there was a tissue of truth in the accusations, as there undoubtedly is in the criticism levied against some of the sects in Japan's current crop of new religions. But unlike today's new-religious sects, which are protected by scrupulously observed freedom of reli-gion laws, the prewar groups had no constitutional or other legal protection to shield them from state interference and persecution. As the new religions soon learned, in prewar Japan religious organizations were legitimate only if the government said they were. Otherwise they had no right to exist at all.

Even though the constitution in force in the 1930s allowed for freedom of religion, it was always a carefully qualified right. The constitution stated that no religion could prejudice peace and order or conflict with a citizen's duties as a subject of the state. Eventually the government got around even this limited freedom of religion by declaring the new sects to be "false religions" to which the constitution did not apply.

By the mid-1930s, senior officials had decided that the new religions were trouble. Launching a nationwide campaign aimed at "eliminating the evil cults," the government quickly established a nationwide network of "religious police" that in the late 1930s and early 1940s moved aggressively to quash the new sects, forcing a number of the larger groups to disband. The government's tough measures were supported by a large portion of the Japanese public, especially the educated classes who regarded the new religions as purveyors of superstition. Many of the new prewar sects, however, were the spiritual ancestors of the new religions flourishing in Japan today.

In an article recently published by the *Los Angeles Times*, Princeton University professor Sheldon Garon noted a striking resemblance between the prewar Omoto Kyo sect and Aum Shinri Kyo. The charismatic patriarch of Omoto Kyo organized paramilitary groups from his membership, and like Asahara's creation of his own Household Agency, flirted with lese majeste. He openly mimicked the sacrosanct emperor while reviewing the troops from atop a large white horse similar to that ridden by Emperor Hirohito during formal military reviews in the prewar years. Garon writes that Omoto Kyo's eeriest resemblance to Aum lies in its belief in an impending apocalyptic war with the United States, a war that would destroy all of Japan except for the sect's compounds.

Omoto Kyo, then, was a fascist sub-state, and the sect's headquarters was the first to be raided by police in the government's crackdown on the new religions. After jailing nearly a thousand leaders and followers, Omoto Kyo was officially disbanded and the police ordered wrecking crews to smash the sect's holy buildings into pieces smaller than a foot in size, fearing anything larger could be used to rebuild the shrines.

This brutal treatment of the new religions did not go unnoticed by the American military occupation government that took control of Japan in 1945.

Charged with turning militaristic Japan into a democratic nation, the American occupiers first eliminated the status of Shinto as the national cult, though it was allowed to remain as a non-official religion. This required only the stroke of a pen; a more difficult objective was to ensure freedom of religion for all Japanese citizens. To achieve that, the American occupiers reached back into their own history and decided that religious organizations must be given adequate, enduring protection under the constitution and law. Thus, when framing the 1947 draft of the Japanese constitution, they wrote in the strong, unambiguous guarantees of religious freedom that exist to this day.

Following the firm guidance laid down by the Americans, the Diet enacted the Religious Corporation Law in 1951, further strengthening the rights of religious organizations by giving them tax exemptions and unusually strong protection from state intrusion into their affairs. Both these developments have given postwar Japan's one hundred eighty-five thousand legally registered religious groups unprecedented legal protection and a high degree of practical and psychological autonomy. But as history repeatedly demonstrates, even the most well-intended legal protections can be abused, and when they are, it is almost always to the detriment of the public they are intended to serve.

It is ironic that the American drafters of the Japanese constitution believed, based on their own experience, that the state and its police apparatus were the primary threats to religious freedom in Japan. In many respects, the American occupiers were ignorant of the intensely bureaucratic nature of the culture which they were intent on reforming. It never occurred to them that future generations of Japanese officialdom would obey their legal dictums about freedom of religion and the sanctity of religious organizations so literally. Once it was inscribed into law that officially sanctioned religious groups were to be treated with deference and not interfered with, Japanese authorities at all levels generally complied without dissent. Though the new religions were prosecuted for criminal activities on several occasions, overall such instances were rare.

It is ironic that forty years later, Aum Shinri Kyo, a minor Japanese religious sect headed by a half-blind, soft-spoken man, would shelter securely for years under the constitutional legacy of religious freedom drafted by the Americans he so despised. Beneath the American-inspired legal umbrella that kept Japan's police at bay for many critical months, the guru would introduce religious terror to Japan and ultraterrorism to the world.

When the terrorists of the new-religious sect Aum Shinri Kyo launched the sarin attacks in the streets of Matsumoto and in the subways of Tokyo, it became the first group ever to use chemical warfare on a mass population. As Bruce Hoffman of the Center for the Study of Terrorism and Political Violence at Saint Andrews University in Scotland recently put it: "We've definitely crossed a threshold. This is the cutting edge of high-tech terrorism for the year 2000 and beyond. It's the nightmare scenario that people have quietly talked about for years coming true."

The sarin attack on Matsumoto was a precedent-shattering episode in the history of modern terrorism, but no one, either inside Japan or out, seemed to attach much significance to the fact that a highly deadly World War II–era nerve gas, an agent all but unknown in Asia, had been unleashed with deadly results in a remote mountain town in central Japan.

U.S. intelligence officers in Tokyo noted the initial news reports in the Japanese media and, after a brief flurry of interest because of the sarin angle, apparently classified the incident as a domestic Japanese issue. Instead of actively pursuing the case to learn more, they decided to wait for the Japanese authorities to tell them what had happened. And they waited. And waited. And waited. Eventually this "minor," local-interest intelligence item dropped off their radar screen altogether. Their decision to allow Japanese police to investigate and then review their findings was probably correct, as far as it went. But when no Japanese report appeared, not even an informal verbal update on the situation, U.S. intelligence should have immediately examined other options to find out what happened. The key words, after all, were *sarin nerve gas*. One easy way for American intelligence to learn more about the incident would have been to monitor the Japanese news media, which continued to hammer away at the Matsumoto story.

Nine months would drift lazily by before Japanese authorities, U.S. intelligence, and the world finally learned that in the Matsumoto attack a new and horrific threshold had been crossed in the world of terrorism, a threshold beyond which lay the potential for inflicting deaths and injuries on a scale so massive it could, in a single attack, dwarf all the combined terrorist casualty counts that had gone before.

Matsumoto was the dawn of the use of chemical weapons in terrorism, a development that had been long anticipated and feared by terrorism experts and government intelligence services around the world. Ironically, the event arrived unheralded because the terrorists who made the attack kept their silence, and the Japanese police did not immediately appreciate the gravity of the startling evidence that was mounting daily before their eyes. But in terrorism, as in much other criminal activity, there is an axiom that states if an operation is successful, it is worth repeating. The gas attack on Matsumoto was all too successful, and it was soon repeated.

Kyle Olson, an authority on chemical- and biological-arms control and counterterrorism, was the first American specialist to visit the scene of the attack in Matsumoto. His investigations into the case began months before U.S. and Japanese intelligence and international experts on terrorism even realized there was a case. Called to testify at hearings conducted by the U.S. Senate Permanent Subcommittee on Investigations in late October 1995, he was characteristically blunt about the meaning of the Matsumoto and Tokyo gas attacks. "From a security planning perspective," he declared, "I believe we must assume we have entered a world in which the chemical and biological, and perhaps even the nuclear cards are in terrorist hands. I do not believe it is coincidental that in the weeks after the Tokyo attack, terrorists in the Philippines and in Chile both threatened the use of chemical weapons."

After learning of the Matsumoto gassing, Olson was invited by a Japanese television network to visit the scenic mountain city to investigate what seemed to be a mysterious incident. On a bleak winter day in December 1994, Olson inspected the site of the gassing, interviewed witnesses and local authorities, and eventually reached a disturbing and novel conclusion: The seven Matsumoto dead were killed in a terrorist attack. Though he did not describe them as such, the Matsumoto dead and injured were, in fact, the world's first victims of ultraterrorism.

In reviewing the totality of the circumstances surrounding the Matsumoto gassing, Olson also concluded that the attack was a field test of a new sarin weapon rather than a full-blown terrorist strike. History, of course, has proven him right.

Kyle Olson was the first Western specialist to peer into the dark abyss of ultraterrorism and understand exactly what he saw. By the time he left Matsumoto, he was a different man. For him, it was apparent that the future of political violence and terrorism had irreversibly changed, and for the worst. The January 1995 report on his findings in Matsumoto contained a number of startling conclusions and predictions, all of which would prove to be deadly accurate. Again, however, this seemed to produce no sense of urgency in Japan or in the West.

"I concluded that an organized terrorist group had—for the first time—demonstrated the ability and willingness to use a weapon of mass destruction," Olson told the Senate subcommittee. "It was clear to me that the persons behind that first attack would likely strike again, and that the next target would be much higher profile. In my report, circulated in January of this year [1995], I also pointed out the symbolic and tactical vulnerability of the Tokyo subway system at rush hour to a nerve gas assault."

But while Olson had viewed the nerve-gas attack in Matsumoto with perfect vision, Japan and the rest of the world urgently needed an eye test. Until the attacks in Matsumoto and Tokyo, the specter of a terrorist group using chemical or biological weapons against a mass population was, as Bruce Hoffman stated, only a quietly discussed possibility, one that seemed more hypothetical than real given the scientific and technical complexity of successfully producing the poisonous agents and the systems needed to deliver them.

Intelligence reports of groups showing interest in such devices did come in, if infrequently, but up until Matsumoto there was no credible evidence to suggest that a terrorist group—at least none monitored by U.S., Japanese, and other intelligence sources—had actually developed chemical weapons. Aum, unfortunately, had never appeared on the intelligence "radar screen." Given the sect's history, none of which was secret, it is almost impossible to understand how Aum managed to avoid being included on one or more of the terrorist watch lists maintained by intelligence agencies around the world.

Prior to both sarin attacks, Aum's *public* activities included a strident doomsday philosophy; vitriolic anti-American rhetoric; extraordinary purchases of chemicals and sophisticated laboratory equipment from around the world; extensive connections with former Soviet weapons scientists, politicians, and military figures; unusual interest in acquiring data and research on weapons of mass destruction; the acquisition of conventional weapons technology and the machinery needed for weapons production; the purchase of a civilian version of a military helicopter and several drone aircraft; the lease of a ranch in a remote section of Australia where it mined for uranium and conducted sarin tests on sheep; the arrest of a number of Aum members for burglaries of weapons-research centers in Japan; plus numerous other criminal complaints made to the Japanese police, including murder.

Despite this disturbing list, Aum Shinri Kyo as a terrorist organization remained undetected—indeed, largely unknown—for most of its active life. During that time, it managed to build a worldwide organization and accumulate a financial fortune that was used to develop and deploy, in Matsumoto, Tokyo, and other locations, the most powerful arsenal of mass-death weapons ever possessed and used by a terrorist group.

How one small, relatively obscure religious cult operating out of Japan managed to produce some of the deadliest weapons known to man, and remain undetected while it did so, is more than just a fascinating story of modern terrorism. It is a case study of a new kind of modern terror that must be examined for the lessons it teaches. The questions posed by Aum Shinri Kyo are many, but key among them are these:

How extensive was the threat posed by the cult's religious zealots?

How did they manage to become the world's first ultraterrorist group in such a short period of time?

What did they believe, politically and spiritually, and more important, exactly what were they trying to achieve?

Finally, how prepared are governments around the world to deal with the new threat of ultraterrorism that now confronts them?

The answers to these questions, and many others, are slowly unfolding in Japan and the United States. What the world is learning from Aum Shinri Kyo about the future of terrorism is uniformly grim. Japan's police force, in many respects one of the most efficient and effective law enforcement agencies in the world, is on the cutting edge of acquiring knowledge and insight into the nature of ultraterrorism.

Aum Shinri Kyo's shadowy rise and its highly successful efforts to obtain and use weapons of mass destruction raises questions that extend well beyond the specific threat posed by Asahara and his disciples. The incredible ease with which the cult recruited a dedicated and well-trained nucleus of scientific experts is troubling, but even more troubling is the ease with which those scientists were able to gain access to the vast international supermarket of weapons and weapons technology to advance their prophet's prediction of Armageddon. How much they acquired and how much more they could have obtained remains a mystery. How much the next group of ultraterrorists can accomplish is one of many pertinent question now facing the world.

Another is the vexing problem of collecting critical intelligence in a democratic society. Central to meeting any terrorist threat is knowing that one exists, and if the deadly work of Aum Shinri Kyo demonstrates anything, it is that the West with all its democratic freedoms is uniquely vulnerable to ultraterrorism. Despite all of Aum's overt, far-flung activities, not a single Japanese or U.S. law-enforcement or intelligence agency perceived them as a terrorist group until the attack on the Tokyo subway system, eight months after the relatively more innocent Matsumoto gassing.

Undoubtedly there are a number of constitutional and cultural reasons why this was the case, but the fact remains that Aum was not very good at concealing its presence or its intentions. If an amateurish, untrained, and largely unprofessional group that left big footprints practically everywhere it went can operate so long with relative impunity, what does that say about the potential of smaller, more disciplined and professional terrorist groups who may now be tempted to adopt the more "profitable" course of ultraterrorism?

Equally disturbing is another sobering truth that must be confronted. In his testimony before the Senate subcommittee hearing on Aum Shinri Kyo, Olson made this statement: "We do not presently have the capability in place to defend our cities against a clandestine attack involving chemical and biological weapons. In the case of biological weapons, it is unlikely we would even know we had been attacked until people begin to fall. We do not have adequate vaccines on hand, nor do we have adequate planning in place at the local, state and federal levels to manage the effects of even a small, relatively unsophisticated biological warfare attack. We would probably fare somewhat better against chemical warfare, but more because of the localized nature of the weapon's effects than because of any efforts on our part. In the absence of a commitment to civilian defense, the only organized response we can realistically hope to offer the victims of a terrorist biological warfare attack is a form of triage: bury the dead, comfort the wounded, and pray for the survivors."

Aum Shinri Kyo: Where the One-Eyed Man Is King

S hoko Asahara's real name, the name he was given by his parents and recorded by them in the official Japanese family registry, is Chizuo Matsumoto. Born in 1955 in the small rural village of Yatsushiro on Japan's main southern island of Kyushu, Asahara entered the world afflicted with infantile glaucoma, a disease that left him blind in one eye and with diminished vision in the other. He was the sixth of seven children in an impoverished family living in a tiny house. His father struggled to earn a living as a craftsman who made tatami mats, the tightly woven rice-straw mats used as floor coverings in traditional Japanese homes. At age six, Asahara was sent to join an older brother, who was totally blind, at a government-funded boarding school for the blind in the city of Kumamoto, some thirty miles from his home. The family's decision to send the youngster to the government school was based strictly on need. At the school the government would fund his education and provide him with free room and board. In the late 1950s and early 1960s, times were hard in rural Kyushu; the nation's economic miracle had yet to reach the southern countryside.

As he grew older at the boarding school, Asahara discovered that his limited vision gave him an advantage over the other sightless students. In the country of the blind, the one-eyed man is king, and the adolescent Asahara quickly realized that he was king absolute. In the dark world of his fellow students, he possessed the power to shed light, to be the one others depended upon to interpret their surroundings and to guide them to places they could not find by themselves. But perhaps the most important lesson Asahara learned in the school for the blind was that power over others could be easily translated into personal influence and money. People sought out his favors and some paid to share his precious vision. If a group of students wanted to go off campus to have dinner at a local restaurant, he would guide them, but only if they agreed to pay for his meal. It was heady stuff for a young teenager obsessed with acquiring power and money. And it was also effective. By the time Asahara left high school, he had accumulated more than three thousand dollars, an extraordinary amount of money for an unemployed high-school graduate.

Asahara's limited vision was not the only advantage he had over his classmates. Teachers remember him as a boy with a well-developed physique who was good at sports, especially judo, which he began in junior high school and continued until he reached the second highest rank of pro- ficiency. Academically, Asahara was rated as better than average by some teachers, who felt he had promise. But other teachers remember a darker side to his personality. They say he was frequently disciplined for picking fights and on one occasion reportedly broke a student's eardrum in a brawl. He was also manipulative and sly when brought to task for breaking the school's rules. A former teacher recalls that after one disciplinary session Asahara lost his temper and angrily threatened to burn down the dormitory in which he lived. When he realized that he was about to be punished again for making the threat, he swiftly changed his attitude and began meekly pleading for leniency, arguing that he should not be disciplined for simply making a statement.

His early tendencies toward violence surface frequently in the recollec- tions of the Kumamoto school staff. One of his housemothers says he was a friendless, arrogant bully who was domineering and aggressively hostile. "He was bossy and violent," she said. "He was very volatile and fought with dorm supervisors whenever he was warned about minor things like switch- ing on the lights at night or taking a bath after the scheduled times."

But it was Asahara's fellow classmates who rendered the most consis- tent judgment of him as an avaricious bully. Down through the years they repeatedly rejected him when he ran for student-body president in elementary, junior high, and high school. As one bold student told him after the high-school elections, "We are afraid of you."

After graduating from high school in 1975, Asahara worked in Kumamoto as an acupuncturist, a traditional occupation for the blind in Japan. Later he became involved in a fight in which several people were seriously injured and was forced to leave Kyushu for Tokyo. Before leaving Kyushu, he confided to his brother that his great ambition was to enter the Law Faculty of Tokyo University—the Japanese equivalent of Harvard or Yale Law School —and then go into politics. A few classmates recall that he often expressed a desire to become prime minister. One of them has a more chilling recollection of Asahara declaring he wanted to create a robot kingdom, where he was supreme ruler.

In 1977, Asahara moved to the Tokyo area where he again found work as an acupuncturist and at the same time entered a prep school to study for Japan's rigorous college entrance examinations. Acquaintances say that during this period he became a devoted reader of the revolutionary philosophy of Mao Tse-tung and taught himself to read and speak Chinese. Whatever the true nature of his ambition, the grueling hours of study necessary to score high marks on the college exams did not pay off. He reportedly failed the college entrance exams and never attended college.

He met Tomoko Ishii, a young college student, on a train in the summer of 1977 while commuting to prep school. He was immediately smitten, and on their second date he announced that he would marry her. Though Tomoko told friends she thought he was "strange," the attraction was obviously mutual. They began living together that summer, were married in January 1978, and then opened a one-room Chinese herbal medicine and acupuncture clinic in the city of Funabashi, southeast of Tokyo in Chiba Prefecture. A year later a daughter was born, the first of six children. The little shop did very well, and one account of his life says he made several hundred thousand dollars selling potions such as orange peel soaked in alcohol.

From his arrival in Tokyo, Asahara began to take an interest in religion. Later he would claim to have had an out-of-body experience at age three, but 1977 seems to mark his first serious attraction to religion, a fascination that grew stronger as his personal circumstances changed. Things happened fast in the big city and in a very short time he found his ambition of attending Tokyo University shattered, plus he had a wife and child to support. Though his small business was doing well, he began to seriously question where his life was going. In his later books, Asahara described himself at this time as beset by a deep-seated anxiety, experiencing a "raging conflict of self-confidence and personal complexes" which made him feel that he "could not go on like this."

To resolve his personal crisis, he began to study traditional Chinese medicine, fortune-telling, and astrology, which are all closely linked to each other and to acupuncture. He read the writings of Shinji Takahashi, founder of the new religion GLA (God Light Association), who claimed to be an incarnation of the Buddha and also incorporated aspects of Christianity in his teachings. Soon Asahara came across the writings of such eminent Buddhist scholars as Hajime Nakamura and Fumio Masutani, in particular their books on Early or, as it is sometimes called, "Primitive" Buddhism.

Early Buddhism was a "new" thing for Asahara, a kind of idealized Buddhism not found in Japan, a Buddhism of sincere seekers who left their homes and devoted their entire lives to rigorous meditation practices aimed at attaining Nirvana, or enlightenment. By contrast, Zen Buddhism, which enjoys so much popularity in the West, elicits little more than a barely stifled yawn from most young Japanese. The same is true for the starchy traditional Buddhism practiced in Japan. To many young people the image of traditional Buddhism is one of elaborate funeral services held in ornate temples, and most show little interest in the many established sects of Japanese Buddhism.

Asahara was profoundly moved by what he discovered in the Early Buddhist writings, particularly in a group of texts called the Agon Kyo, which were supposed to record the original sermons of the Buddha in the ancient Pali language. "I read Buddhist texts and I meditated," he would later recall. "I realized that everything in the world is sin. When I realized that I myself was also a polluted person, I could not stop weeping. I also learned the spirit of self-sacrifice."

Throughout his early career, Asahara was a passionate autodidact. He loved books, but he hated the authority that a teacher would have over him, so he studied and practiced on his own. His first and only experience as an ordinary member of an organized religion came in 1981, when he joined a new religion called Agon Shu.

Agon Shu was founded in 1978 by Seiyu Kiriyama. It is best known to the general public for the dramatic Fire Ceremony it holds annually, the numerous (nearly fifty at last count) publications of its founder, and the aggressive international promotional campaign that the sect has bought from Japan's leading advertising agencies. Agon Shu is a heady cocktail of many of the elements floating around in the world of Japanese new religions. The first is the Early Buddhism that attracted Asahara. Early Buddhism emphasized eliminating "karmic obstructions"—the bad mental and physical habits that prevent enlightenment—through long, involved, step-by-step meditations. In order to break the cycle of rebirth into a world of suffering and thereby achieve Nirvana, both Agon Shu and Aum place great importance on freeing oneself from bad karma.

A second element of Agon Shu was Tantric Buddhism. Now practiced mainly in Tibet, Nepal, and by small groups of converts in America and Europe, Tantric Buddhism emphasizes visualization of deities; a strong master-disciple link; complicated meditation programs, aided by a series of initiations from master to disciple; the enjoyment, if not the pursuit, of superhuman powers; and in some esoteric and advanced teachings, sexual and other practices that transcend the boundaries of conventional morality. Asahara found all of these concepts highly appealing.

Agon Shu also taught the use of the ancient Hindu system of *kundalini* yoga and Taoist yoga from China. To this Kiriyama added a pseudo-scientific theory of the brain, and his writings are filled with quotes from brain theorists and New Age scientists of many stripes. Kiriyama taught his followers that if they successfully applied all of these "tools" it was possible to become a superhuman being who, literally, would never age or die. Judged against that lofty standard, Aum's early religious goals were modest.

By all accounts, Asahara was a sincere and hard-working member of Agon Shu. He faithfully attended training sessions at one of its centers in Tokyo. In his later writing about this period, Asahara claims that he was deeply involved in Agon Shu practice, particularly a ritual called the "thousand-day offering," which required forty minutes of daily devotional activities carried out over one thousand consecutive days. Asahara would later complain that his Agon Shu practice only increased his "karmic obstructions," but even during the toughest times he maintained the daily devotional cycle to the end of its required three years. During this period he also claims to have experienced the *"kundalini* awakening," a yogic state in which the body's male and female essences are united to produce a higher level of consciousness.

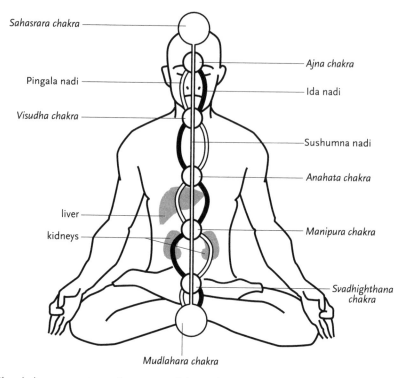

Sahasrara chakra

Ajna chakra

Pingala nadi

Ida nadi

Visudha chakra

Sushumna nadi

Anahata chakra

liver

kidneys

Manipura chakra

Svadhighthana chakra

Mudlahara chakra

The chakras, or centers of energy, and the nadis, or channels of breath, as described in the practice of kundalini yoga (from *The Secret Method of Developing Superpowers*).

Disaster struck in 1982, however, when Asahara was arrested on suspicion of peddling fake Chinese cures—specifically, the magic orange peels soaked in alcohol—which he sold for four hundred to six hundred dollars each. He was jailed for twenty days, after which the court found him guilty of the charge—which he vigorously denied—and levied a fine of two thousand dollars. Friends said Asahara was devastated by his conviction, a criminal felony, and many see it as a major turning point in his life. Following a highly critical local newspaper article detailing his arrest and conviction, his business quickly went broke and he was too embarrassed to face his neighbors. For some time after the trial and bankruptcy, he and his wife lived a hermit-like existence, only venturing outside at night to buy food and other essentials. This dramatic about-face in his life pushed him more forcefully in the direction of religion.

Asahara quit Agon Shu in 1984, taking a dozen or so of the sect's members with him. He blamed the "thousand-day offering" practice for his misfortunes, but during his studies as a member of Agon Shu he discovered something that would be of immense value in the immediate future—a do-it-yourself salvation manual called the Yoga Sutra, an ancient Hindu text that described the stages of yoga practice in great detail. With the small group that followed him from Agon Shu, he opened a yoga training center, Aum, Inc., in Tokyo's bustling Shibuya district. "Aum," often written "om," is a mystic Sanskrit syllable that is often chanted in yogic meditation, or at the beginning and end of prayers; it was a perfectly natural name for a yoga club. Asahara appointed himself managing director, and named his wife and a devoted follower, Hisako Ishii, directors of the corporation. In addition to holding yoga training classes and seminars, the company also sold health drinks and started a small publishing enterprise.

Because of his good physical conditioning, Asahara was an excellent yoga practitioner and teacher who became known among his students for his exceptional control over his breathing technique. He was very different in appearance, too, from the fat, pale, long-haired guru of later years. Photos at this time show a slim, reasonably shorn, muscular young man who may indeed have been a charismatic yoga teacher. According to early members, at this time Aum was a fairly relaxed and casual group without a rigid hierarchy.

"There was no religious atmosphere," one member recalls. "It was a fun gathering, you know, 'Let's all have fun with yoga and acquire supernatural powers.' We were members, not followers, and Asahara wasn't a religious leader, just this guy who was our yoga teacher."

The goal that Asahara held out to his followers was the *kundalini* awakening he had experienced and which was taught in his new guidebook, the Yoga Sutra.

The center prospered during the next two years as its ranks swelled to more than three thousand followers. Sometime in 1985, Asahara began to create a new identity for himself as a charismatic leader of supreme spiritual accomplishments with a divine mission. In the early part of the year he claims to have levitated for the first time. When the popular magazine *Twilight Zone* ran photographs of Asahara levitating, he became a focus of interest for many of Japan's young spiritual seekers. Several members of Aum later recalled that the article in *Twilight Zone* led them to seek out Aum.

Asahara also began to have meetings with the gods about this time. He went to Mount Goyo in Iwate Prefecture in northern Japan to visit a shrine that possessed a text supposedly given by the gods to the prewar historian and rabid anti-Semite Katsuisa Sakai. The text is an account of Armageddon, the catastrophic battle between the forces of good and evil at the end of the world, and there is little doubt that this book planted the seeds of what would later become Asahara's apocalyptic vision of the future.

Asahara also reported that in spring of 1985, while meditating on the beach at Miura in Kanagawa Prefecture just south of Tokyo, he was visited by the Hindu god Shiva, who appointed him "the god of light who leads the armies of the gods" and charged him with building an ideal society made up of those who had attained psychic powers, a society called the Kingdom of Shambhala.

The Kingdom of Shambhala is an ancient concept appearing in Islam, Hinduism, and Buddhism, but Asahara's knowledge of it derived from a Tantric Buddhist text in which Shambhala is portrayed as a hidden valley located somewhere in Northeast Asia—a Shangri-la for spiritual adepts. According to this tradition, at some unspecified future date a messiah-king will appear in Shambhala, defeat the infidels in a final war, and establish a universal reign of Buddhism. Asahara's seaside epiphany was the origin of his claim to be a messiah and his leadership role in the Armageddon, or final war, which would destroy Japan.

It was also in 1985 that Asahara introduced his first "initiation ritual." In Hindu and Buddhist meditation, initiation is a rite that the master performs for his students to speed their spiritual progress. Asahara selected a Hindu ritual, *shaktipat*, which he performed himself. In the rite, the guru places his thumb on the follower's forehead where the yogic "third eye" is said to be located. Aum teachings held that *shaktipat* injected the guru's positive spiritual power into the follower and at the same time triggered a discharge of the follower's bad karma into the body of the guru. In later years, it was widely rumored that Asahara's health was suffering because he had performed the rite so often, and that he would soon stop administering it. Aum's aggressive marketing staff used the rumors to heighten demand for the costly ritual.

"If you want to be emancipated in this life," the sect's bulletins urged, "you must receive *shaktipat*. There are only 595 times of Master's *shaktipat* left. Probably his *shaktipat* will cease this August [1988]. If you want to receive it, earn sixty credits [of training] early."

In addition to the sixty training credits required for eligibility, which members had to pay for, there was the basic *shaktipat* charge of five hundred dollars. In August 1988, Asahara stopped performing the rite after it was reported that he had suffered considerable physical damage. The task then fell to his leading disciples, who required only thirty training credits and a more modest fee of three hundred dollars.

In 1986, the group's name was changed to Aum Shinsen no Kai, or "The Aum Group of Mountain Wizards," and its headquarters moved to Setagaya Ward, a more suburban Tokyo area southwest of Shibuya. It was there that Asahara published his first book, *The Secret Method for Developing Supernatural Powers*, and the relaxed atmosphere of the Shibuya yoga center began to disappear. In its place, the roots of the "Aum Nation" were sprouting.

In the summer of 1986, with the yoga center firmly established and growing, Asahara left Japan on his first journey abroad, an extended trip to India and the Himalayas where he studied Hinduism and Buddhism. During his travels he met with senior Indian and Tibetan religious leaders and visited a number of Tibetan monasteries. Asahara played the role of the "Ugly Japanese" with great success on his travels in India. A young Japanese man studying at one of the Indian ashrams recalls that Asahara and his group came barging into the center very late one evening, uninvited, unannounced, and demanding to be admitted as students. As foreigners, the brusque Japanese were given considerable leeway by the tolerant Indians, but Asahara soon managed to abuse even those polite concessions. In a few days he was heaping criticism on the other meditators, insisting that he was far more advanced than they and demanding that the ashram's guru teach him more advanced practices.

His embarrassed fellow Japanese reports how Asahara built a photo-album resume while abroad, one that would serve him very well when he returned to Japan. When the time to leave the ashram came, Asahara asked to have his picture taken with the guru, who only agreed with a very reluctant "If you insist." As a final insult, Asahara threw his arm over the guru's shoulder just as the shutter snapped even though he knew full well that it was extremely rude to touch a guru. In 1995, when the Japanese police finally arrested him, among his first words were, "No one is allowed to touch the guru's body."

On his return to Japan, Asahara announced that while meditating in the Himalayas, and as a result of eight previous years of ascetic experiences in Buddhism and yoga, he attained Nirvana. He also immediately began work to cash in on his wafer-thin credentials as a self-proclaimed "internationally known authority on religion." An important first step was writing several works on the supernatural and mysticism that he later used to launch a clever public-relations campaign aimed at getting himself and his fledgling sect before the public eye.

Demonstrating an impressive flair for public relations, Asahara leaped headlong into Japan's media mainstream. He soon became a regular guest on late-night television talk shows, on which he appeared with leaders of other new religions and with well-known university professors of religion, several of whom touted him as a sincere and important new religious leader. Some of the professors would later make humiliating public apologies for their lack of judgment and one was pressured to resign his position.

By all accounts Asahara was a brilliant television performer who was able to shift from pronouncements about the future delivered in lofty tones to tears of compassion for all suffering things. He understood that by successfully courting the media's attention, the media would create the public persona he needed to promote himself and his group. His strategy was very effective, and soon increasing numbers of earnest new followers were flocking to the door of his small yoga center in Tokyo.

The year 1987 was crucial for Asahara and his followers. In February he visited Dharmsala, the north Indian center for Tibetan exiles where the Dalai Lama is often in residence. Asahara was able to meet the Dalai Lama, and he described their session together.

"Imagine my delight at being able to meditate with His Holiness, the Dalai Lama," he wrote later. "And in His Holiness's private meditation room! . . . 'I'll sit here where I always sit; you sit there,' he instructed me. 'Let me give you a Buddha image.' . . . After a few minutes of loud, deep breathing, all traces of the Dalai Lama vanished. He must have completely stopped his breath. At that moment, the astral vision of the golden face of Shakyamuni Buddha radiated from my *ajuna chakra*. The vision persisted steadily, without a flicker. 'Ah, this is the Buddha image the Dalai Lama was talking about,' I thought. I continued my meditation."

Asahara also claimed that the Dalai Lama had told him that Buddhism was about to disappear in Japan and that he should spread true religion there. Asahara had his picture taken with the Dalai Lama, and this became the centerpiece of his PR effort. Armed with the books and his photos with the Dalai Lama, he personally made the rounds of editorial offices of a number of religious, New Age, and mass-market magazines. Sensing public interest in an internationally respected Japanese guru, the magazines published the photos and Asahara was on his way. The Dalai Lama, it should be noted, has a different recollection of Asahara's visit. During a 1995 visit to Japan he denied making any endorsement of Aum Shinri Kyo or Asahara.

In July of 1987, Asahara decided it was time to change the name of the group once again, this time to Aum Shinri Kyo, or Aum Supreme Truth. But more importantly, Asahara's popularity and the large influx of new members was putting his ecletic religion to the test. Many of his leading followers were catching up to him in their spiritual achievement, attaining *kundalini* awakening and whatever other new tests he set them to. It was time to change the rules and set higher religious goals for them to aspire to.

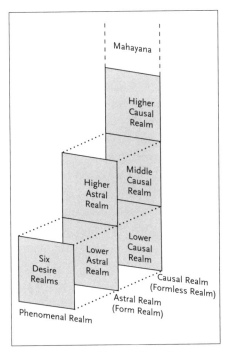

The three levels of being adopted as a guide for meditation practice by Aum Shinri Kyo (from *Mahayana Sutra*).

First, he added several layers of cosmic existence that they would have to work through, then he introduced a new set of practices and goals, all chosen from ancient Buddhist meditation systems. But his disciples stayed hot on his trail. In May 1988, Hisako Ishii, now known by her Buddhist name, Great Master Kheema, attained the *maha mudra,* Asahara's most recently set goal. This put her one step behind Asahara in spiritual accomplishment. It was this pressure from his overachieving disciples and Asahara's determination to keep the place of Enlightened One to himself that transformed Aum from a yoga club into a charismatic religion.

From the beginning Aum, like Agon Shu, linked individual salvation to the salvation of society, and Japan as a whole. But in 1988, Asahara expanded his vision, calling not only for the salvation of Japan, but of the world. In an

Aum recruiting pamphlet published that year, the sect laid out its scheme for bringing happiness to all mankind: "This kingdom (Shambhala), ruled by the god Shiva, is a world where only those souls which have attained the complete truth of the universe can go. In Shambhala, the ascetic practices of messianic persons have made great advances in order to lead souls to *gedatsu* (emancipation) and save them. Master Asahara has been reborn from there into the human world so that he might take up his mission as a messiah. Therefore, the Master's efforts to embody truth throughout the human world have been sanctioned by the great will of the god Shiva.

"Let us take a look, however, at the situation of Japan and the world. Clearly we face a very dangerous situation, due to the rapid growth of egoism. Master Asahara's prophecies, such as a worsening of the trade friction between the United States and Japan, an increase in defense spending, and abnormalities in the Fuji volcanic region and the Pacific Plate have already proved true.

"If we allow the demonic energy to increase, it will be extremely difficult to prevent the slide towards a nuclear war at the end of the century.

"For that reason Aum Shinri Kyo's plan to transform Japan into Shambhala was presented. This plan is without equal in its scope, as it wants to extend Aum's sacred sphere throughout all of Japan, making Japan the base for the salvation of the whole world by fostering the development of multitudes of holy people. This plan cannot be realized without the help of our believers. Please come and join us!

"Wouldn't you like to help to build a society based on truth, and help more and more souls to live the life of truth, leading to *gedatsu* and life in a higher world? Wouldn't you like help the world avoid disaster and build a future of happiness? Let us combine our efforts, and translate into action the great will of the god Shiva and our guru, Master Asahara.

"The plan to transform Japan into Shambhala is the first step towards making the whole world Shambhala. And your participation in this plan will result in great merit and lead you to a higher world."

The pamphlet then provided an "Outline of the Plan," which includes details for the establishment of a type of commune called "The Lotus Village":

"This means the construction of an Aum village, so that everyone can live a life founded on truth. We will build a completely independent society, providing everything from clothing, food, and housing to a place for religious practice, medical and educational facilities, weddings and funerals, and opportunities for employment. We will also establish facilities for medical, scientific and agricultural research, so that it will become a place to create a culture of truth."

This utopian optimism was widespread among Aum members at the time and its appeal to Japan's alienated younger generations, a group estimated by some sociologists to represent ten percent of the nation's youth, was both persuasive and appealing. In the summer of 1988, Aum completed its new headquarters at Fujinomiya, in Shizuoka Prefecture. When Hisako Ishii spoke at the dedication ceremony, she called it Aum's first "Lotus Village." But the purchase of large amounts of land and the construction of other Lotus Villages required considerable sums of money, and Aum set out to raise it—from its members.

The first thing the sect needed was more members, and Asahara instituted a new mechanism for increasing the group's membership. Recruiting new members into the sect became a high-priority spiritual requirement for those who had already joined.

But who were these new recruits, and why did they harken to the call of a half-blind guru with a bizarre plan for saving the world? By the late 1980s, Japan's "Bubble Era" of economic growth was in full swing, boosting the nation's per capita income to the highest level in the world. But the sustained rise in affluence also widened a number of long-festering generational fissures. One sociologist says that those in their their twenties in the late 1980s were the first young Japanese to be free of financial pressures. They were Japan's "fun generation," and their attitudes toward life—borrowing, spending, leisure, and the virtues of hard work and loyalty—were quite different from those of their parents, and worlds away from those of their hardworking grandparents.

But there was also a serious, introspective side to many of these young people. As some of the newer generations graduated from college and entered the work force they began to have ideas and questions that their education had not prepared them for. In examining their own lives and the society in which they lived, many felt lost and wondered whether job security and social conformity were all there is to life. Seeking answers, they often naively reached out to anyone or any group that professed to have a solution or held out the promise of involving them in something bigger than themselves. Earnest and sincere, once they made the leap to a new faith, they wrapped themselves in it with the single-mindedness of people who never intended to be lost again.

But why would young doctors, scientists, and highly trained technicians join a group like Aum Shinri Kyo? Anthropologist and author Sheila Johnson, in a recent artcle published in the *Los Angeles Times,* says the answer seems to be "precisely because they are experts. They are trained in one specific, technical field, but this does not necessarily make them wise. Nor does it necessarily make them happy. These people, when they join such a movement, are among its most dangerous members, because while they may not be the most violent, they may be the most able to plan and carry out dangerous missions."

The recruiting success of Shoko Asahara—and many of Japan's other new sect leaders—was due to the fact that that he understood perfectly that Japan's young were searching for meaning and value in their existence, that in order to be happy, to have real fulfillment in their lives, they needed a spiritual world view they could claim for their own. Asahara knew, too, that in the spiritual world-view business he could conjure with the best of them. By the late 1980s, he was well on the way to proving it.

In establishing his new recruiting policy, Asahara was doubly clever. He not only exploited the free labor of junior members as recruiters, but he actually forced them to purchase the flyers, handouts, and books that they used to bring new members into the fold. With his natural instinct for PR, he also insisted that only attractive and appealing members be assigned as recruiters.

Around this time, the membership was divided into two groups, lay believers and monastics. Lay believers lived and worked in the outside world, and attended Aum seminars, lectures, and practice sessions after work and on weekends. They were strongly encouraged to make large and regular donations to Aum. Anything was accepted, but cash was preferred. In addition, they paid for various religious services and training, including a series of rites of initiation. The *shaktipat* ritual was first offered to members in 1985. As each year went by, Aum's menu of religious aids grew longer and ever more costly.

For example, there was the *purusha,* a small ceramic badge engraved with the Aum symbol and containing "the Master's energy"; its purchase price was one thousand dollars. Then there was the "*Purusha*-model Pandora's Box" for one hundred dollars, designed to "purify the terrestrial elements"

TRAINING COURSES

GENERAL FEES

Registration fee..¥30,000
Monthly fee..¥3,000
Change of course fee...¥5,000

YOGA COURSES

Beginning course (10 sessions)...¥30,000
Intermediate course (20 sessions)...¥35,000
Advanced course (20 sessions)...¥80,000
Correspondance courses
  Part One (60 days)..¥70,000
  Part Two (60 days)..¥70,000
Evening seminar (one 6-hour session)....................................¥6,000
Intensive overnight seminar...¥7,000–8,000

ADVANCED COURSE FOR SUPERNATURAL POWERS

Comprehensive program (two sessions/month)..................¥15,000
Initiation (one session)...¥15,000
Correspondance course..¥15,000
Seminar..¥20,000

INTENSIVE "MADNESS" SEMINAR..¥220,000 and up

SHAKTIPAT

From Asahara...60 credits and ¥50,000
From Asahara's disciples...............................30 credits and ¥30,000

INITIATION RITUALS

Initiation of Love...¥300,000
Bardo Initiation...¥500,000
Initiation of the Blood...¥1,000,000
Secret Initiation..more than ¥1,000,000

RELIGIOUS ITEMS

Purusha-model Pandora's box..¥10,000
Aum seminar videotapes..¥ 15,000
Sandalwood rosary..¥15,000
Miracle Pond (Asahara's bathwater, 200cc).........................¥22,000
Purusha badge...¥100,000
Yoga and training videotape sets.........................¥80,000–400,000
Perfect Salvation Initiation headset..........¥1,000,000 / month rental

A menu of Aum Shinri Kyo's training courses and religious services.

by releasing a perfumed smell. The "Miracle Pond," Asahara's bath water, which members were to drink for maximum effect, sold for one thousand dollars per liter. The "Initiation of Love" was a bottle of Asahara's "cultured DNA," which was priced at three thousand dollars. The most expensive initiation offered was the "Blood Initiation," a small vial of blood, supposedly from Asahara himself, to be drunk by the member. It cost about ten thousand dollars.

Later rituals included the Bardo Initiation. Bardo is the state between death and reincarnation described in the *Tibetan Book of the Dead*. This cost more than five thousand dollars, and according to one member who purchased it, included an intravenous drip. The "Initiation of Christ" involved taking a drug manufactured by Aum—illegal drugs were to play an increasing role in many spheres of Aum religious practice from about 1993 on. Perhaps the most photogenic initiation was the "PSI (Perfect Salvation Initiation) telepathy headgear." This was a helmetlike affair with electric wiring that supposedly synchronized a follower's brain waves with Asahara's. The PSI telepathy headgear could not be purchased, but members were permitted to rent a set for a fee of ten thousand dollars per month. The PSI alone earned Aum something around two billion yen, or about twenty million dollars.

The pièce de résistance was "The Ultimate Donation to the Sonshi." The believer was asked to pledge a total figure that he would donate to Asahara over his lifetime, and then was given the generous option of paying for it in a lump sum or installments.

Constant pressure was also exerted on lay members to become monastics. Asahara claimed that high levels of enlightenment could only be obtained by monastics who left their families and devoted every moment to religious practice in a sect commune. This policy did not, of course, apply to Asahara and his family, who were the very core of the organization. Aum reaped a huge financial reward from each person who became a monastic. This is how they did it.

Each new monastic was required to swear an oath to "trust my mind and body as well as all properties to Shiva and Asahara Sonshi and sever all connections with this world." They also signed a release stating that "Whatever happens [to me], there shall be no responsibility on the part of Aum or Asahara. It is solely my will to choose the path of practice; only I am responsible." The monastics moved into an Aum commune, where they were given room and—very paltry—board. Meals were served once a day and consisted of bland, overcooked, cheap vegetables, with an occasional package of Aum's instant ramen as a treat. They were allowed to bring one bag and two cardboard boxes of personal belongings, mostly clothes. Everything else they owned became the property of Aum.

Once inside, contacts with the outside world ceased; even letters and phone calls to relatives and friends were forbidden. All property, including cash, belongings, real estate, royalties, and any intangible properties were donated to Aum. To insure that nothing of value was overlooked, the sect developed detailed procedures for handing over property, starting with an exhaustive inventory of personal worth: (1) Cash and cash equivalents, such as postage stamps and telephone cards; (2) Bank accounts with amounts, account numbers, PIN numbers, and personal seals; (3) Stocks and bonds, including names, amounts, purchase date, purchase price, maturity date, and current value; (4) Life insurance policies, with full values and cancellation rebates; (5) Real estate, including addresses and values. Aum also required that all debts, such as telephone bills, taxes, and student loans, were to be paid before entering a commune. Immediately after the inventory whatever could be turned into cash was quickly converted.

Once inside, the monastics devoted their days to a combination of "hard practice"—various meditation regimens—and what Aum called "*waaku*," that is, work. This work also brought money into Aum's coffers. In the early nineties the group founded a large number of businesses in which its monastics were used as a free labor force.

With the publication of *The Day of Destruction* in 1989, Asahara offered his interpretation of the New Testament Book of Revelation, or "John's Apocalypse" as it is sometimes referred to, in which he predicted that the Soviet Union would collapse in the year 2004, China would be destroyed at the end of 2004 or the beginning of 2005, and that "the American president elected in 1995 [sic] and the Soviet Party Secretary at that time might lead the world to Armageddon." Of course, the Soviet Union collapsed well ahead of Asahara's timetable, the American presidential elections take place in 1996, and Soviet Communist Party Secretaries are now a subject for historians. The book also predicted that Europe would survive Armageddon and that a "super-human race," origins unspecified, would rule the world.

Apparently pleased with his first venture into apocalyptic literature, Asahara published a sequel later the same year titled *From Destruction to Emptiness: A Sequel to the Day of Destruction*. Gloomier and more pessimistic than the first book, Asahara lamented in this work that despite his best efforts he was running behind schedule and the hour had grown short for mankind. "It will be possible to limit the destruction if Aum works at producing large numbers of people who have reached Emancipation," he wrote. "It will be possible to limit those who die at Armageddon to one-fourth of the world's population. However, right now my plan for salvation is running behind schedule and the percentage of those who will survive is getting lower and lower. It is already impossible to limit the victims to under one-fourth."

Asahara's growing fascination with Armageddon did not mean that Aum Shinri Kyo was on the verge of becoming a millenarian sect. If Aum had been truly millenarian, it would have regarded the approaching end of the world as unavoidable; there is nothing in its public rhetoric that suggests this. As the quote demonstrates, Aum's apocalyptic doctrine had changed from one of prevention of Armageddon to that of assuring the survival of a small number of chosen people. Asahara was clear that prevention of Armageddon was not possible, but he still believed—if one is to take him at his word—that Aum Shinri Kyo could save people outside the sect and intended to do so. Equally clear was the fact that religion alone would not be enough to do the trick. Something more was needed, and as usual, Asahara was not without ideas about how to proceed.

The drive for political power for Aum began at a meeting in late July 1989. Assembled around Asahara were his closest advisers and disciples. The subject under discussion: the future of Aum and its plans to save the world. During the discussion it became apparent to everyone that religious activities alone would not be enough to advance the sect's plan of salvation. This was an astonishing conclusion that confirmed, at a certain level, the failure of the sect's faith system, but that not so subtle point went unremarked by those present.

Asahara had been mulling over this dilemma and was ready with the answer. The sect, he announced, would field a slate of twenty-five candidates in the next election of the lower house of the Japanese parliament. Asahara himself would stand for a seat. He was supremely confident of victory.

Thus it was decided. In August Aum Shinri Kyo formed a political party called Shinrito, ("Truth Party") and large amounts of money were poured into campaign literature and promotion activities.

Asahara could not know that with this bold stride onto the public stage, he was setting a collision course between his sect and the society in which it thrived. There is a famous Japanese proverb that goes, "The nail that sticks out is hammered down." The increased visibility of Aum as it bid for a political role was the beginning of the end, the first step down the path that would lead it to paranoid isolation and ultraterrorism. The first big problem to arise had to do with the parents of the sect's members.

Aum's practice of having its commune members sever all links to the secular world, including contact with their parents, relatives, and friends, aroused anger and suspicion. Parents of the Aum commune members were outraged at being denied access to their children, and they were at least as outraged at Aum's policy of confiscating all the financial assets of members. Parents watched as their children gave up savings that *should* have been used for a wedding ceremony or education; wives or husbands were aghast when their partners disappeared with the family nest egg. In society at large, big trouble was brewing for Aum, and at a particularly bad time.

Aum had applied for recognition as a religious corporation, and to Asahara and his top advisers it seemed as if the government officials were dragging their feet in granting approval. They interpreted this as the work of the unhappy parents of Aum commune members and a sympathetic Diet member who had been won over to their cause. The sect's response was to stage a series of vigorous protest demonstrations outside the government offices during which they charged officials with religious persecution and oppression. On August 25, 1989, the Tokyo Metropolitan Government reluctantly gave in and recognized Aum Shinri Kyo as an official religion. Though this new official status was a major victory for the sect, its problems with Japanese society were mounting.

In October 1989 Asahara stated that Aum Shinri Kyo had a total of three hundred eighty monastic commune members and approximately four thousand regular members. Also in October, the popular mass-circulation magazine *Sunday Mainichi* began publication of a series of extremely critical articles under the title "Aum Shinri Kyo's Insanity," in which it attacked the sect for its aggressive recruitment activities and solicitation of forced donations. This unpleasant bit of publicity represented a major threat to the sect. Aum may have been given recognition as an official religion, but it had yet to get through a one-year probationary period. A legal setback would doom Aum both in terms of its official status and at the ballot box in February, when the Aum slate of candidates would be running for office in the Diet.

Asahara, as we have seen, panicked and ordered the murder of Tsutsumi Sakamoto, the man he believed was a major threat to the sect and its political ambitions. Following the disappearance of Sakamoto and his family, the parent's organization, The Victims of Aum Shinri Kyo, remained active and would prove a legal thorn in the sect's side for years to come. But it lacked the drive and intelligence that Sakamoto had provided. Asahara, relieved of the threat to his small empire, was now free to concentrate on the coming elections and the fulfillment of his early schoolboy dreams of achieving real political power in Japan.

Countdown to Armageddon

um ran a remarkable political campaign in the first months of 1990 that first amused, then appalled, and finally frightened many in Japan. The campaign began with a kick-off rally at a rented auditorium in Nakano Ward, Tokyo. Shoko Asahara and the other twenty-four Aum candidates were lined up across the wide stage, but the only speakers at the rally were Asahara himself and his wife, who gave a short introductory speech. Durga Seitashi—Asahara's eldest daughter, named after the Hindu goddess of death and destruction—presented her father with a bouquet of flowers, in the hallowed Japanese campaign tradition.

It was odd indeed that none of the other candidates spoke, especially given their glowing resumes touted in Shinrito (the Aum political party) campaign literature: so many elite universities, so many bright young people. Young is the keyword. The average age of the Aum slate was a little less than thirty, at least three or four decades younger than most Japanese politicians. Another distinguishing feature of the Aum candidates was that they were all running under their "holy names": Maitreya, Mahakassappa, Ajita, Jivaka, Milarepa, Naropa. Most of these were names of the Buddha's leading disciples, taken from the ancient scriptures of Early Buddhism; others

HOLY NAME	DISTRICT	SEX/AGE	EMPLOYMENT/EDUCATION
1. Shoko Asahara	Tokyo 4th	M (34)	Sect founder Kumamoto Prefecture School for the Blind
2. Maha Kheema	Tokyo 3rd	F (29)	Nissan Fire and Marine Insurance Company Industrial Efficiency Junior College
3. Maitreya	Tokyo 5th	M (27)	Aerospace Development Group Waseda University (Engineering)
4. Maha Angulimala	Tokyo 11th	M (29)	Nishin Pharmaceutical Company Onoda Industrial High School
5. Milarepa	Tokyo 7th	M (25)	Marusan Ai, Inc. Aichi University School of Law
6. Sakula	Tokyo 11th	F (28)	Nissan Fire and Marine Insurance Company Bunka Women's Junior College
7. Kisa Gotami	Tokyo 7th	F (35)	Clerical worker Jissen Women's Junior College
8. Punna-mantaniputta	Saitama 3rd	M (37)	Acupuncturist Tokyo Acupuncture High School
9. Machig Lapdrön	Tokyo 8th	F (29)	Illustrator Fukui Prefectural Ashiba High School
10. Manjushrimitra	Tokyo 5th	M (31)	Kobe Copper Works Osaka University (Engineering)
11. Mahakasappa	Tokyo 10th	M (34)	Designer Asagaya Art School
12. Kankha-Revata	Tokyo 1st	M (28)	Hitachi Manufacturing Waseda University
13. Marpa	Tokyo 2nd	M (38)	Real estate Chiba Industrial College
14. Naropa	Tokyo 9th	M (28)	Daiwa House Shibaura Industrial College
15. Uruvela-kasappa	Tokyo 6th	M (30)	Musician Tokyo College of Music
16. Siha	Saitama 1st	M (31)	Dance school Nihon University (Science)
17. Vangisa	Saitama 2nd	M (31)	Tosho Printing Company Hokkaido University
18. Sukka	Tokyo 2nd	F (25)	Waseda University
19. Jivaka	Chiba 4th	M (29)	Kyoto University Graduate School
20. Ajita	Kanagawa 2nd	M (25)	Tokyo University of Fine Arts and Music
21. Tissa	Tokyo 10th	F (34)	Hair stylist Iwamizawa Barber & Beauty School
22. Dharmavajiri	Tokyo 9th	F (26)	Freelance announcer Kyoto College of Education High School
23. Vajiratissa	Kanagawa 3rd	M (27)	Doctor, Osaka Railroad Hospital Kyoto Prefectural School of Medicine
24. Bhaddakapilani	Tokyo 6th	F (28)	Teacher Toyama University
25. Sanjaya	Saitama 5th	M (25)	Waseda University Master's Course

The Shinrito slate for the Lower House elections in spring 1990.

were the names of famous Tibetan monks of ages past. To get an idea of the equivalent, it was as if a U.S. political party ran of slate of candidates with names like Peter, Paul, Luke, John, and Mark, with a few Marys, Magdalenes, and others thrown in.

Asahara gave one of his typically rambling speeches, in which he laid out the five main points of the party platform: (1) the repeal of the new sales tax; (2) educational reform; (3) increased welfare benefits; (4) medical reform; and (5) democratization of the political system. The guru's speech was followed by the appearance of about thirty members wearing giant Asahara masks, who then danced to a song called the "Asahara March."

Why did Aum run twenty-five candidates? Because Japanese election law accords special privileges to a party with that minimum number, privileges such as permission to make election speeches in public places, drive loudspeaker cars through the streets blaring campaign promises, put up posters and hand out pamphlets, and distribute campaign literature in public buildings. All of these were also ideal methods for publicizing Aum Shinri Kyo and its message to a broader public, and Shinrito literature placed more emphasis on Aum than on its slate of candidates.

Some question whether Asahara really expected to win the election. Shoko Egawa, a journalist who has followed Aum since the late 1980s, suggests that the whole thing was no more than a massive public relations campaign for Aum, the real intent being an increase in membership and, with it, the all-important donations that kept the Aum juggernaut running. It can certainly be said that if Asahara truly expected to win, he was already so far divorced from everyday reality that there was no turning back.

The Aum candidates campaigned in the diaphanous white robes of the sect (except for Asahara, who showed a preference for imperial purple under a gauzy gold overrobe), which was a picture in itself given the conservative gray suits preferred by Japanese politicians. But what attracted the most attention—and finally turned the most people off—were the groups of Aum followers who gathered in front of subway stations and danced about wearing huge papier-mâché heads of Asahara Shoko, singing the Shinrito election song:

Shoko, Shoko, Shoko-Shoko-Shoko, Asahara Shoko
Shoko, Shoko, Shoko-Shoko-Shoko, Asahara Shoko

Japan's Shoko, the world's Shoko, the earth's Shoko, Shoko, Shoko
He rises now, shining brilliantly
Let's put ourselves in the hands of this youthful ace
To protect our Japan, we need his strength
Shoko, Shoko, Asahara Shoko

The sight of the giant, bearded heads bobbing around may have amused Japanese voters at first—Japanese campaigns are pretty dull and predictable stuff—but in the end the whole thing smacked so powerfully of a twisted idolatry of Asahara that the effect was decidedly chilling.

In February 1990 the results at the polls were as predictably humiliating as in the days when Asahara ran for office at the school for the blind. Not a single Aum candidate came close to election. The entire slate garnered a mere 1,783 votes. Asahara immediately cried foul, heatedly denouncing the vote as rigged, and stated that Aum was considering the legal option of contesting it. But the undeniable truth was that Aum had from the beginning only the barest chance of electing any of its candidates, and even those low prospects were dimmed by its bizarrely misguided campaign antics.

Asahara was not the only one disappointed by the election results. The campaign had been a major drain on Aum's finances, and the ridicule to which Aum exposed itself resulted in a major drop in membership. In an attempt to rally, unify, and increase the membership—especially of the communes—Asahara dreamed up the infamous Ishigakijima Seminar in April 1990. First he made a dramatic doomsday prediction that an unspecified disaster was about to occur in Japan, with the approach of the Comet Austin. The word was put out that he would divulge the details of the disaster at the seminar, and that only those who attended would be saved, throwing many Aum members into a panic.

The seminar was described as free—with a travel fee of three hundred thousand yen (some members have testified that the travel fee was originally announced as thirty thousand yen, but after the seminar they were charged ten times that amount). Members were picked up at various Japanese ports by a ship, but any indication of their destination was withheld. Finally they found themselves landed on the tiny island of Ishigakijima, one of the Ryukyu Islands (which include Okinawa), so far to Japan's southeast extremity as to be only miles from Taiwan.

The Aum forces occupied a public campsite on the beach, blocking off the area to all outsiders. Though sect leaders had reserved facilities on the island for the seminar, they had done so under a false name, and had also committed so many other violations of the rules that they were denied use of the buildings. The more than one thousand two hundred members ended up camping out on the beach in cheap vinyl tents—which were promptly blown away by a gale-force rain storm that arose that night. After taking shelter wherever they could find it, including horse trailers and old shipping containers, the attendees eventually found lodging in small family-run inns in the area. Meanwhile Asahara and his retinue flew off in a private plane to luxurious quarters farther inland.

The seminar on Ishigakijima was finally canceled, and everyone was loaded back on the boat. There Asahara delivered his message to the faithful, several of whom found it not worth the trip. One member relates, "All he said was that with Haley's Comet in 1986 and Comet Austin this year, something was going to happen. And we paid three hundred thousand yen to hear that, plus took off work. Some even quit their jobs." But to the faithful, the message got through: The end was coming, and only Asahara could save them.

Organizational disaster that it was, the Ishigakijima Seminar is still widely regarded as a turning point for Aum Shinri Kyo. From that time on, many members complained, all one heard from Aum was a double drum beat of "money, money, money" and "members, members, members." It also marked an increasingly dark turn in Asahara's apocalyptic thought. That same month, Asahara published a digest of his Ishigakijima message in an Aum magazine. The world was rushing headlong toward Armageddon, he wrote, and cited as proof the crisis in the Middle East, the arrival of Haley's Comet (yes, again), the appearance of saucer-shaped UFOs, the democratization of the Soviet Union, and the unification of Europe. It was out of Aum's hands, Asahara said.

"And what will happen after Armageddon?" he wrote. "That will probably be the beginning of the division of those souls which will head for heaven from those heading for the true hell.

"And there is nothing we can do about it. We are truly helpless. That is why we have to explore now what it is we can do to protect ourselves against this danger, how we can control ourselves in order to enter heaven, or even better, how we can enter Maha Nirvana. We have to enter a protective mode right now.

"So, what kind of protective actions will Aum Shinri Kyo take? First, we have to secure a place where we can protect ourselves from bodily harm, where we can live and continue our ascetic practice, no matter what kind of weapon, whether that be nuclear weapons, or bacterial weapons, but where we will be protected no matter what kind of weapon is thrown against us. We are beginning those preparations now. Around May 17, a place . . . will be ready. We have been preparing this place as quickly as possible.

"Next, right now we are working to acquire another piece of land of about thirty-seven acres. This land is almost completely flat, and will be used as another place where Aum can carry out its communal lifestyle. I would like to include a more perfect nuclear shelter on this land.

"From this day, from this moment on you'll have to dedicate yourselves to even stricter practice, and quickly raise yourselves to the stage where you are prepared for death at any time."

In these passages, Asahara made a major leap away from his earlier message of bringing happiness to the world. He conceded the inevitability of Armageddon, Aum's helplessness to prevent it, his desire for "a more perfect nuclear shelter," and the need for members to train harder and be ready for death. Fueling this significant change in tone was the sect's growing alienation and its inability to cope with the continuing difficulties the sect was experiencing with Japanese society. But fueling those difficulties was the group's own behavior—its aggressive recruiting; persistent solicitations for donations; barring sect members from contacts with the outside world, including relatives; and publishing severe criticisms of others while vehemently denying any criticisms leveled against itself. All of these traits are characteristic of exclusionary and closed groups, and to some degree they had marked the behavior of Aum from its earliest days.

Aum added a new weapon to its antisocial arsenal with its "invasion" of Namino Village in May 1990. While typical of the sect's arrogance toward outsiders, it also reveals what was to become an ingenious fund-raising scheme that Aum practiced on several occasions: purchasing land in a community, threatening to move in and take over, and then negotiating a buyout at double the price.

Namino is located in Kumamoto Prefecture on the southern island of Kyushu, where Asahara was born. In May, Aum filed the papers required by the Japanese government for any land transaction, reporting the transfer of ownership of a fifteen-acre field to the sect as a gift from the owner. By the end of the month the sect had begun construction of a training camp to house as many as six hundred of its members. Namino is a small, conservative country village. Its residents were alarmed at the influx of so many outsiders who not only showed no inclination to respect local civilities and customs, but about whom frightening rumors were flying in the national and local press. They watched with growing apprehension as trucks carried construction materials to the site at all hours of the day and night, smashing into buildings and damaging public roads on the way; the fact that Aum members chased any visitors to the site away, and made videotapes of any cars that even passed their property, jotting down license numbers, didn't make the people in Namino feel all warm and neighborly, either. And the sight of bearded, half-naked commune members slapping together their jerry-built structures—as always, Aum saved money by putting its members to work—was equally scandalizing.

What really set the alarm bells ringing, though, was the sudden appearance of forty-five members at the town hall in June, there to register as Namino residents. The villagers now knew the wolf was at the door. Hundreds of Aum followers would flood the village rolls, taking control of their local government and their lives. With the homegrown shrewdness that Japanese peasants were forced to cultivate over the centuries as a survival technique, the village officials quietly accepted the applications, as they were required to by law, then simply forgot to process them. Now began a long wrangle between the village and the sect. The village residents formed a "Protect Namino Village Association" and called in prefectural officials to investigate a possible Aum violation of the land-use laws. Aum, in turn, sued the village for not processing its members' residency applications.

The village hit the first home run. In a police crackdown, Aum attorney Yoshinobu Aoyama was arrested for filing false papers concerning the land purchase—for indeed that is what it had been, not a donation. But the Aum team won the game. The Kumamoto District Court handed down a judgment against the village in January 1993. The Aum members should have been registered as they demanded. By now the villagers were desperate to get rid of Aum, and in August 1994, they agreed to a settlement. Aum had purchased the property for five million dollars; they now demanded four times that— the entire annual budget of the village, or seventeen thousand dollars per household! Eventually the two sides settled on a little over nine million dollars, five million the first year and the rest in three annual installments.

The results of this little caper encouraged Aum to try it again. In similar cases in Tomizawa-cho, Yamanashi Prefecture, they demanded ten million dollars to relinquish land purchased for two hundred thousand dollars. In Kumamoto, they asked for one million dollars for land that cost two hundred eighty thousand dollars. Both of these generous offers to get out of town were rejected.

Aum's history of extortion can be traced back to the shaking down of its members for donations, which had begun very early on in its history. Though not made public until much later, it turns out that it also had a surprisingly long history of lethal violence. Some say that the decisive step toward violence had come in November 1989 with the murder of the Sakamoto family, but in fact Asahara had ordered earlier murders, and his followers had dutifully carried them out. They committed their first murder sometime during 1988 (the precise date is still unclear), when a young devotee "accidentally" died while undergoing what was later described as a "severe religious training session" in a sect bath house.

While the exact circumstances surrounding this "training accident" may never be known, several Aum members who confessed to the police in 1995 confirmed that the incident did occur, although they were vague about the details. The dead man was a twenty-five-year-old member who they characterized as "extremely insecure" and in need of "special training." According to members who were present during and after the training session, the young man "drowned" in an Aum bath, and efforts to restore his heartbeat and breathing failed. Though police may never learn how the member really died, it is worth noting that the sect's "special bath training sessions" were normally administered to recalcitrant members who had fallen out of line with the sect's practices, or to members who express a desire to quit the sect and leave.

As described by former Aum members who witnessed it, the "bath training technique" consisted of immersing trainees in extremely hot water. Though Aum has never explained the spiritual benefits of a scalding bath, modern medical science is replete with warnings about exposing the body to hot water. Unless a person is in unusually good physical condition, total immersion in extremely hot water can quickly bring on shock and a fatal heart attack. In Japan, the steamy bath is a national passion, and each year a number of elderly and even middle-aged people die from heart attacks associated with soaking in water that is too hot. But in this case the water temperature was raised to near-scalding temperatures for strictly punitive reasons.

After it was confirmed that the young man was dead, the news was conveyed to Asahara and his top aides. The death constituted a major crisis, and the guru immediately summoned four of his closest advisers. According to one aide who was present at the meeting, it was not so much the death of the young member that disturbed Asahara as how it might affect the sect's public image. Actually, Asahara and his leadership were faced with a much more immediate problem than public relations: how to dispose of the obviously scalded body. Even though the death could be superficially explained as an accidental drowning, notification of the police—a legal requirement in all deaths in Japan—might result in a very nasty investigation, even an autopsy, especially after police and relatives of the dead man caught a glimpse of his parboiled body.

Little imagination was required to figure out where all that might lead. In such an obvious case of physical abuse resulting in death the police would have no choice but to pursue the matter to its end, and in the process ask Aum's leaders a lot of knotty questions they'd rather not answer. Asahara ordered his close advisers to burn the young man's body and scatter the ashes in the lava gravel covering the ground of the compound.

With the evidence thus destroyed, it will probably never be known whether Aum Shinri Kyo's first serious crime was a deliberate murder or an accidental death caused by severe physical abuse. But it is beyond all doubt that Asahara and his top lieutenants conspired to cover up the young man's death, and in that conspiracy they forged a powerful bond of criminality at the very apex of the Aum Shinri Kyo leadership. This only made it all easier the second time around.

In the early fall of 1989, Hideo Murai informed Asahara that he had uncovered information strongly suggesting that a young Aum monastic at the Kamikuishiki commune was planning to kill him. According to confessions made to the Japanese police, several members of the top leadership believe Murai, who they described as a "vicious troublemaker" who often exaggerated things to ingratiate himself with the guru, deliberately distorted the young man's problem to alarm Asahara. The young adherent had also angered the supreme master by violating a strict taboo forbidding Aum monastics from having sex with each other. This young man had been caught having an affair with a young Aum woman, also a monastic, and when Murai informed Asahara of that transgression the guru exploded in a jealous rage.

According to one senior leader who was close to Asahara, the sect leader believed that all Aum women "belonged to him exclusively, they were his property." Again the senior advisers were called into a meeting where Asahara ordered them to kill the young man and burn his body. Five of the guru's top aides cornered the victim in a sect building and one of them strangled him with his bare hands. His body was also burned and the ashes spread across the lava gravel in the compound. To date, police investigations and testimony of Aum members have turned up thirty-three members who were murdered or so severely physically abused that they died. The number is likely to grow as the police continue their investigations into the fates of at least twenty other members who are currently listed as missing.

The increasing tensions with Japanese society outside and mounting violence inside the sect seem to have fed each other. The sect began a campaign to persuade all of its followers to join Aum's communes, the well-guarded compounds in which they could be shut off from outside contact and information. Recruiters stressed the impending Armageddon and urged followers to break ties with their families, give all their personal wealth to Aum, and devote themselves to ascetic practice as soon as possible. Only then would they attain the salvation Asahara promised as the world around them went up in the flames of Armageddon. But this pressure to enter communes did not produce results, and the number of followers who actually became commune members in 1991 and 1992 was disappointingly small.

Aum responded in two ways. First, it emerged again with a number of initiatives aimed at improving its image with non-commune members and with the public at large. Aum devised its own ceremonial system, mostly to attract new lay members. These included a birth ceremony, to name and bless a newborn child; a wedding ceremony; and ancestor worship, which is a strong and familiar component of religion throughout East Asia, including Japan. It also developed a memorial rite observed on the forty-ninth day after death, replacing a traditional Japanese Buddhist memorial. Rituals to mark the important events of followers' lives such as these were designed to comfort lay members at life's important junctures and make Aum Shinri Kyo seem more like other, more familiar religions.

Other efforts to improve Aum's image included public theatrical and dance performances, produced with professional help. Aum-sponsored works such as "Death and Transmogrification" and "Creation" attracted general audiences, some of whom went on to become members. The sect also began a translation project aimed at translating the entire canon of Early Buddhist literature into modern Japanese, and widely publicized these efforts. They pointed to this as an indication of their seriousness and devotion to "pure" Buddhism, using the project to counter media images of Aum as a wild fringe group—much as they used photos of Shoko Asahara with the Dalai Lama.

Aum was even able to turn the Namino Village incident to their advantage, finding some scholars of religion who sympathized with Aum in the struggle with the conservative villagers. Aum leaders cleverly cultivated these supportive voices and set up interviews between them and Asahara, which were then published in mass-market magazines, again casting Aum in a favorable light for a wider Japanese audience.

Second, Aum took increasingly drastic steps to keep those who were presently commune members from leaving. Leaving Aum, never an easy task, now became impossible. Guards were posted at all exits, and only the most trustworthy members were allowed to leave the compound. All mail was opened by sect leaders, and passed on to members only if it was deemed innocuous. Special permission was required to make a telephone call, and even then the presence of a senior member within hearing distance was required. People who managed to escape the sect's communes were tracked down by special strong-arm squads who seized them, then quickly brought them back to the commune. Escapees were sometimes drugged and thrown into waiting cars. The Aum leadership produced a manual that included techniques for luring apostates back to the fold. It suggested arranging a meeting at a restaurant and then slipping something into the escapee's drink before hustling him out to the car in the guise of assisting a sick friend. Those who were recaptured often faced extended periods of "special training" in the black boxes, the small, dark isolation chambers where they underwent drug-induced "meditation." More lethal punishments, such as the bath-training session, also awaited recalcitrant members. Psychological pressure was especially intense. Asahara and his top executives repeatedly warned Aum members that those who left the sect would eventually end up in a "special hell" where the tortures awaiting them were beyond imagination.

At the same time that Aum was clamping down within its ranks, it was reaching out to the world. First on the domestic front, and later worldwide, Aum began in 1992 to establish or purchase several businesses. Aum's commercial activities were wide-ranging and included restaurants, a chain of *bento* (boxed lunches) shops called "It's Good! It's Cheap!," a fitness club, a baby-sitting service, noodle shops, dating services, travel agencies, hospitals and medical clinics, laboratories, real estate, pharmaceuticals, computer stores, and a very lucrative personal-computer manufacturing business that undercut most of the competition in Japan.

The PC company, Mahaposha or Maha Posya, assembled and sold PCs in six outlets across Japan for about eight hundred sixty dollars—a real bargain since PCs of the same general quality usually go for twice that and up. The PCs were assembled in factories in Osaka, Nagoya, and Tokyo and delivered direct to the sales outlets, cutting out the expensive Japanese distribution system (another little advantage to being a religion). They got their parts from Taiwan and Hong Kong and bought their semiconductors wholesale in Japan. In Taiwan Aum had an import-export agency, and in Sri Lanka it operated a tea plantation. All in all, Aum owned and operated more than thirty-five companies and agencies located in Japan and, later, the United States, Australia, Sri Lanka, and Taiwan. Overhead operating expenses for many of these companies were low since they were located in sect-owned buildings and manned by sect members, many of whom worked for little or nothing, as part of their spiritual training.

While the publishing companies and hospitals were publicly identified as Aum companies, the more usual practice was to set up dummy companies that pursued Aum's larger ends while covering up any trace of the sect's involvement. For example, Hasegawa Chemical, Tokyo, and Beck, Inc., in Yamanashi Prefecture, were set up in 1993 and placed under the direction of the Science and Technology Ministry. Their purpose was to purchase the chemicals the ministry needed for its weapons programs without calling attention to Aum.

Many Aum watchers believe the person behind the sect's business success was Hisako Ishii, Aum's Minister of Finance and one of Asahara's oldest and most accomplished disciples. A former insurance company employee, she was only a couple of years out of junior college when she met Asahara and began attending yoga sessions at his studio in Shibuya Ward, Tokyo. Described by Aum members as one of the guru's most devoted followers, she was said to be a tireless worker at building the sect's financial resources. Exactly how she managed the sect's money is not known at this time, but there is little doubt she was effective.

Aum began to extend overseas for the same reason, setting up branches and offices in several countries, most of them minor operations. Two areas where the sect's activities were not minor, however, were Russia and the United States. The first links to Russia were forged in 1991, shortly after the sect's decision to begin militarizing. The major proponent of the sect's expansion into Russia was Asahara's primary deputy and most trusted confidant, Construction Minister Kiyohide Hayakawa. Like Finance Minister Ishii, Hayakawa had made the long march with Asahara from the very earliest days, and when the sect's militarization began after the humiliating defeat at the electoral polls in 1990, he was the mastermind of Aum's attempts to arm itself and a keen promoter of expanding the sect's beachhead in Russia. In total, Hayakawa visited Russia twenty-one times from 1992 to 1995, spending more than six months there. From November 1993 to April 1994, he visited Russia regularly, between one and two times each month.

Aum devoted most of its overseas propagation energies to Russia, where it recruited vigorously among disaffected university students. As in Japan, it specifically targeted persons with scientific and technical backgrounds. Finding new members was not difficult. After more than seventy years of state-imposed atheism, any religious group using slick marketing campaigns to offer spiritual salvation could easily attract thousands of Russian young people. In 1995, a Russian government investigation into the sect's activities estimated that its membership stood at thirty-five thousand, with up to fifty-five thousand lay followers attending the cult's seminars on a sporadic basis. The Russian sect reportedly had five thousand five hundred "full-time monks" who lived in Aum accommodations, usually housing donated by other members. Overall, Aum had eighteen branches in Russia, seven of which were located in Moscow.

In 1992, as part of an effort to spread its message and maintain a visible presence in Russia, Aum signed a three-year contract for radio air time from one the three largest radio stations in the nation, the state-run Mayak Radio. The total cost of the contract was 2.4 million dollars, and Aum broadcast an hour-long daily program which was relayed via a sect-owned radio tower in Vladivostok to Japan every evening. Aum television programs were also broadcast on Russia's "2X2" television station.

But almost from the beginning it was clear that one of Aum's primary interests in Russia was technology, weapons, and military training. The religious side of its work there was little more than an elaborate cover for its more serious militarization program. The sect sent a delegation to Russia to discuss laser weapons with a top Russian expert in the field, and it smuggled submachine-gun-manufacturing blueprints and other weapons data back to Japan for its conventional-arms program. From notebooks and other evidence obtained by the Japanese police, there are clear indications that Aum was also interested in buying Russian rockets and nuclear weapons.

Documents taken from Hayakawa after his arrest in 1995 indicate he had information about a gas laser weapon. The Japanese press reported that other notes referred to the name of a Russian city "where there is a weapons market" and noted its distance from Moscow. Most ominously, Hayakawa's documents also contained references to the desired purchase of nuclear weapons. One contained this question: "How much is a nuclear warhead?" and lists several prices. It is unclear whether the references are reflections of actual discussions or negotiations.

Aum's connections with Russian military, scientific, and political figures and institutes extended to the highest levels. Asahara led a delegation of some three hundred members to Russia in March 1992. While there he met with Parliament vice-president Alexsandr Rutskoy and former Russian parliament speaker Rusian Khasbulatov. The premier nuclear research facility in Russia, the Kurchatov Institute, had Aum followers as employees. During 1992 and 1993, Aum leaders visiting Russia approached science officials to seek laser and nuclear technologies. Secretary of the Russian Security Council, Oleg Lobov, received anywhere from five hundred thousand to one million dollars from Aum. This relationship started in December 1991 and continued through 1995.

All of the Russian officials denied allegations that they helped Aum in any way. But U.S. Senate investigators found photos in Aum publications that showed Rutskoy, Khasbulatov, Basov, and Lobov with Asahara. Lobov would later admit to meeting with Aum officials but claimed that he was duped by them due to his "charitable nature." He said that neither the Russian Ministry of Foreign Affairs nor the intelligence services warned him away from the sect.

Another of the cult's more intriguing overseas ventures occurred in Australia, where it purchased a five-hundred-thousand-acre sheep ranch in a remote, isolated location some three hundred seventy-five miles northeast of Perth. In the area there is a known uranium deposit. While inspecting the property, the group indicated they wanted a remote site where they could "conduct experiments of benefit to mankind." The Aum officials who visited the sheep ranch included Construction Minister Kiyohide Hayakawa and Intelligence Minister Yoshihiro Inoue.

During their tour of the site they conducted several tests using a lap-top computer and electrodes that they placed in the ground. After purchasing the property through a front company, Aum members met with an Australian geologist in early September 1993 and discussed with her the possibility of exporting uranium ore from the ranch to Japan via ship. The following week, Shoko Asahara arrived in Perth accompanied by twenty-four followers from Japan, including five females under the age of fifteen who were traveling without their parents. The group had with it an assortment of chemicals and mining equipment on which they paid thirty thousand Australian dollars in excess baggage fees and fifteen thousand Australian dollars to customs. Among the baggage was a mechanical ditch digger, picks, gas generators, gas masks, respirators, and shovels. Because of the large amount of excess baggage, Australian customs searched the entire group and seized a wide assortment of chemicals that were not listed in the customs declaration or were mislabeled. Two Aum members were subsequently charged with carrying dangerous substances on board an aircraft and fined one thousand seven hundred fifty Australian dollars each by an Australian court.

At the ranch the sect began explorations for uranium and it set up a laboratory complete with computers and various types of digital equipment. Shortly after the Tokyo attack, the sheep ranch was sold. Australian police investigations into the sect's activities indicate that while they were interested in obtaining uranium ore, they also conducted sarin experiments on sheep at the ranch. Australian Justice Minister Duncan Kerr said that Aum tested sarin in Australia before the Tokyo subway attack. He said that tests on wool and soil samples taken from the ranch confirmed traces of the nerve agent being present. This finding may explain the sighting on the ranch of a number of Aum members in protective clothing and gas masks.

The full extent of Aum's operations on its remote sheep ranch in southern Australia remains unknown and, to a certain degree, a mystery. The cult's activities in the United States, however, are a good deal clearer.

Aum Shinri Kyo officially arrived in the United States in late 1987 when it incorporated in New York City under the name Aum U.S. Company, Ltd., a not-for-profit corporation. Although the Manhattan office purported to promote book sales and recruitment of new members, its primary function was to act as a purchasing agency for the sect's attempts to obtain high-tech equipment, advanced computer software and hardware, and other items needed in Aum's militarization program. Additionally, in the 1990s the sect used a purchasing agent in California to facilitate similar acquisitions along with military equipment such as gas masks. The total extent of Aum's efforts to buy equipment and technology in the United States is unknown, but some of the items bought were never delivered because U.S. company representatives became suspicious of the sect and the purported end-use of the products. Other purchases were preempted by the gas attack in Tokyo, which exposed the sect's terrorist nature to the world. In numerous instances, however, Aum was able to legally buy sophisticated technology, the use of which is still unaccounted for. U.S. government investigators have also concluded that the full scope of advanced technology purchases may never be known because shortly after the Tokyo subway attack a sect member apparently took a large number of the New York office records back to Japan.

The equipment Aum sought in the United States included a Mark IVxp interfrometer manufactured by a firm in Connecticut. The Mark IVxp is a laser measuring system that has dual commercial and military applications including the measuring of plutonium. Additionally Aum requested a vibration isolation table, which with modest reconfiguration can be used to measure spherical surfaces, including those of plutonium used in nuclear weapons. The sales were never completed because the firm became suspicious and contacted export-licensing officials. In 1994, Aum bought thirty-two thousand dollars worth of HEPA media, which is used for air filtration in "clean rooms." At their production facilities in Japan, Aum constructed "clean rooms" to facilitate the handling of sarin, VX, and other chemical and biological weapons.

From a company in Oregon, Aum bought molecular-modeling software that enables chemists to experiment with synthesizing molecules on a computer screen rather than through more expensive and timely laboratory methods. Other major purchases that were not consummated or delivered included extremely advanced lasers for industrial and scientific cutting and welding; and molecular-design software to develop new therapeutic drugs in the preclinical design phase. The latter could also be used to research and develop biological toxins. On the West Coast, Aum agents wanted to purchase thousands of serum bottles, hundreds of mechanical fans, and equal amounts of camcorder batteries, along with military-style gas masks.

In addition to acquiring technology and equipment in the United States, Aum was also able to obtain helicopter-pilot licenses for two of its members at an aviation school in Florida. The two fledgling pilots were Aum Defense Agency Director Tetsuya Kibe and member Keiji Tanimura. After taking the required number of flight lessons and passing written and flight tests, they each received a private pilot rating for rotor-craft helicopters on October 31, 1993. Soon afterward, the cult purchased a Russian civilian version of a military helicopter and brought it to Japan.

Aum Shinri Kyo was not a success at recruiting new members in America. Some U.S. government sources have estimated Aum's total United States membership at slightly less than two hundred, but there is no evidence to support that figure and a recent Senate inquiry determined that in the New York City area—its main base of operations—the sect had only a few dozen followers. Part of the reason for this low figure may be that Aum Shinri Kyo never viewed its American branch as anything more than a purchasing house for its militarization program. It may have realized that its doomsday message—with the United States as the archenemy—would not go down well with most Americans.

Asahara's growing obsession with Armageddon in the 1990s was rapidly replacing yoga and meditation practice and world salvation as the glue that held his group together. Though the sect was not yet fully consumed with apocalyptic prophecies, Asahara, in his writings and speeches, was moving it steadily in that direction. He published in the early 1990s a number of books on doomsday themes, among them *The Truth of Humanity's Destruction*, *The Secret Prophecy of Nostradamus*, *Declaring Myself the Christ*, and *Declaring Myself the Christ, Part II*. In October and November of 1992, Asahara made lecture appearances at several top universities around the country—the Tokyo College of Engineering, Shinshu University, Osaka University, Chiba University, Yokohama National University, Kyoto University, and Tokyo University. By now his apocalyptic vision had grown even darker, and the Armageddon he presented to students and faculty was one in which atomic, biological, and chemical weapons of mass destruction would be used to wipe out more than ninety percent of Japan's urban populations. Armageddon would occur by the year 2000.

By this time, Asahara no longer talked of Shambhala or a Lotus Village. Instead, in order to survive the horrors that the guru predicted, one would have to become a "superhuman" through the sect's ascetic practices. Asahara told his audiences that among the several projects that Aum planned as aids for survival was the construction of an underwater city. Later, he would reach even further by claiming that those who entered the sect and followed its ascetic practices would earn a special immunity to the weapons of mass destruction that would rain down on Japan during Armageddon.

As if gearing up for Armageddon, Aum Shinri Kyo's practices took on the hard, even desperate edge of extreme and punitive asceticism. Practitioners spent days in the isolation and confinement of the black box, often without food or water, while videos of Asahara's sermons played continuously at a roaring volume. In a variation on this grim exercise, the person in the box was bombarded, for days on end, with videos of the most grisly and gory scenes and sounds of death and destruction; this was supposed to drive home the point that everyone dies, and the only glory is giving one's life to the guru.

The black box was "inspired" by a practice of extended solitary meditation in Tibetan Buddhism, as was another, much more athletic practice introduced at this time in which members threw themselves prostrate on the ground and picked themselves up, over and over again. This went on from sixteen to twenty hours a day, while the practitioner recited: "I take refuge in Aum, in the Guru, and in Shiva. Please lead me quickly to enlightenment."

In this same period, Asahara began to emphasize what he called Tantra Vajrayana, or "the Secret Diamond Vehicle" to salvation. Although he borrowed the term and some practices from Esoteric forms of Tibetan Buddhism, he gave it a distinctive twist. Asahara's Vajrayana emphasized the absolute power of the guru—that is, himself. Followers were to empty themselves completely of their own selfhood so that they could be filled with the spirit of the guru. Their only religious practice was to do whatever the guru instructed, and the guru was always right.

The sect published a pamphlet entitled "The Vajrayana Vow" that members were encouraged to recite "a thousand, a million, a billion times":

I take refuge in the Tantra Vajrayana! (repeated four times)
What is the first law?
To be mindful of the Buddha.
And in Tantra Vajrayana, the Buddha and the Guru are identical.
I take refuge in the Guru! (repeated four times)

What is the Guru?
The Guru is a life form born to *phowa* all souls.
Any method that leads to salvation is acceptable.
My life will come to an end sometime.
It makes no difference if the end comes in twenty years, thirty
    years, or eighty years,
It will come regardless.
What's important is *how* I give my life.
If I give it for salvation, eliminating all the evil karma I have
    accumulated, freeing myself from all karma, the Guru and Shiva
    and all winners of truth will without fail lead me to a higher realm.
So I practice the Vajrayana without fear.
The Armageddon taught in the Bible approaches,
The final battle is upon us.
I will be among the holy troops of this last great battle
And *phowa* the evil ones.
I will *phowa* one or two evil ones.
Phowa is the highest virtue
And *phowa* is the path to the highest level of being.

Obviously, *phowa* is a key term here. Though the original Tibetan means to lead a soul to a higher level of being, usually at the moment of death, for Asahara and many of his key followers, it had become a euphemism for killing, and the Tantra Vajrayana became a very effective form of brainwashing that successfully convinced many of the guru's followers murder was acceptable if Asahara ordered it.

Beginning in 1994, and perhaps earlier, hypnotic drugs were also used widely, both as punishment and in initiations. One member who successfully fled from the group reported that by 1994 many members had "lost their minds" because of drug experiences, were disoriented, didn't know who they were, and wandered helplessly around the compound. In one form of initiation often used by the sect, the member was hospitalized for days hooked up to an IV bag from which a cocktail of chemicals dripped. He or she was kept at the margins of consciousness as Asahara's cassette tapes were played continuously in the room.

Aum also found pharmaceuticals of certain sorts to be a most lucrative sideline. Police sources suggest that illicit drug manufacturing may have provided the sect with millions of dollars in revenue. In their investigations, which are still ongoing, the police found evidence that Aum used its chemical expertise to manufacture illegal stimulants and other drugs for the Japanese underworld. Japanese government officials concluded that the sect produced and sold through its underworld connections a large amount of the potent hallucinatory drug LSD. Shoko Asahara reportedly dispatched one member to Russia to purchase materials for making LSD and another to the United States to find out how to produce it.

One report indicates that after a good start, Aum's quality control may have faltered badly—eventually the word from the street in Japan was that the sect's drug products were "garbage." But their first efforts at making the hallucinatory drug apparently resulted in very potent LSD. Cult members who were present when Asahara sampled the initial batches of the Aum drug say the guru had intense hallucinations, saw what he believed was the origin of the universe, and then "pissed in his pants."

It was probably not an accident that this darker course Aum Shinri Kyo was adopting on all levels also coincided with Asahara's expanding visions of impending apocalypse. One factor that undoubtedly informed and added impetus to Asahara's Armageddon-obsessed thinking, and perhaps was spurred on by his top cadre of scientists, was the Gulf War in early 1991. Here was the world's first real threat of modern chemical warfare. The televised scenes of missiles slamming into Allied-troop installations in Saudi Arabia and falling on defenseless civilians in Israel, interspersed with images of frightened journalists, soldiers, and civilians donning gas masks in the event the missiles carried chemical warheads, were a rich infusion for the guru, who was already possessed by dire visions of the future.

The Gulf War had demonstrated the awesome potential of chemical and biological weapons, and it took no particular genius for Asahara to realize that his small core of scientists could easily manufacture some of the weapons. All that was needed was the technology for making them; the best places to obtain these were the former Soviet Union, economically shattered by the implosion of the communist system, and the United States, where data and equipment were available for the asking. By early 1992 Aum was well entrenched in Russia and working on weapons procurement out of its New York and West Coast offices. The prospect of acquiring the weapons necessary for fighting the final war was suddenly within reach, and Aum pursued it with single-minded determination.

One of its first steps was to obtain the technology for manufacturing AK-74 submachine guns. The AK-74 is the modern version of the Soviet AK-47 submachine gun used so effectively by the Viet Cong guerrillas and the North Vietnamese during the Vietnam War. The technology for AK-type weapons has been around for decades, and the Chinese have manufactured them by the millions for domestic use by their armed forces and for export to less developed countries. By arms-manufacturing standards, making AK-74s is a relatively simple business. But Aum never seemed to get the hang of it.

After receiving the plans for making the weapons from Russia, it did not take the sect's technical experts long to go into production. By July 1994, more than one hundred Aum members were busy turning out parts for AK-74s with the aid of computer-controlled machinery in its Kamikuishiki complex, but reports indicate only a small number of the weapons were finally produced and there were serious doubts about their overall reliability. When Japanese police raided the Aum facility in March 1995, they discovered completed submachine guns, additional gun parts, used rocket launchers, and other military equipment. The AK-74 production program—like so much else in Aum's aggressive conventional militarization program—never hit high gear, but there is little doubt that had the cult been given a few more uninterrupted years its determined technicians would have achieved the same success with the Russian submachine guns it had in creating chemical weapons.

At the same time they were trying to manufacture AK-74s, Aum scientists were also pursuing an interest in "Star Wars" technology, specifically information on the development of laser weapons. An Aum scientific team traveled to Moscow to interview Dr. Nikolay Basov, a 1964 Nobel Prize winner for his research on the principle of laser technology and the nation's number-one authority on laser weapons. That the meetings took place is beyond doubt; sect publications later printed photographs showing Basov meeting with Shoko Asahara. What ensued from those discussions is not known, but in November 1994, several cult members were arrested for breaking into the offices of Nippon Electronics. The purpose of the burglary was to steal information on laser technology from the company's laserbeams laboratory near Yokohama. One of those arrested was a member of Aum's intelligence ministry, on whom police found sketches and maps of the interior layouts of facilities at six other major electronic firms. Also seized were lists containing the names of dozens of Aum members who worked for major electronic and chemical firms in Japan. The arrests didn't even slow the sect down. By the end of December 1994, several Aum members were arrested for breaking into the Mitsubishi Heavy Industries Research Center in Hiroshima Prefecture. In their investigations, Japanese police discovered the group had broken into the center on a number of previous occasions in an attempt to steal documents and research data on laser beam research.

In March 1995, documents on laser technology, including blueprints for a laser gun, were seized by police from an Aum member; in the same month data on laser devices was found buried in the ground of the sect's Kamikuishiki compound.

Aum's research-center burglaries raise the possibility of another, much more secret tie with Russian officialdom. In 1995, Russian parliamentarian Vitaliy Savitsky, chairman of the Duma's Religious Affairs Committee, complained to fellow members that "his committee seriously suspected that Aum Shinri Kyo had been assisted in its penetration into Russia by Russian intelligence services." Savitsky's suspicions about Russian intelligence involvement with the sect could explain a great deal of Aum's unusual access to senior Russian political and military figures and the relative ease with which it obtained weapons technology, possibly including the formulas for sarin, tabun, soman, and VX nerve agents. There have been unconfirmed reports that the formula and process Aum used to produce sarin was similiar to chemical-warfare technology developed by the former Soviet army.

Historically, Soviet, and now Russian, intelligence-collection efforts in Japan have never been very effective. After the implosion of Soviet communism, the new Russian government undertook a sweeping reorganization of the former Soviet intelligence service. The old Soviet KGB was stripped of a number of its duties, and what emerged in its place was a streamlined Russian intelligence service, again known by a three-letter acronym, called the SRV. The old Cold War intelligence-collection agenda used by the KGB was also streamlined and modernized. Top Russian intelligence officials publicly announced that the new SRV would concentrate its spying in the areas of economics, science, and technology, all things Japan had in abundance. Shortly after the new SRV agenda was announced in the early 1990s, Aum Shinri Kyo arrived in Moscow to establish its religious centers, recruit new members, and begin a rather overt, amateurish—but ultimately effective—campaign to acquire weapons technology. Russian intelligence is highly suspicious of religious groups, especially foreign sects proselytizing among its disaffected young people, and Aum probably attracted the interest of the SRV from day one.

As they watched the sect's operations in Russia, the SRV must have realized that Aum, with its technical and scientific cadre, its unrelenting animosity against the Japanese government, and its urgent quest for weapons technology, would be easy to exploit for its own intelligence collection. Certainly the types of information that Aum sought in its break-ins at Japanese research centers would also be of interest to the SRV. By allowing Aum to operate relatively unimpeded in Russia, and by supplying it with some of the weapons technology it wanted—all things the SRV could easily do on its own turf—it might reasonably extract a quid pro quo share of the technical and scientific data the sect stole from Japan's research centers, the addresses of which the SRV would be only too happy to provide.

From an intelligence perspective, managing the operation without leaving SRV fingerprints would be simple. Aum's top leaders in Russia, like Asahara himself, were unsophisticated when it came to the arcane business of clandestine intelligence collection. It is entirely possible that the sect was used and manipulated by the SRV without ever being aware of it. It is also possible that at least some top members of the sect may have been willing accomplices working with the SRV. There are intriguing rumors, none of them confirmed, that Aum received funding from foreign sources. Its operational costs in Russia were extremely heavy, a burden the SRV could have alleviated if properly motivated.

Aum was also highly interested in so-called seismological or "doomsday weapons" capable of shattering the earth. In Construction Minister Kiyohide Hayakawa's notebooks seized by Japanese police, there are numerous references to nuclear and seismological weapons. There is also reliable evidence that Aum sent a team to the former Yugoslavia to research the work of Nikola Tesla, the controversial discoverer of alternating current, who also experimented extensively with the theory of seismic weapons—weapons which have the ability to create massive earthquakes—before he died in 1943. Tesla, according to one official familiar with his work, was once quoted as saying that with his seismic weapon technology he could "split the world in two." While in Yugoslavia, the Aum members studied Tesla's work on high-energy voltage transmission and wave amplification, both of which Tesla believed could be used to create major seismological disturbances.

Even though its conventional war program was largely a failure, Aum's efforts to produce chemical and biological weapons was extremely success-ful. Their deadly trek into the poisonous gas business began in 1992, shortly after the Gulf War, which some cult scientific members confessed to police was the inspiration for their interest in military chemical weaponry. Certainly it was at that time that the cult's scientists started research on sarin and other related nerve agents such as tabun and soman. The Japanese police believe that the cult chose sarin as its first nerve-gas agent because while it was extremely deadly, it was still "old tech—low tech" and therefore relatively easy to produce. Aum also took an avid interest in the Ebola virus which broke out in Zaire in 1992. Several cult members traveled to Zaire under guise of a "medical mission" to assist in treating Ebola victims, but govern-ment officials believe the real purpose of the visit was to obtain a sample of the Ebola strain and bring it back to Japan for cultivation. Underscoring this claim is a 1994 speech made in Moscow by Seiichi Endo in which he dis-cussed the use of Ebola as a potential biological warfare agent.

Aum not only prepared for global warfare; Asahara was already plan-ning for the time after Armageddon, when only Aum members would remain unharmed—and ready to rule Japan, at the very least. In 1994 the religion adopted a double organizational structure, one spiritual and the other political, with Shoko Asahara occupying the top position in both as Founder and Sacred Ruler. On the spiritual level, members were classed according to seven ranks of "enlightenment" and all pledged complete alle-giance to Asahara, the Sonshi. Below him were five "Seitaishi," or True Great Masters—Asahara's wife Tomoko Matsumoto; his third daughter, Umabalavati Achariya; Hideo Murai; Fumihiro Joyu; and Hisako Ishii. The next rank down was called "Seigoshi," or True Enlightened Master, of which there were nine, including Asahara's eldest daughter, Tomomitsu Niimi, Kiyohide Hayakawa, and Yoshinobu Aoyama. Next in rank were three ranks of lesser masters, then the *swami*, or "yogic adept." Holy names were bestowed on those from the rank of *swami* on up. Below the *swami* were the monastics, or *shamana*. Lay members formed the base of the pyramid.

But unlike other religions in Japan, Aum also organized itself along the same political lines as the Japanese government, complete with ministries, departments, and agencies. The assumption was that after Armageddon, the

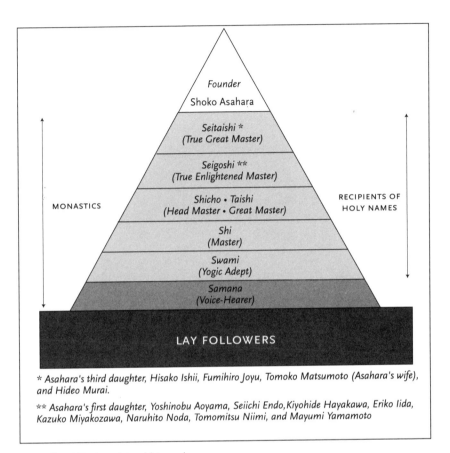

* Asahara's third daughter, Hisako Ishii, Fumihiro Joyu, Tomoko Matsumoto (Asahara's wife), and Hideo Murai.

** Asahara's first daughter, Yoshinobu Aoyama, Seiichi Endo, Kiyohide Hayakawa, Eriko Iida, Kazuko Miyakozawa, Naruhito Noda, Tomomitsu Niimi, and Mayumi Yamamoto

Aum Shinri Kyo's spiritual hierarchy.

sect would be ready to step in and fill the role of the government of Japan. Almost exactly paralleling Japan's government, the political organization of Aum Shinri Kyo included twenty-four separate ministries and agencies, all of them comparable to the government with similar functions and responsibilities. Aum had ministries of Defense, Health and Welfare, Science and Technology, Education, and many more. Although the cult had nearly three times more members in Russia than in Japan, all the highest positions were held by Japanese citizens. Furthermore, after Armageddon, Aum was apparently preparing to replace more than just Japan's government. In a telling move that bordered on lese majeste—and which said a lot about the sect's

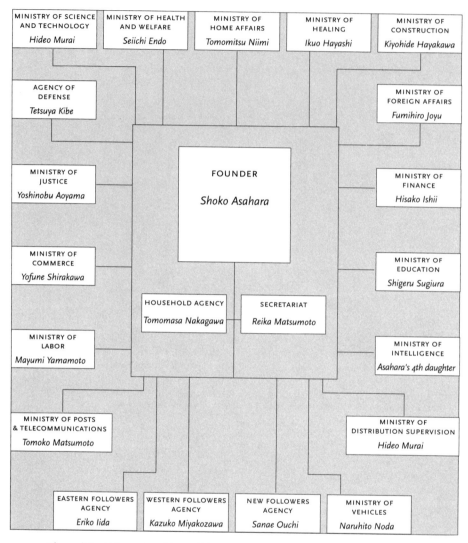

The political hierarchy of Aum Shinri Kyo.

vision of the future of Japan's Emperor—Asahara ordered the establishment of a Household Agency for himself and his family like the one that manages the daily administrative details of the Japanese emperor and his family and provides security and medical care for Japan's first family. Among the many lofty dreams Asahara had for himself in the post-Armageddon era, Emperor of Japan was surely among them. On a less regal level, the guru also formed a Secretariat, which was headed by his eleven-year-old daughter, Reika. The ministers in Aum's shadow government along with the head of his Household Agency formed Asahara's inner circle of advisers. Unlike the tens of thousands of devotees who were unaware of the sect's true nature, the inner circle knew the full extent of the cult's criminal activities.

By the spring of 1994, the sect, urged on by Asahara's increasingly shrill accusations, began to claim that Japanese and American aircraft were unleashing chemical and biological weapons on them. The drift toward becoming a closed religious sect was now almost complete. Ties with outside society, which they now viewed as their enemy, were severed. At the same time, aggressive new efforts to recruit as many new members as possible from the outside society continued. These new members would become soldiers in the group's preparation for a war that would feature both conventional armaments and weapons of mass destruction.

In his inner councils, Asahara was now preaching an extreme doctrine that held Aum must actively defend itself against the growing array of enemies confronting them, and that in order to survive they must fight. It was a classic paranoia in the making, striking out at an imagined enemy before the enemy has a chance to strike first.

But for Asahara and Aum Shinri Kyo, the agenda never seemed to stay on track or follow the timetable they laid down. So it was with the predictions for Armageddon in 1997, a date that had been chosen for numerological reasons. The importance of the mystic date 1997 was shoved aside sometime in 1994, perhaps late in the year after the Japanese police began to press their investigation of the Matsumoto gassing, and a new date for Asahara's cataclysmic war was established: November 1995. Exactly why this date was selected is still shrouded in mystery, but Japanese government sources confirmed to a U.S. Senate investigating committee that they became concerned after analyzing cult materials that Aum's leadership had decided "to speed things up" by starting their predicted war between Japan and America two years early. This may be a polite Japanese bureaucratic way of saying they were troubled because the date coincided with the scheduled visit by President Clinton and seventeen other world leaders to Osaka, Japan, for the annual Asia-Pacific Economic Cooperation (APEC) from November 16 to 19. In any event, President Clinton did not attend the meeting because of pressing budget problems with the U.S. Congress.

The security precautions planned for the meeting were not exaggerated, especially given Asahara's long history of anti-American rhetoric. In early 1994, he accused the United States of masterminding and carrying out a series of chemical attacks on himself and Aum facilities in Japan. In the same year the cult produced a video titled *Slaughtered Lambs*, which it claimed documented the American poison-gas attacks. In this video, an Aum narrator calmly reassures his audience that the sect was not the producer of sarin gas, but the victim of it. He charges that in the past few years some two hundred forty Japanese and American aircraft, including everything from helicopters to military jets, have swooped low over Aum's compound spraying the deadly gas.

The narrator claims that by using Russian gas-detection equipment (a system, incidentally, that can also be used in the production of nerve gases), Aum's medical staff has found samples of poisonous gas in the compound, including sarin and mustard gas. The video states that at least eighty Aum monastics were sickened by the gas, and the medical staff was forced to inject all the stricken members with atropine, the antidote for sarin. Near the end of the tape, in a voiceover, the charismatic Asahara speaks: "Aum survives these [gas] attacks because it is a mystic religion that transcends the boundaries of life and death. Aum is a mighty obstacle to the evil that rules this world. I am suffering the effects of mustard gas. I am now facing death."

The strident anti-Americanism—and the mystery surrounding the selection of the November 1995 date for the new Armageddon—continued in January 1995 when the cult's monthly publication, *Vajrayana Sacca*, printed an article asking "Will Clinton Be Assassinated?" In it the sect editors noted: "Clinton will be without doubt a one-term president. At best, he will not be reelected. At worst, it would not be strange if he were assassinated, in a way that appears accidental." The same publication contains an article raising the possibility of planned terrorist assassinations of various Japanese officials. A number of prominent Japanese officials are listed as "black-hearted aristocrats who have sold their souls to the devil." Included is Daisaku Ikeda, the honorary president of Soka Gakkai International (who Aum had earlier tried to kill in what was its first, unsuccessful attempt to use sarin), a major Japanese religious group that Asahara despised and regarded as his biggest religious rival in Japan; Yukio Aoshima, the governor of Tokyo; and Ichiro Ozawa, head of the New Frontier Party, who was labeled by Aum as the "king of darkness" for his close ties with the United States; and Crown Princess Masako, an "agent of American business."

There are other unconfirmed reports that President Clinton was also named on a separate, similar list of assassination possibilities circulated by Aum. The cult's death list gained increased significance on May 16, 1995, the date of Asahara's arrest, when Tokyo Governor Aoshima, who had publicly called for disbanding Aum Shinri Kyo and who was prominently mentioned on the January assassination list, received a mail bomb which exploded, blowing off a number of fingers on one hand of his secretary outside the governor's office. The governor, in another office, was not injured in the bomb's detonation.

Whether Aum's hostility toward America would have resulted in attacks on U.S. population centers is uncertain, but such attacks were being actively considered by the sect's top leadership. Reliable Japanese press reports indicate that Aum's chief doctor, Ikuo Hayashi, confessed to police that as early as November 1994 Aum was planning to mail packages of sarin nerve gas to unnamed locations in the United States. Hayashi was quoted as saying that the sect's intelligence chief, Yoshihiro Inoue, wanted him to travel to America and receive the parcels for local delivery. U.S. Senate investigators confirmed that Inoue kept a number of detailed diaries in which he jotted down random thoughts and plans concerning future Aum operations. Seized by the Japanese police, these diaries outline a plan to conduct indiscriminate nerve gas attacks in major US cities, including New York City.

If America was Aum's number-one target, the world's Jewish community came in a close number two. There seems little motivation for the group's belligerent anti-Semitism (though the same could be said of the bizarre strain of anti-Semitism that has been a conspicuous and growing social problem in Japan for a number of years). There are few Jews in Japan, and those there are represent not the slightest threat or mildest challenge to the Japanese, on either an individual or a group level. If anything, many have commented on similarities among the two peoples. Yet Aum's anti-Semitism is a well-established fact. In January 1995, for example, the sect formally declared war on the Jewish people, which it described in a special edition of *Vajrayana Sacca* entitled *Manual of Fear* as "the hidden enemy" and "the world shadow government": "On behalf of the world's 5.5 billion people, *Vajrayana Sacca* hereby formally declares war on the 'world shadow government' that murders untold numbers of people and, while hiding behind sonorous phrases and high-sounding principles, plans to brainwash and control the rest. Japanese awake! The hidden enemy's plot has long since torn our lives to shreds."

Quoting liberally from a number of anti-Semitic works, the Aum tract blames the Jews for the mass murders in Cambodia by the Khmer Rouge, the massacres of Serbs and Croatians in Bosnia, the tribal killings in Rwanda, and for masterminding a sinister international plot of similar massacres which will reduce the world's population to three billion people by the year 2000. In its literature Aum tied Jews to its enemies in Japan, the "black aristocracy" of Japanese "internationalists" that included a large number of current and former politicians and statesmen. Aum also targeted in its rhetoric many persons that it identified as "Jewish Japanese," people who were not Jewish but rather cosmopolitan Japanese, government officials and members of the Tokyo and Osaka business communities who personified Aum's perception of the internationalism and materialism that were destroying Japan.

Aum Shinri Kyo's transformation from a new-religious sect to a criminal cult devoted to bringing about Armageddon through the use of ultraterrorism had entered its most deadly stage. Leading the way, of course, was the guru Asahara Shoko.

Sarin: Old Wine
in a New Battle

I ts chemical name is not sarin, but the heftier isopropyl methylphosphono-fluoridate. Benign in physical appearance, sarin is colorless and odorless in its pure liquid state. But don't be deceived by appearances. It will kill the average human being in five to fifteen minutes if less than a minute drop of it penetrates the pores of the skin. That is what it is designed to do, the only function it has—to kill people.

In the deadly world of nerve gases and military chemical warfare sarin has a code name that's straight out of James Bond. It is one of a series of what are called "G-agents." But unlike the high-tech stuff Bond uses, sarin is now so old that it is from another time, an early-model typewriter in the age of advanced word processors. And like the old typewriter it still works; the ultraterrorist can still use it to pound out a grisly modern masterpiece of mass death and injury.

Today chemists say there are more than one hundred ways in which sarin can be produced, most of them fairly simple processes that would not tax the abilities of an average graduate-level chemist. Probably the most troublesome step in the process is finding the formula, but because sarin is old technology that is no longer difficult at all. In England the best place to start looking is the patent office. In the United States, the chemical formula for sarin is readily accessible to anyone who knows what he's looking for. Most universities with large chemistry departments have it somewhere in their reference libraries, and if it can't be found there it's always available on the wackier fringes of the Internet, where its deadly secret has been spelled out in detail with disturbing regularity.

Sarin takes its name from an erroneous acronym of its German chemist inventors, Schrader, Ambrose, Rudriger, and van der Linde. According to one source, the four accidentally discovered the nerve gas in 1938 while trying to produce an agricultural insecticide using organo-phosphorous chemicals, the same chemicals found today in many modern pesticides. Their lethal discovery was turned over to Third Reich officials, who refined it as a chemical-warfare weapon. There are unconfirmed reports that German scientists tested the effectiveness of sarin on inmates in the Nazi death camps. Though the Nazis produced an arsenal of sarin and other nerve-gas weapons, they never used them against the Allied troops during World War II, probably out of fear that the Allies would use their own chemical weapons to retaliate against Germany's vulnerable urban population centers.

In addition to sarin, the Nazis produced a number of nerve gases in the late 1930s. The first was tabun, coded "GA," which was discovered by Gerhard Schrader, the same chemist who accidentally codiscovered sarin, coded "GB." Tabun is a colorless liquid in pure form; when converted to a vapor it gives off a faint odor. Like sarin, the tabun vapor is relatively "nonpersistent," a chemical-warfare term that means it tends to disperse into the air over time. This makes it a short-term threat in large, open spaces but an extremely deadly one if released in enclosed areas where it lingers longer in concentrated form and does not dissipate as rapidly as it does in the open air. Another gas in the G-agent strain is soman, or "GD," which is heavier, more poisonous, and more persistent than sarin. Soman, considered an ideal chemical-warfare weapon by Soviet defense scientists, was put into mass production by the Soviet army during the Cold War, but there is no evidence it was ever used.

Chemical weapons have been employed on the battlefield for more than two thousand five hundred years, but it was during World War I that chemical warfare entered its modern phase. Germany was then the world's leader in chemistry and the German army turned to the nation's chemists to provide them with a weapon that would break the stalemate of trench warfare on the Western Front. The first weapon they introduced was chlorine gas, a powerful choking agent that attacks the lungs. Under the right circumstances chlorine can be fatal, as the Allied armies of the West soon discovered.

April 22, 1915, dawned as a beautiful spring day over the quiet battle-front at Ypres, Belgium, when British and French troops, crowded in trenches several miles long, were suddenly startled by a loud hissing noise coming from the German lines just across the way. The hissing sound they heard came from more than six thousand chlorine-gas cylinders spraying their lethal contents upwind of the Allied forces. Looking over the edge of their trenches, the Allied soldiers saw a long cloud of white mist emerging from the German lines, heading directly toward them. An excerpt from McWilliams and Steel's book, *Gas—The Battle for Ypres, 1915*, describes the terror inflicted by the choking agent when it engulfed the British and French positions: "Shrieks of fear and uncontrolled coughing filled the poisonous air. Terrified soldiers clutched their throats, their eyes starting out in terror and pain. Many collapsed in the bottom of their trenches and others clambered out and staggered to the rear in attempts to escape the deadly cloud. Those left in the trenches writhed with agony unspeakable, their faces plum-colored, while they coughed blood from their tortured lungs."

Caught completely unprepared for the German chemical attack, the Allied forces in one day suffered more than fifteen thousand casualties. But the German chlorine gas was only the opening curtain in gas warfare. Yet to come was mustard gas, the most horrific chemical agent used in the Great War and still considered by chemical-warfare specialists as one of the most gruesome gases in their arsenal.

In 1917 the German army fired more than one million artillery shells filled with mustard gas into the French city of Armentières, killing or wounding most its residents. Mustard gas is a brown, garlic-smelling liquid which inflicts unusually painful burns on any part of the body it reaches, including the eyes, ears, throat, nasal passages, and lungs. There is no anti-dote for mustard gas and it is extremely persistent. Science writer Malcolm W. Browne of *The New York Times* reported that "even 40 years after World War I, tree stumps in France contaminated with mustard gas still caused casualties when farmers sat on them to rest." Browne goes on to note that even though only six hundred of the one hundred twenty-six thousand Americans killed in action died of mustard-gas poisoning, a far larger number were permanently disfigured or disabled by the substance. In the 1930s and 1940s, veterans whose faces were pitted by scars and who spoke in croaking voices through vocal cords seared by "King Mustard" were a familiar sight in America. Nor is King Mustard's long march through military history over. Today chemical warfare researchers have refined the agent into a much more toxic "sulfur-mustard" weapon, which Iraq manufactured in the 1980s and used in its war against Iran.

Though world opinion condemned the use of chemical agents in warfare and their use was banned at the Geneva Convention, today more than twenty nations continue to develop and stockpile the weapons or possess the capability to manufacture them. World opinion and diplomatic accords are no match for the hatreds engendered by nations at war. In the 1960s, Egypt used poison gas against Yemen, and during the war between Iran and Iraq that lasted from 1980 until 1988, United Nations officials documented the use of chemical weapons by both sides with casualties totaling more than forty-five thousand. In 1988, the Iraqi regime demonstrated its willingness to use chemical warfare against innocent civilians when it unleashed sarin against the villages of its rebellious Kurdish minorities, producing thousands of victims, most of them women and children.

While most of the major deployments of chemical weapons have taken place during wartime in Western Europe and the Middle East, Asia has also experienced its share of modern military chemical and biological horrors. Strangely, one of the least-publicized facts of World War II is that Japan was the only nation in the conflict to employ chemical warfare against both military and civilian targets in several Asian nations, the most horrific example being China. In fact, Japan is the only nation in the modern history of Asia that has resorted to this practice.

Whether the Nazis passed along any of the technology for the G-agent nerve gases to their Japanese allies during World War II is still an open question, but it is a matter of historical record backed up by considerable concrete evidence that the Japanese Imperial Army had a very active chemical-warfare department that produced lethal gases used to indiscriminately kill tens of thousands of people in its military campaigns in China.

Today the Japanese military remains as capable of producing chemical weapons of mass destruction as it was in the 1930s and 1940s. Annually the Japanese Self-Defense Forces produce a limited amount of chemical weapons for "research purposes" at the Japanese army chemical school in Saitama Prefecture, north of Tokyo. Japan Defense Agency officials state that the weapons are produced "for use in the development of protective gear and

Shoko Asahara, the founder and "holy emperor" of Aum
Shinri Kyo, giving a lecture in Yoyogi Park in February 1995.
KYODO NEWS.

RIGHT:
Kiyohide Hayakawa was Asahara's second in command and the sect's Minister of Construction. He participated in the Sakamoto murders and personally engineered Aum's entry into Russia and its militarization program.
KYODO NEWS.

LEFT:
Hisako Ishii, Aum's Minister of Finance and a driving force behind the sect's accumulation of wealth. One of Asahara's original disciples, she quickly achieved a high rank in the sect's spiritual hierarchy.
KYODO NEWS.

RIGHT:
Fumihiro Joyu, a graduate of prestigious Waseda University, became the sect's public spokesman and, for a short time, a charismatic media star with a following of young female fans.
KYODO NEWS.

LEFT:
Attorney Yoshinobu Aoyama, was a vigorous defender of Aum against Sakamoto's charges that the sect was defrauding its followers, and his aggressive tactics served Aum well in several other cases as well.
KYODO NEWS.

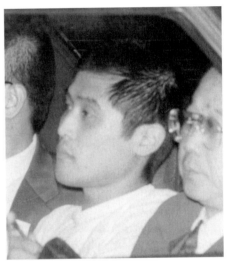

RIGHT:
Masami Tsuchiya, a doctoral-level researcher in organic physics and chemistry at Tsukuba University, played a central role in Aum's manufacture of sarin.
KYODO NEWS.

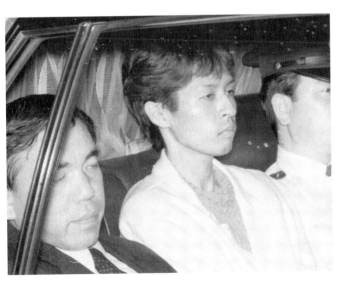

LEFT:
Yoshihiro Inoue was head of Aum's Intelligence Ministry and was a key figure in the kidnapping of Kiyoshi Kariya, which triggered the police response against Aum.
KYODO NEWS.

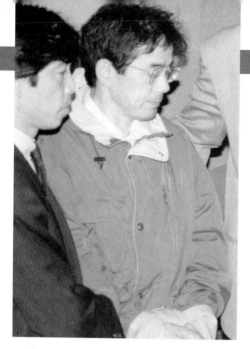

ABOVE:
Attorney Tsutsumi
Sakamoto with his
wife Satoko and son
Tatsuhiko. All three
were murdered by an
Aum hit squad.
KYODO NEWS.

LEFT:
A cold rain fell on
September 11, 1995, as
investigators contin-
ued their inspection
of the site in Nagano
Prefecture where the
body of Sakamoto's
infant son Tatsuhiko
was found.
KYODO NEWS.

The scene of the Matsumoto
sarin attack. Kono's house on
its wooded lot is in the center.
KYODO NEWS.

Yoshiyuki Kono, at a press conference on June 19, 1995, after
receiving apologies from Self-
Government Minister Nonaka.
Kono, one of the victims of the
Matsumoto sarin attack, was at
first falsely identified by police
as the prime suspect.
KYODO NEWS.

ABOVE, LEFT:
The full advertisement
for "Asahara Shoko's
Siddhi Course,"
promising to be "the
key to developing
superpowers, and the
opening chapter on
a wonderful life."
KYODO NEWS.

ABOVE, RIGHT:
The Dalai Lama and
Asahara, from an Aum
pamphlet.
KYODO NEWS.

Shoko Asahara in
December 1987 de-
monstrating his mas-
tery of levitation, in
a detail from an Aum
advertisement to
attract new followers.
KYODO NEWS.

真理党次期衆議院選挙出馬表明式
麻原彰晃党首と24名 ...

必勝！真

Asahara and twenty-four other Aum
candidates campaign for seats in the
House of Representatives.
KYODO NEWS.

An Aum follower wearing the sect's
PSI (Perfect Salvation Initiation) headgear. Photo taken during the police
raid on the sect's facilities in Kamikuishiki at the end of March 1995.
KYODO NEWS.

Asahara with ¥220 million in Aum funds that went temporarily "missing" during the 1990 election campaign. After reporting to police that the money had been stolen by a follower, Asahara suddenly located it again and called a press conference to confirm that the money had been found.
FOCUS, SHINCHOSHA.

Followers meditating on the beach during the Aum seminar at Ishigakijima in April 1990.
KYODO NEWS.

Asahara and his wife, Tomoko Matsumoto, on a visit to Moscow.

KYODO NEWS.

Followers pray at the Moscow branch of Aum Shinri Kyo.

REUTERS / KYODO NEWS.

Aum followers in meditation at Aum headquarters in Fujinomiya on May 19, 1995, three days after the arrest of Asahara.

KYODO NEWS.

Aum facilities at Kamikuishiki, with Mount Fuji rising in the background. The building in the foreground is Satyam Number 7, where the sect is believed to have manufactured the sarin gas and illegal drugs.

KYODO NEWS.

Aerial view of the scene on March 20, 1995, outside Tsukiji Station on the Hibiya Line, as victims of the sarin attack receive emergency medical treatment.
KYODO NEWS.

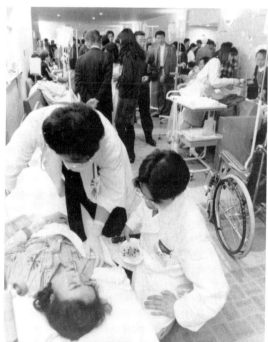

Outside Tsukiji Station
soon after the sarin attack.
KYODO NEWS.

Shortly after the subway
gas attack began, Saint
Luke's International
Hospital near Tsukiji
Station was overwhelmed
by victims, many of whom
received emergency treat-
ment in the halls and
corridors.
KYODO NEWS.

Investigators in protective gear remove bags of chemicals from an Aum facility in Kamikuishiki during a police raid on March 23, 1995.
KYODO NEWS.

The massive air purification system at Aum's Kamikuishiki compound.
KYODO NEWS.

The civilian version of a Russian military helicopter purchased by Aum sits idle in the sect's Kamikuishiki compound.
KYODO NEWS.

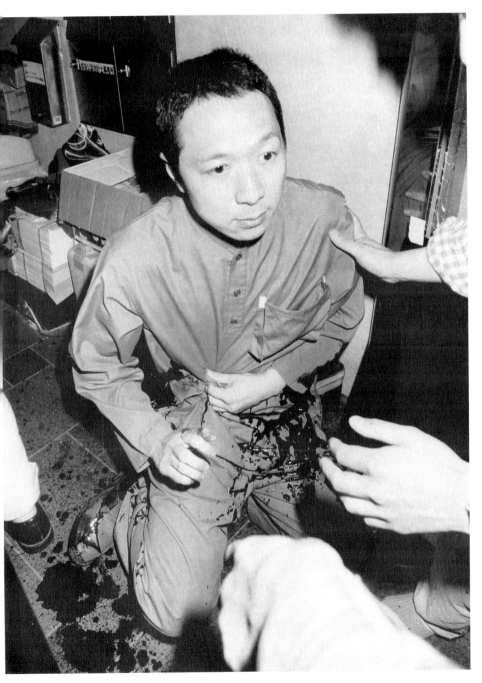

Murai Hideo immediately after his fatal stabbing on April 23, 1995.

Asahara in police custody after his arrest on May 16, 1995.

KYODO NEWS /
YAMANASHI NICHINICHI NEWS

By late October, huge mug shots of fugitive Aum followers were prominently displayed in railway stations—here, the JR Tamachi Station—as police sought their arrest.

KYODO NEWS.

gas masks." It also confirms that mustard gas and other poisonous gases are made at the site, including one hundred milligrams of sarin. Left unsaid is the fact that this annual production of chemical weapons allows Japan's defense establishment to maintain state-of-the-art production knowledge in the event it is ever needed.

The physical effects of the various agents used in chemical warfare—and now by ultraterrorists—vary with the type of agent deployed and the circumstances under which it is used. Like artillery shells, grenades, and bombs dropped from aircraft, gas weapons do not discriminate among their victims. James A. Genovese, head of the Chemical/Biological Counterterrorism Team of the U.S. Army's Chemical and Biological Defense Command, recently described the vulnerability of the human body to chemical warfare agents: "There are three methods for producing chemical casualties within human beings: through inhalation; through skin effects which include both absorption through the skin and dermal wounds; and through ingestion of hazards through the digestive tract. These methods are called routes of entry."

He cited hydrogen cyanide, chlorine, and sarin as examples of chemical inhalation agents. Hydrogen cyanide—which Aum Shinri Kyo also produced in its laboratories—is a "blood agent" that directly inhibits breathing by interrupting a key enzyme responsible for producing energy in the body. Chlorine and sarin we have met before. The relative toxicity of each of these three varies widely. Genovese said that a container with forty-eight ounces of chlorine can produce up to five thousand lethal casualties. Some twenty-five ounces of hydrogen cyanide would have the same effect. A mere third of an ounce of sarin is all that is needed to kill the same five thousand. Each of these examples is based on the assumption that the weapon is disseminated with maximum effectiveness.

One of the most dangerous gases relying on the skin exposure route of entry is VX, another agent that Aum successfully produced and used to kill its opponents. V-agents are highly persistent and have a low rate of vaporization. An oily, non-volatile liquid, VX can linger in place for weeks or longer, posing a continuing threat to anyone in the area where it was dispersed. Extremely toxic, it enters the body through the skin, and in the case of one Aum victim it produced a lingering, painful death.

The final route of entry for chemical agents is through ingestion. Cyanide is a common poison that is readily available as sodium or potassium salts. It works on the same principle as hydrogen cyanide, by aggressively attacking the body's respiratory system. The effectiveness of cyanide has been demonstrated on numerous occasions, the most dramatic being the mass suicide of more than eight hundred followers of the Reverend Jim Jones in Guyana in November 1978.

In analyzing human vulnerability to chemical weapons of mass destruction, it is also important to consider the volatility, or evaporation rate, of the agent. Hydrogen cyanide, for instance, dissipates so rapidly that its use outdoors is very limited; in an enclosed space, however, it is extremely effective. Persistent chemical agents, those that linger for lengthy periods such as mustard gas and VX, are not as volatile, and when sprayed or poured onto large open areas will linger for long periods, causing death and serious injury over that time.

Though much of the history of chemical warfare has been public knowledge for decades, Aum Shinri Kyo's intense interest in chemical weapons did not surface until the Gulf War in 1991, when the top leadership saw first hand the extraordinary potential nerve gas had for inflicting mass casualties and spreading fear in heavily populated areas. By that time the sect's scientists were already hard at work trying to produce biological weapons.

Chemical- and biological-arms-control expert Kyle Olson states that Aum had a "dedicated laboratory as early as 1990, in which they produced biological toxins." But while culturing lethal biological organisms is comparatively easy, turning them into effective weapons is much more difficult, a dark science that Aum never really mastered. Prompted by the Gulf War television coverage and their failure to quickly produce an effective method for disseminating their lethal biological agents, Aum's scientists turned to chemical warfare as an alternative, one that finally hit pay dirt for them.

Aum's chief chemist and the head of its chemical-warfare team was thirty-year-old Masami Tsuchiya, a devout member of the sect who received his doctoral degree from Tsukuba University in organic physics and chemistry. Tsuchiya would later claim that he first produced sarin in his own personal lab in November 1993, and that the experiment was "nothing but a scientific interest" that had no specific purpose. His "personal laboratory" was a small but sophisticated facility adjoining the main laboratory in the Aum Kamikuishiki compound. Given Asahara's darkly apocalyptic mood at the time, the sarin experiments known to have been conducted on sheep in Australia in September 1993, and the very chemicals with which he was working, Tsuchiya's assertion, to put the most generous face on it, is highly dubious. Though he successfully pioneered the development of sarin for the group, Tsuchiya was not the only Aum chemist to make the nerve gas. In order to insure that the sect had a core of scientists with sarin-production knowledge, Asahara also assigned the task of making the nerve gas to bio-chemist Seiichi Endo, thirty-four, the head of Aum's Health and Welfare Ministry, and to Kazumi Watanabe, thirty-six, a computer specialist who was the number-two man in the Science and Technology Ministry under Hideo Murai. Working in their own separate lab facilities like Tsuchiya, both men were able to produce the agent. Now that Aum's scientists had mastered the chemistry involved, they needed a laboratory large enough to mass produce the nerve agent. Asahara assigned the overall project to mass produce sarin to Murai, and he in turn placed Watanabe, the computer expert, in charge of creating the lab.

By late 1993, Watanabe had work well under way on a modern chemical laboratory in a building called Satyam (Truth) Number 7 located in the Kami-kuishiki compound. Designed and constructed to produce large quantities of nerve gas, illegal drugs, and other chemicals, the lab in Satyam Number 7 was connected to several external cooling towers by a web of piping leading inside the building. Entry to the building was tightly controlled and its door was made of steel. Aum's leaders told members not associated with the project that the lab was the sect's "science and technology agency," a highly secret place which ordinary sect members were not allowed to enter.

The lab itself was an extremely sophisticated setup in which advanced computerized chemical equipment was used to synthesize sarin, tabun, VX, and other chemical weapons. During its short lifespan, which extended from late 1993 through the fall of 1994, Satyam Number 7 grew like Topsy as advanced equipment purchased in the United States and Japan began to crowd Aum's secret laboratory. Eventually the lab became so cramped that a small building had to be constructed next door to house hundreds of thousands of dollars worth of optical-analysis equipment used to measure gases. Experts estimate the cost of the laboratory exceeded a million dollars and, judging from the huge amounts of chemicals stored nearby, Aum clearly intended to use the facilities to mass produce sarin and other chemical weapons of mass destruction that would be deployed against the Japanese people—and perhaps Americans—to trigger Shoko Asahara's Armageddon prophecies.

But despite the best efforts of Murai, Watanabe, Tsuchiya, and their scientific and technical staff of more than three hundred followers, they were never able to mass produce sarin or any other chemical weapon in the sect's shiny new laboratory. This was because the hardest part of the process was to create the gas without killing the people making it. Head chemist Tsuchiya would later confess to Japanese police that he had tried to mass produce sarin in the facility but that during the process there were repeated leaks of toxic substances. He said a number of Aum's lab technicians inhaled the deadly fumes and suffered varying symptoms of sarin poisoning such as vision problems, nosebleeds, and muscular spasms. As Tsuchiya said, the leaks of sarin inside the facility were often massive, sometimes escaping the building and spreading beyond the carefully guarded perimeters of the sect compound to the nearby farming village of Kamikuishiki. Understandably, this only added to the problems the sect was having with its neighbors.

The villagers of Kamikuishiki actively disliked the behavior of the religious sect and wanted Aum to leave almost from the moment it arrived in 1989. But far from leaving, the sect was growing, and the villagers watched in dismay as building after building rose in the closed compound, finally totaling thirty-four in all. Aum members wore weird electronic headgear and blared their sacred mantras over the loudspeakers late at night. They were also untidy, a flaw considered unforgivable by conservative rural Japanese, and littered the ground inside their compound with empty chemical containers and other debris. Then there was the march.

One evening the villagers were startled when a procession of more than three hundred Aum members clad in ghostly white gowns left the compound's buildings and began a solemn march across the hills and down through the little village. It scared the hell out of the children.

But it was when their dairy cows stopped producing milk that the villagers knew something was terribly wrong inside the religious compound. In the spring of 1994 they began to detect foul odors. Some said the smell resembled burnt plastic. Being farmers who lived close to the earth, they also noticed that patches of vegetation and leaves on the trees adjacent to the Aum compound had suddenly wilted and died. Certain that something suspicious was taking place in the mysterious sect compound, they called the police and demanded an investigation.

In early July the Japanese police arrived at Kamikuishiki, heard the complaints of the villagers, made notes in their books, and before leaving took soil samples from around the strange patches of dead vegetation. Several months later police chemical analysts learned that the soil samples they had collected contained chemical compounds used to make the nerve gas sarin, the same compounds that had been taken from the soil following the sarin attack in Matsumoto in late June.

But while the police were making this discovery, Tsuchiya and his superiors in the Science and Technology Ministry of Aum Shinri Kyo were reaching some conclusions of their own. In its present state, the chemical laboratory located in Satyam Number 7 was riddled with toxic leakage and other problems that made it unsafe, and until those problems were solved it was not going to produce the large quantities of nerve gas needed to initiate Asahara's Armageddon. That would take time, the one thing Aum no longer had. By now the sect's leadership was growing uneasy, fearing that the Japanese police, though moving at what seemed like glacial speed to its critics, were closing in on them. Sometime in late 1994, Asahara told Tsuchiya and his cohorts to shut down the Satyam Number 7 laboratory. The young chemist later told police that he made sarin only four times after his first successful experiment with the nerve gas in 1994. His total output in both his own smaller lab and the bigger one adjoining it amounted to only thirty liters of the deadly agent. But though the nerve gas laboratory in Satyam Number 7 never realized its deadly potential, its role in Aum's surreal drama was far from over.

Satyam Number 7 underwent a major overhaul beginning in early January 1995 after Asahara was shocked by press reports that sarin-related chemicals had been discovered in the soil near the Kamikuishiki compound. Fearful that the police might raid the building and find the laboratory, he summoned Hideo Murai and Kiyohide Hayakawa to a hasty meeting in which he ordered the two to quickly remodel Satyam Number 7 and turn it into a worship hall. At the same time they were also to begin removing any evidence that sarin or other chemical weapons and drugs were produced there. But in his haste to disguise the laboratory, Asahara either forgot or ignored the tons of incriminating chemicals that were stored all around the buildings. Nonetheless, the work started immediately, and among the first incriminating items to go were the chlorine and distillation equipment and drug stockpiles. Disguising the building was another matter.

Murai and Hayakawa adorned the interior of Satyam Number 7 with two religious sculptures that they believed would lend credence to its new sacred status as Aum's highest religious sanctuary. One sculpture was a gold-colored, three-foot figure of Buddha; the other a cheap-looking, fifteen-foot polystyrene image of the face of Shiva, the Hindu god of destruction and re-creation and Aum's chief deity. As part of its new cover, Aum members were told that Satyam Number 7 was now the sect's highest place of worship, a holy sanctuary that supposedly contained some of the remains of Buddha that Asahara had brought back from Sri Lanka during one of his pilgrimages there.

The remodeling was completed in February 1994, and in an effort to publicize its new image Aum invited a number of religious authorities and selected members of the news media to inspect the newly opened "sacred hall of worship." Aum spokesmen told the media representatives that the building was so holy that all visitors were now required to change into blue gowns before they could enter. The visitors complied with this odd request, not realizing that on the other side of the wall, cloaked in darkness behind the cheap foam mask of Shiva, lay the partially skeletonized remnants of the world's first ultraterrorist nerve-gas laboratory. The next outside visitors to breach the silence of Satyam Number 7 would be also be wearing blue, but it would be the rough blue uniforms of the Japanese police and in their hands they would carry small cages containing yellow canaries.

Why Aum Shinri Kyo's scientists chose sarin as their nerve gas of preference is difficult to answer. One certain influence was the Gulf War; another was the ease with which they were able to acquire the technical data, equipment, and chemicals for making it; and a third may have been its relative cheapness to produce. Certainly the sect's chemists were working on the development of other, more deadly gases—VX, tabun, and mustard gas—and if events had not closed in on them so rapidly, they might have developed and used one of those deadlier agents as their primary weapon. But for their immediate purposes, sarin was the easily available choice, and as a weapon of terror it was highly effective.

Relatively easy to produce in small quantities, as Tsuchiya and others demonstrated in their labs, sarin was highly impressive in its Matsumoto field test against actual human targets. Though not as deadly as tabun, soman, or VX, sarin still packed a reliably lethal and easy punch, a major consideration for Aum's leaders. Whatever else could be said about it, they knew that sarin was effective. It killed.

In describing the toxic effects of sarin on human beings, chemical warfare experts resort to technical language that largely disguises what it does to the human body. One expert describes it like this: "an inhalation hazard that inhibits the enzyme cholinesterase which facilitates nerve transmission and muscle coordination." But that prosaic insider's language is intended to mask a terrible truth.

Here's what really happens when the average person takes in a lungful of sarin. The first thing he will notice is a dimming of vision caused by gradual contraction of the pupils. Then uncontrollable vomiting occurs as the mouth salivates excessively and blood starts to pour from the nose. Within in a few minutes the next phase begins: sudden, wracking, involuntary muscular spasms grip the body, a certain sign that the sarin is shutting down the voluntary nervous system. The ability to think logically begins to decline as the chemical reactions in the brain that make human beings rational are gradually closed down. Finally, assuming a sufficient dose, the lungs and heart stop functioning.

The timing of death? It all depends on a lot of variables, but in the worst case all of the above can happen more or less simultaneously and death can occur in minutes. In situations where the exposure is not so severe, it can take up to hours. Some victims may not die but lapse into comas from which they never recover. Doctors make no promises about the future health of those who survive a sarin attack because medical science has no reliable data on the aftereffects of this toxic gas.

Many of the sect members who were involved in making the deadly gas are now claiming in court that they were unaware of how it would be used, and that they had no idea what horrible effects it had on people. But the most damning evidence of the chemical team's knowledge of the nerve agent occurs in a manual dated December 30, 1994, which the police recovered from an Aum facility. In the manual is the chemical formula for making sarin, plus a song entitled "Song of Sarin, the Magician":

It came from Nazi Germany,
A dangerous little chemical weapon,
Sarin—, Sarin—
If you inhale the mysterious vapor,
You will fall with bloody vomit from your mouth,
Sarin—, Sarin—, Sarin—
The chemical weapon.
Song of Sarin, the Brave.

In the peaceful night of Matsumoto City
People can be killed, even with their own hands,
The place is full of dead bodies everywhere,
There! Inhale Sarin—, Sarin—
Prepare Sarin! Prepare Sarin!
Immediately poisonous gas weapons will fill the place.
Spray! Spray!
Sarin, the Brave Sarin.

Sarin in the Subway:
Ultraterrorism's
Brave New Morning

The proximate cause of the Tokyo subway nerve-gas attack was the abduction of a sixty-eight-year-old office manager by the name of Kiyoshi Kariya. A quiet, unassuming man, Kariya ran a notary office in a small building owned by his sixty-two-year-old sister in Tokyo's Shinagawa Ward. In early 1995, Kariya had a real problem on his hands, though at the time he may not have realized just how serious it was about to become. His sister had joined Aum Shinri Kyo in October 1993, and in the intervening years had personally handed Shoko Asahara a small fortune—some four hundred thousand dollars out of a total of six hundred thousand she would eventually donate to the sect. But despite her generosity, some top Aum leaders felt there was a lot more she could do.

In January, Aum members approached Kariya's sister with the suggestion that she renounce the secular world, give the sect her land and building in Shinagawa, along with her vacation home, and then enter an Aum commune to become a monastic. Not keen on the idea and distressed by the high-pressure tactics employed against her, on February 24, 1995 she slipped out of the sect's building in the posh Minami Aoyama section of Tokyo and went into hiding. When the news reached Shoko Asahara that she had fled in the face of Aum's proposal, he ordered Yoshihiro Inoue, the group's twenty-five-year-old Intelligence Minister, and other members to track her down and return her to the fold. His motive was the building and land.

Even for a group that prided itself on the youthfulness and education of its top members, Yoshihiro Inoue was unique, a young man in a class all by himself. Unlike other Aum leaders, he did not have an elite university pedigree, or indeed, a degree of any kind. He dropped out of college after several months to dedicate his life to Aum Shinri Kyo, and by dint of sheer religious devotion and a zealous attitude that was unusual even for an organization filled with zealots, he soon rose through the sect's ranks. His religious fervor was exceeded only by his uncompromising dedication to Asahara; on one memorable occasion he declared to several Aum members that he would willingly kill his parents if the guru ordered it. There was no doubt in anyone's mind that the earnest young man meant what he said.

Born in Kyoto, the cultural capital of Japan, Inoue joined Aum as a high-school junior after being seriously injured in martial arts practice two years earlier—an injury which was reportedly healed by Asahara. Inoue quickly became a fanatic believer who sought out opportunities to promote Aum Shinri Kyo through his personal example. In doing so he was able to recruit many others into the sect, an achievement that brought him to the attention of the group's top aides. His classmates in high school remember him as a skinny kid who would meditate in the lotus position by the side of the hallways during class breaks, a sort of living advertisement for Aum Shinri Kyo. They also recall that he was so articulate and persuasive as a recruiter that he even talked his mother into joining the sect. For these and other acts of devotion he eventually became known within Aum's membership as a "Mini-Asahara," a sobriquet which undoubtedly pleased both Asahara and his unquestioning young disciple.

Four days after Kariya's sister slipped out of Aum Shinri Kyo's compound in Minami Aoyama, he was in deep trouble. He must have known of his sister's plight and wondered what it all meant to him. He was soon to learn. Closing the notary office on schedule, Kariya left the building at 4:30 P.M. and stepped out into the street. There he was seized by three waiting sect members, forced into a small van, and injected with a drug that instantly knocked him unconscious. By early evening the elderly man awoke to find himself a prisoner in Aum's Kamikuishiki compound on the slopes of Mount Fuji, surrounded by a group of hostile people who wanted to know where his sister was. He either didn't know the answer or wouldn't give it to them. Inoue then ordered Ikuo Hayashi, forty-eight, a senior Aum member and medical doctor who managed a sect clinic in Tokyo, to inject Kariya with a "truth serum" called thiopental that the sect had illegally manufactured and often used on its members. In administering the drug, Hayashi was either unfamiliar with the correct dosage, or he failed to understand the effect it might have on the heart of an elderly man. Kiyoshi Kariya lapsed into unconsciousness and died the following day. It was left to Tomomasa Nakagawa, the doctor who was head of the sect's Household Agency, Asahara's personal family doctor, and a murderer of lawyer Sakamoto and his wife and baby son, to perform a medical service at which he was now adept. He pronounced Kariya dead.

As always, Asahara personally decided how the body would be disposed of. When Nakagawa consulted him on the matter he was told to haul the remains to the basement of Satyam Number 2, where a special microwave incinerator had been installed. Once the body was burned, Asahara ordered the ashes dumped into a nearby lake.

The Aum abduction squad's big mistake was one that had to catch up with them sooner or later. When setting out on a criminal operation Aum's usual practice was to rent the cars and vans it used rather than taking its own vehicles or employing the well-worn but effective tactic of simply stealing the vehicles they needed. From a practical standpoint, renting a vehicle for use in a crime is a poor idea because it runs a high risk of leaving an incriminating trail of paperwork and witnesses—the rental forms and the clerks who might later give police an accurate identification of the renter. Aum never seemed to figure this out, and in the case of Kariya it came back to haunt them.

As is often the case in crime, it is the minor actor, the peripheral figure, who unintentionally makes a mistake that gives away the game. In Kariya's kidnapping, that minor actor was a pathetic young Aum member named Takeshi Matsumoto. Matsumoto was a personable young man with dreams of becoming a Grand Prix auto racer. The sect's leaders found this ambition sufficient to qualify him for a spot as the van driver on the abduction team, a position which meant he had to rent the vehicle. In filling out the forms, Matsumoto left his fingerprints all over the many papers he signed. The Japanese police also had witnesses who saw the license plates of the van into which Kariya was abducted, and with that description they made the rounds of rental agencies until they found what they were looking for.

Matsumoto's fingerprints and his identity as an Aum member were the legal pretext the Japanese police needed to raid the sect's compounds and offices across the country. They had been waiting desperately for just this kind of break. Battered for months by the press and politicians for the slowness of their investigation into the Sakamoto murders, the Matsumoto gassing, and the many other accusations made against the sect, the police were all too aware that a good deal more than just the Kariya abduction was riding on the fingerprints of Takeshi Matsumoto. Despite the public criticism and pressure they silently endured, the police had been working hard to crack the case. They had other fingerprints—chemical fingerprints—that were deeply incriminating; but still they did not believe that was strong enough evidence to make a good legal case for raiding a religious sect. They had known since September 1994 that the soil samples from Matsumoto and Kamikuishiki, the farming village near the Aum compound on the slope of Mount Fuji, had yielded the same results after analysis. Each location revealed undeniable traces of sarin compounds and the police strongly suspected that Aum was making nerve gas in one of the buildings of the Kamikuishiki compound. Matsumoto's fingerprints, however, were the solid legal knife into the hide of Aum Shinri Kyo that the Japanese National Police had patiently waited for.

At this point, their biggest gaffe was the steps they took within the department to acquire protective gear to shield their policemen against the chemical threat they knew they faced in the Kamikuishiki compound. In mid-March, the week before their planned raid on Aum facilities, the police asked the Japanese army to supply them with three hundred gas masks and protective suits. This unusual request was picked up by two alert army sergeants who were members of Aum. They proceeded to ask a few questions and then informed the sect leadership via an open computer network that the police raid was scheduled for early the following week, March 22.

The planned police raid was all the embattled Asahara needed to hear. The news media was clamoring for fast action on the Kariya abduction and strongly hinting that Aum Shinri Kyo was behind the crime, and possibly involved in other equally serious matters, such as the gassing at Matsumoto.

Asahara sensed his web was unraveling and he quickly gathered his top aides for a war council. A quick fix was needed to ease the pressure and stop the police. As always, the Master had the answer. Asahara instructed Hideo Murai to prepare plans for a massive sarin attack on the Tokyo subways, centering on the subway lines running through the busy Kasumigaseki district, an area near the heart of Tokyo that was home to a large number of major government agencies and the headquarters of the Japanese National Police. Every weekday morning, tens of thousands of government workers rode into the Kasumigaseki district on packed trains, ascended the conveyors and concrete steps to the surface, and walked briskly to work in the nearby government buildings. Asahara's terrorist plan was ingenious, but the difficulty was its timing. The guru wanted the strike to take place on Monday morning, March 20. That meant Murai's sarin team had little more than a weekend in which to come up with a plan of action and produce the sarin to carry it out.

It was the biggest challenge the guru had ever handed his Science and Technology Minister, but Murai, like Inoue, was a consummate zealot dedicated to realizing the Master's orders. If the subway attack could be done, he was the man who would do it. Anticipating the short-order sarin production problem, Asahara ordered Seiichi Endo to immediately begin work on producing the nerve gas. Along with Masami Tsuchiya and Tomomasa Nakagawa, Endo set to work. Helpful in the process was a chemical by-product that Nakagawa had left over from an earlier sarin production run and that could be used to easily make the nerve gas. Murai instructed him to bring the chemical to Endo's personal lab, where on the night of March 19 he and Endo made almost two gallons of sarin under the supervision of Tsuchiya.

But there were problems with the final product that disturbed the fastidious Endo. In making the sarin under rush conditions in Endo's small laboratory, a large number of impurities had entered the liquid, and the three men reached the conclusion that its strength was considerably reduced. Endo was concerned that the impurities had diluted the sarin to the point that it might not produce the number of casualties required to successfully carry out the guru's plan. He went to Asahara's personal quarters in Satyam Number 6 and confessed his misgivings to the Master.

"It is completed, but it's still not pure," he said. "It is a mixture [of sarin and impurities]."

"That's OK," Asahara replied, thus approving the use of the impure mixture for the nerve-gas attack and in the process perhaps saving thousands of lives, although that was certainly not his intent. He undoubtedly reasoned that impure sarin was better than no sarin at all, and with time running out, the main thing was to strike back on Monday, the next day, with whatever sarin was available. Chemical analysis would later reveal that the sarin was considerably weaker than even Endo or Asahara suspected. It was estimated to be only thirty-percent pure; by no means harmless, but less harmful than it could be.

Obedient as ever, Endo trooped back to Satyam Number 7 and relayed Asahara's orders to the waiting Murai, Tsuchiya, and Nakagawa. Murai then gave the three men sheets of plastic wrapping and told them to place the liquid sarin inside it. The men cut the plastic into eight-by-eight-inch squares, and using a sealing machine they converted them into bags with each corner specially cut to create an opening. A little over twenty ounces of sarin were carefully poured into each bag, which was then sealed. Eleven bags were made. To prevent the bags from leaking as they were being carried, each was placed inside a larger plastic bag that was ten inches square and completely sealed.

His long work done, Endo carried the eleven bags to Murai in Satyam Number 7, where they briefly discussed the process used to seal the sarin. Murai, who already knew how the sarin would be released on the subway, told Endo to make five similar plastic bags filled with water so he could train the Aum members who would carry out the attack. Endo made the practice bags and took them to Murai, who then instructed Nakagawa to prepare five sarin antidote pills for the sect members who would make the attack. Thus Nakagawa learned to his great relief that he would not be one of those asked to unleash the nerve gas in the subways.

For that deadly deed Murai chose four vice ministers of his own Science and Technology ministry: Yasuo Hayashi, Kenichi Hirose, Masato Yokoyama, and Toru Toyoda. The fifth member was Dr. Ikuo Hayashi, head of Aum's Medical Treatment Ministry. Figuring closely in the planning and execution of the attack was the young Minister of Intelligence, Inoue, who was given the critical task of procuring vehicles, conveying the members to their attack sites, and acting as a conduit for final instructions. On the night the sarin was produced, all members of the attack team already knew they had been selected for the operation and what their role would be. The morning before, Murai fully briefed Inoue on Asahara's plan to gas the subways, and shortly afterward brought the five men into the scheme, telling them they were the ones who were actually going to release the gas.

Although each of the men must have realized the enormous danger they faced in such a desperate, untested operation, all of them readily agreed to participate. On the afternoon of the same day, March 18, now less than two days from zero hour, the busy Murai gathered a small group in his room to plot exactly which subway lines and stations to target. Poring over a map of the city's subway lines he asked, "Where are the exits near the Metropolitan Police Department? If we carry out the attack, places near the MPD are better." Following a discussion of the pros and cons, he ordered the sarin attacks to take place on the Hibiya, Marunouchi, and Chiyoda subway lines, all main arteries that feed into the Kasumigaseki Station, and then confirmed that the nerve gas would be unleashed at 8 A.M. on Monday, March 20, during the height of rush hour.

By March 19, most of the assault team was in Tokyo and ten members of the group met with Inoue at a sect hideout in a condominium in Shibuya Ward to receive their personal assignments. Inoue broke down the attack targets and assigned them to five teams of two men each. One man would enter the subway and unleash the sarin and the other would be the driver of a getaway car that would be waiting at a predetermined point after the attack. Inoue divided the teams and their targets as follows (the first person in each pair would release the sarin and the second would be the getaway driver): Yasuo Hayashi and Shigeo Sugimoto would attack the Naka Meguro-bound train on the Hibiya Line; Toru Toyoda and Katsuya Takahashi would attack the Kitasenju-bound train on the Hibiya Line; Kenichi Hirose and Koichi Kitamura would attack the Ogikubo-bound train on the Marunouchi Line; Ikuo Hayashi and Tomomitsu Niimi would attack the Yoyogi Uehara-bound train on the Chiyoda Line; Masato Yokoyama and Kiyotaka Tonozaki would attack the Ikebukuro-bound train on the Marunouchi Line.

The attack was intended to spread the nerve gas among five subway cars on the three lines going into Kasumigaseki. When the trains stopped to let out and take on passengers, the odorless and colorless gas would spread from the cars and contaminate the station platforms along the way. If all went as planned, five subway cars, each approaching from a different direction and filled with sarin, would crisscross through the busy Kasumigaseki intersection shortly after 8 A.M., leaving behind them a number of poisoned subway stops. Anyone headed toward Kasumigaseki on the three lines shortly before or after 8 A.M. on Monday stood an excellent chance of riding straight into the deadly gas. Tens of thousands of workers going to the numerous stops before and after Kasumigaseki on the three heavily traveled subway lines, all of which served the busy inner heart of downtown Tokyo, were equally in peril.

The five teams left the Shibuya hideaway at about 10 P.M. in cars and proceeded to their respective target stations, where they boarded the subway trains and conducted a personal, on-site surveillance of the places where they would puncture their bags of sarin. Their confidence buoyed somewhat by the stolid familiarity of the subway system, they next met to conduct a carefully detailed review of the equally critical second phase of the operation: the plans for linking up with their drivers after the attack and making a getaway. No one could say what was likely to happen when they jabbed the sarin pouches. Would an observant passenger notice what they were doing and protest? After all, it was bound to seem strange for a passenger to suddenly begin stabbing at something on the floor with the tip of his umbrella, honed ice-pick sharp. If someone noticed, would they call a subway attendant, or worse, a policeman, both of whom were usually somewhere on each bustling station platform? They agreed they'd have to handle this when and if it happened; knowing that a driver and car was waiting outside was reassuring in the face of such unknowns.

The teams confirmed their plans and returned to the hideout, but for five of them the long night was not over. At about 1:30 A.M. on March 20, Murai phoned Yasuo Hayashi at the Shibuya hideout and ordered him to come right away to Satyam Number 7 with the four other team members who would release the sarin. The purpose of this trip in the morning's wee hours was to issue the sarin pouches to the strike force and conduct some last-minute training. The five men piled into two cars and headed out to the Kamikuishiki compound, where they arrived at 3 A.M. While the five were en route, Murai remembered another detail that had been left undone in the rush. He phoned Inoue and told him to buy seven umbrellas, the kind that had long metal points extending out from the top of the roof. It must have seemed an odd thing to the all-night convenience store clerk in Fujinomiya, a tourist city near the Aum compound, when Inoue strode in at two o'clock in the morning and purchased the seven vinyl umbrellas; it was not raining, and cheap convenience-store umbrellas are usually bought by people caught in a sudden downpour.

Speeding back to the compound, Inoue handed the umbrellas to Murai, who had an Aum member sharpen the points. Shortly after 3 A.M., the sarin attack team arrived from Tokyo and entered its final briefing phase. Murai told the group that in order to assure the greatest possible success they must remove the outer plastic bag covering the sarin before they entered the subway trains. The bag containing the sarin was to be placed on the floor of the train, then pierced by sharply jabbing it several times with the tip of the umbrella. Once the pouch was pierced, they were to immediately get off the train. Murai then brought out the five dummy bags filled with water and told the team members to practice piercing them. After they actually tried it, several members of the group remarked that placing a plastic bag filled with liquid on the train floor and then suddenly poking vigorously at it with a sharp-pointed umbrella was bound to stir suspicions among the train's passengers, even during the packed rush hour.

There had to be a less obvious way to go about this. Someone then suggested that the bags be wrapped in a layer of newspaper. Almost everyone carried a newspaper on the subway during the morning, and many left them on the trains, littering the seats and floors. A newspaper containing the sarin bag could be placed inconspicuously behind one's feet, then stabbed several times just as the attacker rose to leave the train. The attackers murmured their consent to the idea and Murai okayed it. Then he handed out sarin antidote pills to the five men, who were instructed to take them two hours before the attack.

The problem of how to divide the eleven bags of sarin among five men was solved by Yasuo Hayashi, who volunteered to pierce three of the bags and let the other four puncture two bags each. On that note of comity the meeting broke up, and shortly afterward the team returned to their Shibuya hideout in Tokyo, arriving just after 5 A.M. There, joined by their drivers, the sarin bags were distributed to the various teams and Ikuo Hayashi gave each of the five subway attack team members hypodermic syringes containing two milliliters of atropine sulfate, a drug effective in treating sarin poisoning. Hayashi cautioned them that if they were accidentally exposed to the nerve gas, either through inhalation or by having it splash on their skin, they were to inject themselves with the drug as soon as possible.

Like the getaway plans, what to do in case of accidental exposure to the gas weighed heavily on the mind of each of the attackers. They were pioneering a new method of releasing sarin and, unlike the field test in Matsumoto, they could not saunter aboard the subway in full protective suits and gas masks. Though it didn't seem likely from the practice with the water dummies, they must have wondered what would happen if the liquid sarin spurted out through the plastic bag and newspaper wrapping, wetting their trouser cuffs, socks, and ankles. One small drop on the skin was enough to kill or incapacitate. A splash big enough to wet your socks was certain death—all of them knew that. The obvious thing to do was keep the feet well back while jabbing, if you could.

The packed subways may have been ideal for claiming the most victims but they also presented a problem. What if they got stuck in the car behind an immovable crush of people, unable to get out before the doors closed, and they were trapped inside as the gas spread? That was a real possibility, as anyone who has traveled the Tokyo subways during the rush hour knows.

Up all night, tired and anxious, at around 6 A.M. the five members of the subway attack team swallowed their sarin antidote pills and then left the hideout with their drivers, clutching their sarin bags and pointed umbrellas. In less than seventy-two hours, the senior leadership of Aum Shinri Kyo had conceived, prepared, and was now on the verge of executing their grotesque act of terrorism.

Sarin squad member Ikuo Hayashi, a medical doctor who earned his degree at Tokyo's prestigious Keio University, was the head of Aum's Treatment Ministry, so it was only fitting that his driver be someone of equal rank: Tomomitsu Niimi, the sect's Home Affairs Minister and a grisly veteran of many of Aum's abductions and murders. Like the others in the attack force, the two left the hideaway condominium in Shibuya at 6 A.M. On the way they stopped for Hayashi to buy a copy of *Akahata*, the Japanese Communist Party newspaper that is must reading among the party faithful and Japan's turbulent body of left-wing intellectuals. Hayashi used a knife to carefully slit open the outer plastic bags covering his two pouches of sarin and then folded them inside the pages of *Akahata*. Hayashi got out of the car in front of Sendagi Station on the Chiyoda Line; he filled his extra time by riding the subway to an outer Chiyoda Line station and then reversing back toward Kasumigaseki. At 7:48, the prompt subway train slowed for its entry into Shin Ochanomizu Station, a point just up the line from Kasumigaseki. Hayashi placed his *Akahata*-wrapped sarin pouch on the floor and glanced around the interior of the car. According to reports published by the Japanese press, it was then that he began to have second thoughts about what he was about to do.

"When I looked around," he was quoted as telling police investigators, "the sight of many commuters leaped to my eyes. I am a doctor and in theory I've been working to save people's lives. I thought, 'In spite of that, if I release

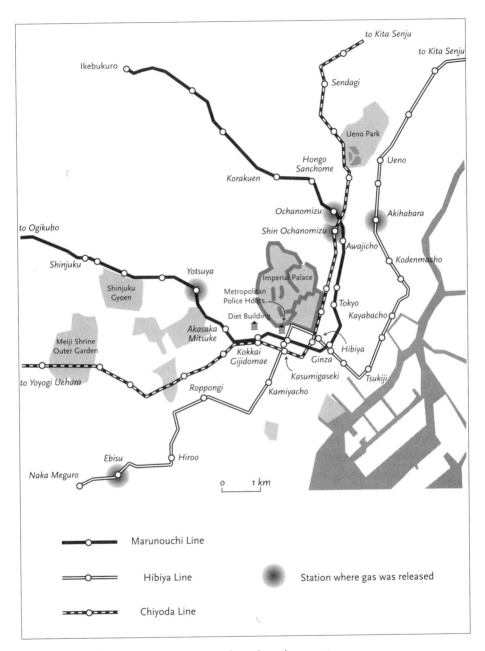

Central Tokyo, showing the nerve-gas attack on the subway system.

this sarin fluid now by puncturing the bag with the tip of my umbrella, many people could die at once.'

"Tormented by pangs of conscience, I hesitated and thought a number of times that I should stop. But I couldn't go against orders."

And he didn't. Despite his humanitarian impulses, on the morning of March 20, Doctor Ikuo Hayashi obeyed the orders of his sect's Sonshi and became a minor footnote in the history of ultraterrorism. When he jabbed the two pouches of sarin at his feet with his umbrella, Hayashi was the first member of the Aum sarin squad to strike the Tokyo subways. But because his heart really wasn't in it, as he later claimed, or because the intense emotion of the moment sapped his strength and distracted his aim, Hayashi's thrusts with the umbrella as the train slowed to make its entrance to Shin Ochanomizu Station only punctured one of the two sarin bags nestled at his feet. Whatever the reason for his failure, it was a small piece of luck for the hundreds of passengers continuing on toward Kasumigaseki. But the thousands of innocents unwittingly trapped by time and the obligation of work in the other trains along the subway lines heading toward Kasumigaseki were not so fortunate.

While Hayashi led the attack by only a few minutes, the four other Aum ultraterrorists were also in place near their various targets, busily puncturing the deadly plastic envelopes of sarin on the trains that were running toward Kasumigaseki. For Toru Toyoda the hardest part was fiddling around on the station platform, waiting for time to slip by and the right train to come along. He left the hideout at 6:30 and had his driver stop on the way to Naka Meguro Station so he could buy a copy of the *Hochi Shimbun,* a popular sports newspaper. In the car he slit the outer bags on his sarin pouches and carefully wrapped them inside the paper. Leaving the car at 7 A.M., he had to wander around the platform for almost an hour before finally climbing aboard the first car of an eight-car train that left Naka Meguro at 7:59. Though Toyoda did not know it, by then Ikuo Hayashi's gassing was already under way on the Chiyoda Line. Soon after the train pulled out of the station at Naka Meguro, Toyoda grabbed a seat near the car door and cautiously slid the newspaper containing the sarin on the floor by his feet. At 8:01, the train began braking to enter Ebisu Station and Toyoda stabbed down hard on the two sarin pouches nestled in the *Hochi Shimbun.* When he walked off the car the nerve gas was seeping from the newspaper and spreading out on the floor. Toyoda was among the first out of the car, and he dashed up the subway stairs

—a common sight during the rush hour and no cause for special notice. Five minutes later he was in the waiting car with Takahashi and they pulled casually away from Ebisu Station, just another featureless vehicle merging into the stream of morning rush-hour traffic.

Monday was not Kenichi Hirose's day; he managed to get things done but there was a lot of heart-stopping angst and confusion along the way. In the first place, he had to go a lot further than the others in order to begin, all the way to Ikebukuro some ten stops from Kasumigaseki on the Marunouchi Line. He left the Shibuya hideaway at around 6 A.M. with Koichi Kitamura at the wheel. Kitamura dropped him off

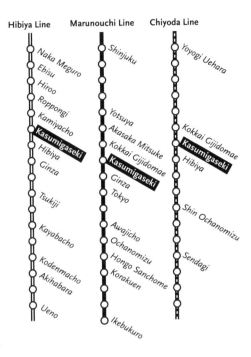

at Yotsuya station, a central Tokyo hub for several lines located across and up the street from the Akasaka Detached Palace, the ornate official state residence where foreign dignitaries often meet when in Tokyo. Toyoda's problems may have started from his own inability to keep things simple. Carrying his sarin pouches in his shoulder bag, he made his way via train to Ikebukuro. On board one of the two trains he took, he slipped into the lavatory, removed the outer bags from his sarin, and wrapped the inner pouches in a sports newspaper he had purchased on the platform. That done, he placed the newspaper containing the sarin back in his shoulder bag. Arriving at Ikebukuro at 7:40 A.M., he got on the second car of a six-car train leaving the station at 7:47. But for some reason things didn't feel right to Hirose on car number two, and after a few stops he got off and moved to car number three. That was an error in judgment, as any early-morning commuter on the Marunouchi Line could have told him. It was rush hour, all the cars going into Tokyo were packed, and all Hirose was able to find was jam-packed standing room crushed against the door. Crowded in by wall-to-wall people and trying hard not to impale anyone with his bayonet-sharp umbrella, he struggled to ease his shoulder bag off so he could retrieve the sarin pouches.

But in the process the newspaper in which they were folded came undone, fluttering at the top of the shoulder bag while he dropped the two plastic bags containing the sarin to his feet. At that point, the hapless Kenichi Hirose probably wondered where he'd placed his hypodermic syringe, a survival tool he was surely going to need in the next few minutes if anyone accidentally stepped on the sarin bags. Panicked, he somehow managed to move the two bags with his feet under the overhang of a corner seat in the car. When the train rolled into Ochanomizu Station, on its way to Kasumigaseki, Hirose punctured both plastic bags. Liquid sarin poured out of the bags onto the train floor as he stepped quickly out of the car and made his escape.

Yasuo Hayashi, the man who volunteered to unleash three bags of sarin, had a pretty smooth run. With his driver Shigeo Sugimoto, he left the Aum hideout in Shibuya at 6 A.M. and headed for his target, the Hibiya Line. On the way they stopped to buy a copy of the *Yomiuri Shimbun,* Japan's biggest mass-circulation daily newspaper, and a pair of scissors, which Hayashi used to slit open the outer bags on his sarin pouches. Wrapping the bags in the *Yomiuri,* Hayashi left the car near Ueno Station at about 7 A.M. and entered the station, where he waited on the platform until 7:46 to board a Hibiya Line train. At about 8 A.M., as the train slowed for its stop at Akihabara Station, the point serving Tokyo's huge electronics retail district, Hayashi stabbed at the three sarin bags encased in newspaper at his feet and sarin immediately began to pour out. He dashed off the train at Akihabara and was met by Sugimoto who was waiting outside.

Like Hayashi, Masato Yokoyama's attack was uneventful. While en route to Shinjuku Station, he had driver Kiyotaka Tonozaki stop and buy a copy of the *Nihon Keizai Shimbun,* Japan's equivalent of *The Wall Street Journal.* Removing the outer bags, he wrapped the nerve gas in the paper and, after waiting for his train, finally boarded at 7:39 A.M. As the train came into Yotsuya Station at 8:01, he punched into the folded newspapers with his umbrella but managed to pierce only one of the two bags of sarin at his feet. The sarin in that bag spilled out of the newspaper onto the floor as Yokoyama made his getaway up the stairs and was picked up by the waiting Tonozaki.

By 8 A.M., the five members of the Aum attack team had struck their targets and were in the process of making their getaway. But for thousands of passengers riding to work on the three major subway lines, the nerve-gas attack was just beginning. On the floors of five subway cars, liquid sarin sloshed out of punctured plastic envelopes, seeped through several layers of newspaper, and then mixed with the heated air inside the trains. It turned into a deadly vapor that partially filled the cars and drifted into the open platforms of the stations where the contaminated trains stopped.

The popular image of a nerve-gas attack is a sudden, mass onset of horrific physical symptoms, followed by panic and hysteria as the victims struggle to escape the scene. Under tightly controlled circumstances, such as the gassing of people in a sealed room, this scenario is possible. But the Tokyo subway attack was anything but tightly controlled. Once the gas (only thirty-percent pure to begin with) was released in the cars, its effectiveness was limited by a number of factors, not

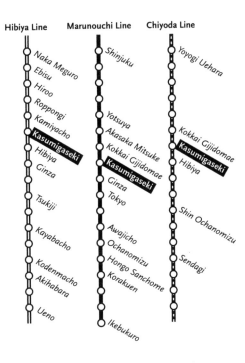

the least of which was the rather haphazard way in which it was dispersed. In the very early stages of the attack, those first minutes when the gas began to form in the stricken cars and people were affected by it, there was little if any panic. First one person, then another became sickened. Some noticed a strange odor, probably caused by the impurities in the sarin. Others had stinging eyes and coughing fits. Some foamed at the mouth, and a few became nauseated and began retching. The degree of injury depended on where people were located in relation to the spreading gas and how much of it they inhaled. Some persons were able to leave the cars and station platforms with only mild symptoms or none at all, while others had odd sensations but felt well enough to proceed on to work, only to be sickened after they were at their desks.

The worst cases, of course, were those who were directly exposed to the gas, either in the cars where it was unleashed by the Aum attackers or on those station platforms where the gas reached high levels such as Kasumigaseki, Tsukiji, Kamiyacho, and Kodenmacho. In some instances, people became ill within minutes of the sarin bags being punctured; for others it took longer. But as chemical-arms-control expert Kyle Olson noted earlier, the extreme danger of chemical weapons is that they work even if you don't use them exactly right. The Tokyo attack is a perfect example of Olson's point.

The Hibiya Line train on which Yasuo Hayashi placed his three bags of sarin left Akihabara Station as the liquid began spreading out on the floor. Two minutes later the train made its next stop at Kodenmacho Station. By then the gas was rising in the car and some people were already sickened by it. A male passenger kicked the nerve gas bags out of the car and onto the platform; then, using his foot, he shoved them near a post. Behind him a woman and a man, seriously poisoned by the gas, staggered from the car and collapsed on the platform. Unaware that anything unusual was happening, the train driver closed the car doors and moved out of the station.

The car containing the sarin on the floor continued to fill with nerve gas and when the train reach Kayabacho Station, a woman stepped out of the train and collapsed on the platform. Three others exited the car then dropped to their knees by a platform bench, unable to go on. Platform attendants moved them to the station office, and, still unaware that the problem was in the contaminated car, allowed the train to proceed. Before the train reached Tsukiji Station, a number of people in the poisoned car were already visibly ill and someone pulled the emergency buzzer to halt the train. After the train stopped at the station and the doors opened, a rush of passengers poured from the car onto the platform and five people crumpled to the concrete floor unconscious. Large numbers complained that they were sick.

Alarmed station officials, now aware that they were confronting a serious problem, but still uncertain what it was, made a hasty search of the train and found three other persons unconscious in the contaminated car. But despite the strange odors and the sudden and visible onset of illness among so many passengers, there was no panicky stampede. Subway officials quickly summoned ambulances to the station and told all passengers to evacuate the train immediately, that its run was suspended. The chief of subway operations, monitoring the reports coming in from the stricken subway line, issued an urgent order to stop all trains on the Hibiya Line at 8:41 A.M.—about thirty-six or thirty-seven minutes after the first sarin was unleashed on Hibiya Line cars by Hayashi and Toyoda. Japanese police later estimated that some fifty ounces of sarin poured from the two plastic bags punctured by Hayashi (Hayashi's third bag, which he failed to pierce with his umbrella, was probably ruptured by passengers who stepped on it in the morning rush).

The Hibiya Line's second attack came from the hands of Toru Toyoda who placed his two bags of sarin wrapped in a sports newspaper on a train which left busy Ebisu Station at 8:02 A.M. The train's next stop was the city's fashionable Hiroo district, where many of Tokyo's most prosperous foreigners reside, and from there it proceeded down the line to Roppongi Station, one of the most popular entertainment districts in the city. As the train sped from Hiroo to Roppongi, the sarin sloshed out of the two bags on the floor of the first coach and then gasified in the warm air. When the train reached Kamiyacho Station—only nine minutes after it left Ebisu—a number of passengers were coughing heavily, others were in various stages of convulsions, and several had collapsed unconscious on the car floor. When the train doors opened, six passengers stumbled out of the car. Unable to continue, they squatted down next to benches on the platform, several of them vomiting uncontrollably. Station attendants called for emergency medical aid and, at the same time, moved passengers in the stricken car to other coaches. But by now a large number of people in the station were complaining that they felt ill. Still, like officials at other stations along the Hibiya Line, the attendants at Kamiyacho had no idea what was causing the illness and at 8:16 A.M., the train left the station, at that point some seven minutes behind schedule. Four minutes later, at 8:20 A.M., it rolled into Kasumigaseki Station, where more stricken passengers tumbled from the cars and collapsed on the station platform. By then forty ounces of sarin had spilled from Toyoda's two plastic bags and the nerve gas was present in every station at which the train had stopped. The officials at Kasumigaseki halted the train's run and asked the passengers to evacuate the coaches.

The Hibiya Line was not the only heavily traveled Tokyo subway line to receive a double dose of sarin—Hideo Murai, Aum's master planner for the

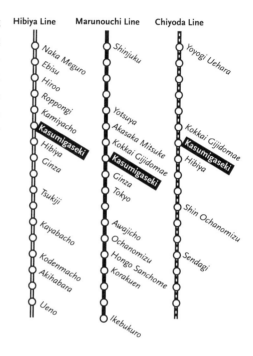

Hibiya Line — Naka Meguro, Ebisu, Hiroo, Roppongi, Kamiyacho, **Kasumigaseki**, Hibiya, Ginza, Tsukiji, Kayabacho, Kodenmacho, Akihabara, Ueno

Marunouchi Line — Shinjuku, Yotsuya, Akasaka Mitsuke, Kokkai Gijidomae, **Kasumigaseki**, Ginza, Tokyo, Awajicho, Ochanomizu, Hongo Sanchome, Korakuen, Ikebukuro

Chiyoda Line — Yoyogi Uehara, Kokkai Gijidomae, **Kasumigaseki**, Hibiya, Shin Ochanomizu, Sendagi three-pronged attack on Kasumigaseki Station also targeted the city's busy Marunouchi Line to receive four bags of the deadly nerve gas. As with the attack on the Hibiya Line, the main target was the government district serviced by the subway station at Kasumigaseki—the station where the Hibiya, Marunouchi, and Chiyoda Lines all intersected and which was heavily used by government employees during the early-morning rush hour. The first team member to strike the Marunouchi Line was the hapless Kenichi Hirose. He punctured his two bags of sarin at Ochanomizu Station, some five stops from Kasumigaseki, and then made his getaway shortly before the train left the station at 7:59 A.M.

At the next stop, Awajicho Station, the liquid sarin was already gasifying, emitting an irritating odor, and people were beginning to get ill. After departing passengers complained of the smell, station officials went into the poisoned car and discovered a male passenger unconscious on the floor. Nearby a woman was foaming at the mouth, staring straight ahead, unable to move. Other passengers complained of feeling ill, and station attendants called in ambulances to provide first aid. During a search of the train, Assistant Stationmaster Shizuka Nagayama came across two plastic bags on the floor of the third coach. One was empty and the other contained half of the original amount of sarin liquid. Nagayama wrapped the dripping plastic containers in newspaper and then took them from the coach to the platform. There Assistant Stationmaster Mitsuaki Shimamura put them in a plastic bag, which he then placed in the station office for safe-keeping before turning them over to the police later that day. It was estimated that about thirty ounces of the liquid sarin leaked from the two bags, and that it had drifted through the stations where the train had stopped.

Like the attack on the Hibiya Line, both strikes on the Marunouchi Line were intended to gas passengers traveling to Kasumigaseki from either direction. The second attack on the Marunouchi Line was executed by Masato Yokoyama, who left two bags of sarin at Yotsuya Station, only two stops from Kasumigaseki. When the train departed Yotsuya at 8:02 A.M. the liquid sarin in one bag seeped out onto the coach floor and turned to gas. Yokoyama failed to puncture the other bag, however, and it remained intact when it was turned over to the police. Incredibly, even though the gaseous sarin drifted inside the car, the train made its journey to its turnaround point at Ikebukuro Station without serious incident. On the return journey to the heart of the city some passengers asked train officials to remove some "strange objects" which were emitting a foul odor.

At the next stop, Hongo Sanchome Station, Assistant Stationmaster Yoshimasa Suzuki used a broom and dustpan to scoop up the two news-paper-wrapped packages containing the sarin bags. Station staffers then cleaned the floor of the car with newspapers, old rags, and mops. When police later examined the two bags, the unopened one contained about twenty ounces of sarin and the other about two ounces. The train was put back in service and continued to make its routine run until 9:27 A.M., when all passengers were asked to leave the train and the run was suspended. Japanese police estimate that nineteen ounces

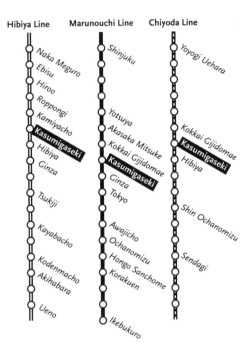

of sarin solution leaked from the punctured bag, gasified, and then made its way into the Marunouchi Line stations at which the train stopped.

The third major Tokyo subway artery pinpointed for attack by Murai was the Chiyoda Line. But unlike the other two lines, the Chiyoda was hit with only two bags of sarin, delivered by Ikuo Hayashi. Wrapped in the Japanese Communist Party newspaper, *Akahata,* Hayashi dropped his deadly packages to the floor of the train that left Shin Ochanomizu Station at about 8:04 A.M. Four stops later, the train reached Kasumigaseki Station at 8:12. The sarin spread out quickly as both bags were pierced and then stepped on repeatedly by passengers getting on and off the coach. Now widely dispersed across the car floor, the liquid sarin rapidly turned to gas, and just before the train reached Hibiya station, the stop before Kasumigaseki, passengers began coughing and complaining of being ill. They informed subway officials at Hibiya Station about the noxious odors and the strange seepage spreading on the floor of the car from a newspaper-wrapped parcel that looked like one of the small lunch boxes frequently carried by Japanese office workers.

At Kasumigaseki Station, Assistant Stationmaster Kazumasa Takahashi had finished his shift but he stayed over to help clean up the mess. He entered the poisoned car, picked up the newspaper-wrapped object, and carried it out to the station platform. He then wiped up the liquid remaining on the coach floor with discarded newspapers. On his hands were a pair of white gloves, standard apparel for most Tokyo subway staffers. Stepping in to help Takahashi was Assistant Stationmaster Tsuneo Hishinuma. Together the two men placed the leaking newspaper packages in a plastic bag and then dashed with them to the station office some fifty yards away. Hishinuma telephoned a senior subway official and reported what the two had done and that the liquid smelled like gasoline. He then noted that he wasn't feeling well and requested someone replace him so he could go to the hospital. A few minutes later, another station official entered the office and found both Hishinuma and Takahashi collapsed in a heap on the office floor, the color drained from their faces and foam oozing from their mouths. The official immediately sought help for the men, but it was too late to purge the nerve gas from their lungs. Takahashi died within a few hours, and doctors pronounced Hishinuma dead approximately eighteen hours later. The sarin bag that had not been pierced contained twenty ounces of liquid sarin while all the liquid in the other bag had seeped out. Though only one bag had been punctured, the lethal gas drifted into all the Chiyoda Line subway stations at which the contaminated car stopped.

The two hours between 8 and 10 A.M. on Monday, March 20, will remain indelibly etched in the minds of the subway passengers caught in the gas attacks on the three lines. The eleven people who died in the attacks—like the seven who died in Aum's earlier Matsumoto "field test"—went to their deaths without the slightest clue as to who or what killed them. But there was one man in Matsumoto who watched the live-television reporting of the victims being carried from the subway stations and knew instantly what had happened. Dr. Hiroshi Morita, who teaches medicine at Shinshu University, stared at the television scenes of people collapsing on sidewalks, blood and vomit pouring from their mouths. He'd seen it all months before in Matsumoto, when he'd been called in to treat the victims.

Before the Tokyo police discovered that the gas used in the attack was sarin, Dr. Morita was on the phone to medical authorities at several Tokyo hospitals strongly suggesting they begin treating the subway victims for sarin poisoning. His early tip undoubtedly saved many lives. But for some no medical intervention could help. One European tourist caught in the attack on the Hibiya Line boarded the contaminated car at Roppongi Station and saw what appeared to be a large spot of oily water on the car floor. It was giving off a foul, irritating smell, and people were backing away from it as others opened windows to try and ventilate the coach. Eleven minutes later the train pulled into Kamiyacho Station, and in one of the closest instances to panic, a large number of people ran out of the train and headed for the station exits. But Shunkichi Watanabe, an elderly retired shoe repairman, was unable to sprint out of the poisoned coach like the others. He had the misfortune to sit down next to the soggy newspaper package, which was now a pool of liquid sarin, spreading out at his feet. When the others fled, Watanabe was already too ill to stand; he had breathed

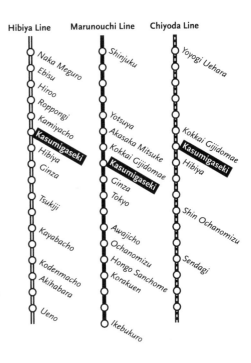

the nerve gas for one or two minutes and now he was alone in the car, dying.

Kamiyacho Station was in the grip of a full-fledged sarin attack and witnesses who saw it described a scene straight from hell. On the platforms lay forty to fifty people in various stages of sarin poisoning: some thrashed their arms and legs about violently as the painful muscular spasms brought on by the gas wracked their bodies. Many others lay on their backs, unable to get up and coughing repeatedly as blood poured from their mouths and noses. A number crawled around in small circles, unable to see, vomiting and foaming at the mouth; some sank to their knees immobilized or sat abjectly against station walls and benches, extremely ill, nearly blind, and afraid that they were dying.

Some people tried to cry out, their faces contorted in pain, but were unable to make a sound because the gas had choked off their vocal cords. Those who could walk or run fled the platform, dodging the prostrate bodies near their feet and charging headlong for the subway-exit stairs and the fresh air in the streets above. But for those who finally emerged into the cold winter morning air, relief was only a brief illusion. The sarin they'd inhaled below was still working its way through their bodies and would eventually produce the effects they had seen below. The horrific suffering at Kamiyacho was repeated at more than a dozen stations up and down the Hibiya, Marunouchi, and Chiyoda lines, and it all happened in less than an hour after the gas was released.

Ambulances from Tokyo's hospitals, along with fire trucks, rescue squads, and police emergency vehicles descended on the stricken subway stations within minutes after subway officials and medical personnel reported their suspicions that the trains had been deliberately gassed. The city's complex and lengthy subway system—a system that daily transports more than six million passengers—was now paralyzed. All three of the major lines were shut down and more than twenty-six subway stations were closed to the public. Saint Luke's Hospital, located in central Tokyo and near hard-hit Tsukiji Station, was quickly overwhelmed with hundreds of patients. Soon it was taking only severe emergency cases and placing patients in hallways, lobbies, and other common areas.

Japanese police working with firemen and Japanese military personnel trained in chemical warfare identified the gas used in the attack as sarin. But doctors at the major hospitals had conducted medical tests at their facilities and were already administering atropine to seriously ill patients. Others were hooked up to intravenous drip bags, which increased the need to urinate and thus helped cleanse the body of the gas. Gradually, the enormous medical rescue effort did its work, and late that afternoon Tokyo's subway system was back up and running. Transport officials said the trains were packed as usual.

Given the hurried planning and preparation that went into the gassing, the attack was a model of precise timing and execution. All five members of the Aum team managed to unleash their sarin pouches within three to five minutes of the 8 A.M. target. If the sarin had been seventy- or eighty-percent pure, instead of the thirty percent reckoned by analysts, it would have taken Japanese rescue squads several days to decontaminate the subways before they could begin the onerous task of hauling out the thousands of dead.

8

The Empire Strikes Back

Within hours of the Tokyo subway gas attack, "Aum Shinri Kyo," "sarin," and "Matsumoto" suddenly became household words throughout Japan. Japanese stared at their television screens in stunned disbelief as cameras panned past suffering victims sprawled on the sidewalks outside the subway entrances. Asahara's scheme to deflect police attention from Aum Shinri Kyo by gassing the subway lines serving the National Police Agency headquarters and other major governmental offices at Kasumigaseki had failed miserably. Even though the news media were initially careful not to directly tie Aum to the gassing, by mid-afternoon practically everybody in Japan had a good idea who did it.

Anyone with access to a television set or one of the special "extras" hurriedly rushed into print by the major newspapers could easily read between the lines and draw the proper conclusion. Since the first of the year, when the *Yomiuri* broke the story of sarin at Matsumoto, Aum Shinri Kyo had become one of the news media's major domestic drums, and they hadn't hesitated to beat it. Now their worst suspicions were confirmed.

But until the police turned up more evidence the media's suspicions remained only that. It was a time for public caution. The top echelons of the Japanese National Police along with leading legal authorities gathered in a series of urgent meetings at their headquarters in Kasumigaseki to plan the next move. There was little doubt in their minds who the culprits were and what had precipitated the attack. Aum's chemical fingerprints were everywhere in the subways and it took no particular genius to tie them to the attack in Matsumoto and the chemical samples gathered outside the sect's Kamikuishiki compound.

Still, the evidence from the chemical analysis was not thought solid enough to make an air-tight case against a religious sect. At best it was circumstantial. The missing link was physical evidence tying Aum to the sarin, and the police were convinced the proof they sought was located in the Kamikuishiki compound. How could they get in? The cautious tactical consensus was to fall back on the strategy the police had drawn up before the subway attack: the search warrants they already had for the investigation into the kidnapping of notary Takeshi Kariya. After all, from the beginning the Kariya search warrants were nothing more than a legal pretext for searching Aum facilities across the nation with the main objective of turning up evidence about the sect's production of sarin.

To give themselves some extra legal insurance, the police agency added to its national "most-wanted" list the name of Takeshi Matsumoto, the driver in the Kariya kidnapping whose fingerprints had started it all. The police charged him with suspicion of abducting Kariya in conspiracy with three or four others. In the event the raids produced nothing incriminating—a distinct possibility considering the time the sect had to clean up its compound and other facilities—the Kariya investigation provided the police with a sound legal defense against the loud and public fuss that Aum's attorneys were sure to raise in the courts afterward. Even with eighteen dead and a staggering six thousand injured in the sarin attacks in Matsumoto and Tokyo, the police and legal authorities pursued their investigation with the calm and deliberation demanded by a criminal justice system that allowed no rush to judgment, one that permitted arrests only when the evidence needed for conviction was irrefutable.

At dawn on Wednesday, March 22, less than forty-eight hours after the subway assault, one of the largest national police raids in recent Japanese memory got under way. More than two thousand five hundred police descended on twenty-five offices, compounds, and complexes belonging to Aum Shinri Kyo. Armed with search warrants justifying the operation as part of the investigation of the February 28 abduction of Takeshi Kariya, the largest contingent of policemen in the nationwide raiding force, more than one thousand men transported in a convoy of one hundred gray police vehicles moved out to the Aum Kamikuishiki complex. The compound was well lit by large red lights and mobile spotlights, a combination that cast a surreal glow over the sect's austere buildings. Adding to the effect was the whapping sound of a small armada of helicopters circling above. Manned by television camera crews and news reporters, they beamed live coverage of the raid into millions of homes. What the viewers witnessed was a series of action vignettes that collectively pointed the finger of guilt squarely at Aum Shinri Kyo. If there was any lingering doubt in the Japanese public's mind who was responsible for the Tokyo subway sarin attack, it all disappeared as the red sun rose on the National Police force swarming through the Aum Shinri Kyo compound.

The first force of police to enter marched resolutely up the compound driveway in a column formation of three abreast, their riot shields held high, evoking the image of warriors from Japan's feudal past. In another area of the compound, a raid on a warehouse was about to get under way. Cameras rolled as a group of two hundred police halted before the building to strap on their gas masks before receiving the order to enter. They had real reason to fear what they might encounter inside—some of them had assisted the victims of the subway gassing—but not a man hesitated. Supporting the police as they swept past the compound gates were eleven Japanese Army officers trained in chemical warfare, along in case help was needed in handling toxic chemicals and to provide technical advice to the police commanders on the scene.

Though Kariya's abduction was the legal pretext for the raid, it was obvious that the police were looking for something other than evidence related to his kidnapping. Some members of the strike force were outfitted in heavy protective gear complete with state-of-the-art gas masks obtained from the Japanese military, while others went into the compound carrying yellow canaries in blue cages; the birds were to serve as sacrificial early-warning alarms in case the investigators encountered toxic gas or chemicals. The only arms the police carried were pistols. Though the hour was early, the police were met with belligerent shouts and derisive noises from Aum commune members, who gathered in the compound in small clusters, all of them fully dressed and behaving as if they were expecting the raid.

Which, of course, they were. Aum's offices throughout Japan communicated with each other via phone, e-mail, and fax. In the early morning hours of March 22, the Aum branches in Japan received an urgent e-mail warning of the police raid along with a cautionary order not to physically obstruct the police—exceptionally good advice under the circumstances. Some Aum members carried video cameras that they used to record the police actions. Aum's chief lawyer, Yoshinobu Aoyama, his face a frowning mixture of contempt and disdain, stood near the main entrance with a portable loudspeaker, through which he blared out protests against the raid. The feisty lawyer shouted that the police were committing a number of legal violations, such as manhandling sect members and searching their personal belongings. He claimed that the police had refused to allow senior sect officials to be present when they searched the compound buildings.

But Aoyama was preaching to the choir, and his solitary melodrama was ignored by the police, who, shortly after they entered the compound buildings, began discovering precisely what they were looking for. In buildings adjacent to Satyam Number 7 they found and seized a large quantity of chemicals, some two tons in all, much of which could be used to make sarin. Among the cache were thirty to forty bottles of a solvent called acetronitrile, an organic cyanide compound that can be used to dilute sarin and make it portable. Acetronitrile was one of the chemical fingerprints collected in the aftermath of the Matsumoto and Tokyo sarin gassings.

Other chemicals seized by the police included isopropyl alcohol and sodium fluoride, both commonly used in manufacturing sarin, and the lethal poison sodium cyanide. The busy officers were seen removing numerous drums labeled ethyl alcohol, a common chemical solvent that can also be used to make other types of deadly poisons. Police also hauled out a large volume of documents, among them a sect publication in the early production stages declaring that deadly gas attacks and other unspecified disasters would kill more than ninety percent of the people living in the world's major urban centers in the coming years and that the end of the world would occur in 1997. The publication noted that cities like Tokyo would be wracked by disease, earthquakes, or poisonous gases, and it asked specifically whether the capital could survive a sarin gas attack.

Along with the documents, police also carted away a large number of gas masks and other protective equipment. The chemicals were removed from the compound to police laboratories where chemists were standing by to begin immediate analysis. Though the chemicals provided a link to Aum, they were still not the conclusive evidence that would bring a conviction in a

Japanese court. The solid legal tie-in the police needed was still missing because, ironically, there was no Japanese law which made it illegal to own or stockpile the chemicals the police had seized. Even worse, it was legal to make and possess sarin itself, primarily because the government had never passed a law making it illegal.

In another part of the compound, police specialists gained entry to Shoko Asahara's personal safe, where they found more than seven million dollars in cash and twenty-two pounds of unassayed gold bars. In the compound chapel they discovered some one hundred Aum followers, fifty of whom had been fasting for more than a week and were suffering from malnutrition. A number of them lay unconscious on the floor or were too mentally confused to answer police questions. Police removed all of the stricken people from the commune and sent them to a nearby hospital. Ambulances carried six persons to the hospital for emergency treatment, among them a middle-aged man and woman who were listed as critically ill by doctors.

Six other members between the ages of twenty-five and seventy-nine were found confined in small dark cubicles, a discovery that led police to arrest four Aum members, three of them doctors. Police later said that the arrest of the four was also connected with the abduction of Takeshi Kariya and other Aum members. Also taken into protective custody during the raid was a twenty-three-year-old woman who told police she had been locked in a small, windowless isolation cell since mid-January. She said she had been taken to the Aum compound in December and ordered to sever all ties with her family and the outside world. Her pleas to be released were ignored by sect leaders and she remained confined to the small cell that she said resembled a freight container. On the day before the raids, sect leaders told her police would search the compound the next day and moved her from the isolation cell to a building where many other people were gathered. On Tuesday night, sect officials forced her and the others to take medicine in the form of pills or by hypodermic injection. She said she pretended to take the pills given her, but others were not so quick-thinking. Doctors at the hospital where the fifty ill people were taken for observation and treatment said many of them showed symptoms of severe narcotic poisoning.

The harvest of evidence collected in the first raid proved only the tip of an iceberg. Much more awaited the methodical police searchers. In the months before the raid, many incriminating documents and much of the sarin-processing equipment had been removed from the compound by members of Aum's Science and Technology Ministry. That was not the only effort made to erase the sect's poisonous past. In mid-March, when Asahara and his top advisers were tipped off by an informant of the impending raid, a second hasty attempt was made to sanitize the nerve-gas facilities in the compound. Shortly before the subway attack, some one hundred members of the Science and Technology Ministry fled the compound in a bus and a number of vans, carrying with them key evidence of their work on sarin and other poisonous gases. At about the same time, a large number of mid-rank to top-level Aum members also vanished from smaller, related facilities in Tokyo and other parts of Japan.

Gone to ground too was Aum guru Shoko Asahara. The man left to defend the sect in the immediate wake of the Tokyo gassing was the energetic and articulate Yoshinobu Aoyama. At a news conference called on Tuesday, March 21, he assumed for the sect a posture of total denial of involvement in the subway gassing and baldly accused the Japanese government of making the attack to frame Aum's leaders. "Aum Shinri Kyo has absolutely nothing to do with this current sarin incident in the subways," he declared. "The mass media describe us as a secretive, closed, and suspicious group that is involved in weird activities. They have created such images of us, and I want to clearly deny their truth.

"Aum has suffered from being under suspicion," he continued in his rambling statement. "The parties who staged the incident must be receiving some benefit from it. The only logical conclusion is that the [Japanese government] authorities are the perpetrators of this incident."

Aoyama told the news media that terrorist murders were a direct violation of Aum's primary Buddhist teachings against killing. Asahara was said to be such a firm adherent of this rule that he would not even allow the killing of mice and insects in the group's facilities. On Wednesday evening the guru himself surfaced to address the public in a prerecorded radio broadcast transmitted to Japan from Russian stations in Vladivostok and Sakhalin in which he stressed the need to "face death without regrets." The dark, threatening nature of his remarks did nothing to allay growing public fears that another attack similar to the one on the subways might be in the offing. On Thursday morning Asahara made a second recorded radio statement in which he strongly criticized the police searches of Aum properties and noted they had failed to find any sarin. He said the reason no sarin turned up was because the sect did not have any.

But like the television cameras the day before, the headlines in Thursday morning's newspapers told the nation all it really needed to know. Typical was the headline that appeared across the front page of the well-informed English-language daily newspaper, *The Japan Times*: SARIN RAW MATE-RIALS SEIZED IN RAID, POLICE STORM DOZENS OF FACILITIES RUN BY AUM SHINRI KYO SECT.

On the same day as Aoyama's press conference, the police also called a meeting with the news media at which officials said the sarin used in the Tokyo subway attack was apparently produced in the same manner as the gas found at Matsumoto and in the village of Kamikuishiki. The ring was slowly closing.

By day two of the search of the Kamikuishiki Aum compound, the police had uncovered several hundred tons of sarin-related chemicals and the remains of the sarin-production laboratory located in Satyam Number 7. Police sources said they confiscated more than thirty types of chemicals in the compound, most of them stored in metal drums. A major discovery came when police raided a sect warehouse near the city of Kofu, some twenty miles from the Kamikuishiki compound, and found an estimated five to six hundred drums of phosphorous chloride, another primary ingredient necessary for making sarin. Japanese newspaper reports said that if all the chemicals seized by the police were used to make sarin they would produce enough of the lethal nerve gas to kill an estimated four to ten million people. The press reports did not cite a source for the estimate or explain how they arrived at the figures, which were speculative at best, since the police were not certain of the exact amounts of chemicals they had seized during the ongoing raids. At the same Kofu warehouse, police found drums and paper bags containing the raw materials for making five or six tons of nitroglycerine, a common liquid explosive used to manufacture dynamite.

On Friday, Shoko Asahara, still in hiding, appeared on the government-sponsored NHK television network in a prerecorded video tape and again vehemently denied any connection with the sarin attack and the disappearance of Kariya. He said Aum was using the chemicals to produce pottery, and for agricultural use and fertilizer production. He also stated that the chemicals confiscated by the police "are not ones used for synthesizing sarin." Later that day a similar video message was shown at Aum Shinri Kyo's branches and communes throughout Japan.

By day three of the massive raids, the National Police Agency was pressing its investigation of Aum Shinri Kyo on all fronts. Though his whereabouts remained unknown, the agency made public its intention to question Asahara about the sect's huge stores of chemicals. At the same time it instructed police across Japan to begin actively investigating more than one hundred complaints lodged against Aum in various parts of the country and to place the movements and activities of the sect's leaders under close surveillance. Senior government officials also began turning up the heat. Education Minister Kaoru Yosano and Tokyo Governor Shunichi Suzuki dropped several broad hints implying the government might take action to strip Aum Shinri Kyo of its official religious status when the police concluded their investigation.

On Saturday, five days after the subway gas attack, hundreds of elite riot police in full combat gear stood silent guard as trucks and forklifts began the hazardous job of transferring the bulk of the confiscated chemicals out of the Aum compound to government warehouses on the edge of Tokyo. Truck company logos and license plates were partially covered to protect the businesses against reprisal from Aum members, who looked on from the windows of a nearby building, several of them videotaping the event. The police also leaked word that sarin residues taken from the subway, Matsumoto, and Kamikuishiki were identical and that the incidents in all three locations involved the same terrorist group.

The police had reached another equally profound conclusion, one they were preparing to act on the following morning. Based on the chemicals already seized, plus the laboratory discovered in Satyam Number 7 and the ingredients for making nitroglycerine, they concluded that the facilities at the Aum compound were indeed used to produce sarin. On Sunday morning they would raid the compound again, only this time the charge was the suspicion of "preparation for murder" and not the Kariya abduction. This charge is normally brought in situations where there is possession of toxic substances or lethal weapons with the specific intent of killing or injuring persons. Considered a lesser charge under the penal code, preparation for murder carries a sentence of less than two years in prison. For the harried Japanese police, who still had not found the smoking gun that positively linked Aum to the Tokyo gassings, the charge was another legal foot in the door and a step closer to naming the sect as the sarin terrorists.

On Sunday morning, March 26, some one thousand policemen clad in camouflage uniforms again struck at the sect compound, which was now shrouded in winter snow. Equipped with hydraulic shovels, power saws, and sledgehammers, the raiders fanned out and began entering the compound buildings, including Satyam Number 7. They found it now completely covered in large white sheets put up by commune members to prevent outsiders from looking into their "holy building." The searchers found several pieces of advanced laboratory equipment, including an infrared spectrophotometer designed for chemical analysis and a gas chromatography device used to separate chemical compounds. Police-lab analysts took samples of Satyam Number 7's air and collected residues in the building's ventilation shafts, fresh air intakes, and an adjoining air purifier.

The laboratory behind the wall of the Buddha image and the huge image of Shiva was uncovered and police scientists again collected residues and air samples for comparison with the samples taken in the subways and at Matsumoto. Within forty-eight hours, police chemists confirmed that one of the residues collected was a secondary by-product of sarin, and had been found in the subways and Matsumoto. The chemical compound, a tongue twister called methyl-phosphoric acid diisopropyl ester, does not exist in nature and is usually generated as a by-product in the final stages of sarin production. Its discovery gave police chemists more insight into the chemical process used by Aum to produce sarin. But as the raids continued on sect facilities across Japan, Aum retaliated with a vengeance against Japan's National Police Agency.

The morning of Thursday, March 30, was cold and a rainy mist was falling almost straight down out of the gray clouds overhead as Takaji Kunimatsu, chief of the Japan National Police Agency and the nation's top police officer, came out of his residence in Tokyo at 8:25 A.M. and walked briskly toward his waiting government sedan. As he was about to enter the car, a man waiting behind an electric utility pole twenty yards away raised a .38 caliber pistol, took careful aim, and rapidly fired four shots, three of them striking Kunimatsu. Watching his victim fall to the pavement, the gunman quickly climbed on a bicycle and pedaled away in the rainy mist.

The shooting had taken less than ten seconds and the assailant was obviously well trained in using a pistol—Kunimatsu was struck in the right leg, stomach, and right breast. While being rushed to the hospital in an ambulance he told aides he heard four shots but did not see the gunman. At the hospital the fifty-seven-year-old Kunimatsu underwent more than six hours of emergency surgery to remove two bullets and stabilize his condition. Although his wounds were serious, attending doctors said his life was not in danger. Police later recovered one of the spent bullets at the scene and tests indicated that the pistol used was a U.S.–made Colt .38 revolver. Finding the gunman, however, would take a lot longer.

Embarrassed police officials immediately assumed the attempted assassination was a terrorist challenge to law-enforcement authority and set up a special squad of one hundred investigators to determine if the attack was linked to the continuing raids on Aum Shinri Kyo or to organized crime. Since his appointment in July 1994, Kunimatsu had waged a crackdown on organized crime, and he also was the principal officer in charge of the raids on Aum. The special investigation team had little information to go on. Kunimatsu's secretary, walking a half-step behind him when the police chief was shot, did not see the gunman. There were other witnesses, however, who described him as approximately forty years old, of medium height, wearing a black coat and trousers, a cap, a white surgical mask, and carrying a small sports bag. White surgical masks are quite common in Japan during the winter. People with colds and sore throats frequently wear them to protect others from their ailments; they also hide much of the face. Police speculated that after the gunman pedaled away from the scene he was either met by an accomplice in a car or got on a train.

The shooting of Kunimatsu, whose position as director general of the National Police Agency is roughly equivalent to that of director of the FBI, was the second severe criminal jolt to the people of Japan within ten days. For the average citizen it posed a number of frightening questions. The *Yomiuri Shimbun* led its Thursday evening edition with a large headline asking WHAT HAPPENED TO OUR SAFE SOCIETY? Although police were careful not to make any comments publicly connecting the shooting of their chief with the investigation of Aum Shinri Kyo, the media and others were a good deal less circumspect. Many noted the timing of the incident—less than ten days after the first police raids on Aum—and others pointed to Asahara's public writings and speeches in which he demonstrated an almost paranoid hatred for the National Police Agency.

There was also growing public sentiment that the police were moving too slowly in the case against Aum. The more the public and the mass media considered police activities the less they found to like. There was harsh criticism that the police had bungled good opportunities to solve the case earlier. The massive raids on Aum facilities were fine, many said, but why weren't they conducted earlier? More than nine months had passed since the sarin poisoning in Matsumoto, and in that case the police concentrated their investigation on an innocent man, even after it was established he couldn't produce sarin with the chemicals discovered in a shed in his backyard. Since the late summer of 1994 they had known about sarin residues near the sect's Kamikuishiki compound.

Then there were the anonymous warnings and the manner in which the police responded to them. In September 1994, an eleven-page letter was sent to the media and a number of government offices in Tokyo describing the Matsumoto gassing in detail and noting Aum Shinri Kyo's links to violence. It warned that new sarin attacks could occur in Tokyo's subways or concert halls. In January, American chemical-arms-control expert Kyle Olson accurately observed that the Matsumoto gassing was a trial run by terrorists who might launch more serious attacks that could have as their target the Tokyo subway system. But despite all this and the mountain of chemical evidence uncovered in the recent raids, no arrests had been made. Now the nation's top law-enforcement officer lay in a hospital recovering from serious wounds he'd received in a bold daylight shooting in which the gunman, adding insult to injury, made his getaway on a bicycle.

Even though the criticism increased in the weeks ahead, the Japanese police stuck to their tried-and-true investigative methods by mounting a massive surveillance of key Aum figures and concentrating their energy on finding the link between Aum Shinri Kyo and the sarin terrorism. Though the nation was visibly jittery and rightfully worried that another attack might occur, neither the police nor the government fell into the tempting trap of curtailing civil liberties by imposing such measures as curfews, random searches of citizens, and massive roundups of persons suspected of involvement in the attacks. Other, more logical steps were taken, including stripping the subways of trash containers and receptacles that might be used to hide terrorist devices; increasing the number of police and attendants in the subways; and cautioning passengers to be alert for suspicious-looking packages that were unattended or abandoned.

All in all, the month of March 1995 proved a devastating watershed in the way average Japanese regarded themselves and their society. No longer could they point to their island nation as a place free of the violence that often plagued the rest of the world. Implicit in that recognition was the worst of all realizations: Well-educated young Japanese, some of the country's best minds had, in the name of religion, of all things, betrayed the country, its culture, and the Japanese people. Aum was a home-grown terrorist organization, a pure product of the proud culture in which it took root and thrived to maturation and ultimate evil. In sum, Aum Shinri Kyo was uniquely Japan's problem, and correcting that problem would require uniquely Japanese solutions. The coming months provided a severe test for the police and the government as they struggled to accumulate the evidence needed to arrest those responsible.

By the end of the first week in April, the police, both in response to public pressure and as a result of their own investigations, began arresting Aum members, including a number of the sect's highest officials. By the end of April, more than ninety Aum members had been arrested on various charges ranging from suspicion of murder to abduction, trespassing, and resisting police questioning. Included in the haul were Seiichi Endo, chief of the Health and Welfare Ministry; Ikuo Hayashi, head of the Medical Treatment Ministry; Tomomitsu Niimi, Home Affairs Minister; Tetsuya Kibe, director of the sect's Defense Agency; and Masami Tsuchiya, Aum's top chemist. The arrests occurred in Tokyo, Osaka, and several Japanese prefectures, including the island of Okinawa, suggesting that the top Aum leaders scattered out across the nation when they fled the police raids that began on March 22. The whereabouts of the sect's remaining senior officials were unknown, police said.

The rapidly growing national tension produced a rash of complaints from a population that was now having to contend with violent threats to its collective safety. April wasn't a week old before people in Shinjuku reported noxious odors coming from an apartment believed to be an Aum hideout. Residents in the area complained of eye irritations and sore throats. A week later more foul odors were reported in a Yokohama train station, with more than twenty people saying they had sore throats. On April 13, in a television interview, an Aum member warned of a impending disaster that would be more devastating than the Kobe earthquake earlier that year, which had killed more than five thousand five hundred people. Then on April 15, the entire country was put on alert because of rumors that Shoko Asahara had predicted something terrible was going to take place on that date. Though nothing happened, more than twenty thousand police were deployed in full riot gear, bulletproof vests, and gas masks throughout Tokyo. Fearful of an Aum nerve-gas attack, many stores in the capital shut down and large numbers of people stayed away from work or avoided the subway system.

Four days later, on April 19, in what appears to have been a copy-cat attack, more than five hundred people were sickened and taken to hospitals complaining of stinging eyes, nausea, sore throats, coughs, and dizziness after inhaling a mysterious gas released in three different places in the Japan Railway's Yokohama Station. Most were released from the hospital the same day and the police later arrested a non-Aum member for the crime. This did not alleviate the public grumbling about the police and their slowness to make arrests.

On the political front there was some good news. The Japanese parliament plugged a major legal gap in the nation's law books by passing a law against the possession of toxic chemicals such as sarin. The new law banned the use, production, possession, or import of sarin and other deadly chemical substances. It imposed a maximum penalty of life in prison for dispersing sarin or other lethal chemicals, and up to seven years in jail for anyone caught "making, importing, or distributing such substances" with intention to disperse.

The next major shock to sweep Japan came on April 23 when Hideo Murai was stabbed to death on the streets of Tokyo in full view of a large number of television cameras and news reporters, who recorded the act. The assault came as Murai was heading to the sect's five-story Tokyo headquarters in Minami-Aoyama, walking in an unhurried manner in and around the assembled news reporters on the sidewalk who had been awaiting his arrival since early afternoon. The reporters were drawn to the scene by rumors that the police were about to begin making arrests of high Aum leaders, including Murai. As he neared the headquarters entrance, a man dressed in jeans and a sweater jumped from the crowd and slashed him on the wrist with a long knife, in full view of the reporters and cameras. Murai stared at the wound, then kept on walking in the same unhurried manner. Before anyone could move, the attacker leaped at Murai again, stabbing him in the torso. During the brief scuffle that followed the attacker dropped his bloody knife on the sidewalk, then waited patiently for police to arrive and arrest him. Murai was rushed to the hospital bleeding heavily from his arm and upper abdomen. Hospital surgeons worked to save his life, but he died six hours later from loss of blood and severe internal injuries.

Police later identified the assailant as thirty-year-old Hiroyuki Jo, a South Korean who resided in Japan. News reports later quoted Jo as telling police that he wanted to punish Murai for the trouble the sect had caused Japan. It was later established that Jo was a low-ranking member of an organized-crime gang headed by Kenji Kamimine, who was affiliated with Yamaguchi-gumi, Japan's largest organized-crime syndicate. Jo later confessed to police that his boss, Kamimine, had ordered Murai's death. Kamimine denied the accusation.

As in the shooting of police-agency chief Takaji Kunimatsu, speculation quickly arose that the killing was linked to Aum Shinri Kyo. Certainly there was good reason for wanting Murai permanently silenced. Both as head of the sect's Science and Technology Ministry and one of Asahara's closest aides, Murai was a pivotal figure in the production of Aum's nerve-gas weapons, the attacks in Matsumoto and the Tokyo subways, and the manufacture of illegal drugs which were supplied to organized crime for sale and distribution. Another theory held that the murder was ordered by Japanese gang members as a warning to the Aum senior hierarchy not to divulge to police what they knew about the sect's connection to organized-crime figures and the illegal-drug business. In mid-November 1995, a Tokyo district court sent Hiroyuki Jo to prison for twelve years for killing Murai. Kenji Kamimine was arrested in connection with the killing and placed on trial separately. The police were not able to link the crime directly to Aum Shinri Kyo, but continued to investigate that aspect of the case. Murai died before police could question him. That was a major loss to investigators, as he took a wealth of insider information about Shoko Asahara and Aum's terrorist operations with him to the grave. But before he died, Hideo Murai managed to hatch a couple of plots that would come to fruition after his death.

Worried that Aum leader Shoko Asahara was on the verge of being arrested, Murai gathered sect Intelligence Minister Yoshihiro Inoue and other senior officials to a meeting in early April in which he gave orders for two attacks to be carried out in the event the arrest of Asahara seemed imminent. The theory behind the attacks was the same as that in the subway gassing—to disrupt the police investigation and thereby delay any actions planned against the sect leader. Both attacks were to be carried out in May, the month in which Murai believed Asahara would face the greatest danger of arrest. He based his estimate on the fact that Ikuo Hayashi and Tomomitsu Niimi had already been arrested and that growing public pressure would soon force the police to take action. The first attack he outlined was to take place at the Shinjuku subway station, Japan's largest and busiest, and would involve a new chemical weapon, sodium cyanide. The second attack ordered by Murai was a package bomb to be sent to newly elected Tokyo Governor Yukio Aoshima. The governor, who took office on April 9, had publicly stated he would seriously considering disbanding Aum Shinri Kyo. On April 27, officials of the National Police Agency ordered a nationwide manhunt for missing sect leader Shoko Asahara. Reaching out from the grave, Murai's answer to this threat against his guru was not long in coming.

The assault on Shinjuku Station took place on May 5, just as Murai ordered. The chemical device used was a simple binary weapon consisting of two plastic bags, one containing some two quarts of powdered sodium cyanide and the other more than a quart of sulfuric acid. Planted in a men's room in the station, both bags were ablaze when they were discovered. Had they broken open, a chemical reaction would have occurred producing a huge cloud of deadly hydrogen cyanide gas. Chemical experts have estimated that the amount of gas released from the reaction would have been enough to kill between ten and twenty thousand people.

As if things weren't bad enough for the weary Japanese public, a group of four American lawyers now descended on Tokyo, all expenses paid by Aum Shinri Kyo, to publicly warn that the police might be trampling on the group's religious freedom. *Washington Post* Tokyo correspondent T. R. Reid said in a dispatch filed from the capital that the Americans spent three days talking to Aum officials and others but were not permitted to visit the sect's chemical factories or its headquarters. Reid said the Americans held two press conferences at which they suggested Aum was innocent and a victim of excessive police pressure. One of the lawyers, Los Angeles attorney Barry Fisher, a former chairman of the American Bar Association's Subcommittee on Religious Liberty and a current member of its Individual Rights and Responsibilities Section, called on Japanese police to "resist the temptation . . . to crush a religion and deny freedom." Contacted by the media, ABA officials in Washington, D.C. made it clear Fisher was not representing the Association on his trip to Japan. The irony of this strange episode was that while the American lawyers were imploring the Japanese police to exercise restraint, the police themselves were the target of a public ground swell of criticism for that very reason. In the end both police and public ignored the Americans, and the search for Asahara—last seen in public on March 3— and twenty-one top sect leaders greatly intensified.

At the beginning of May, police increased their watch over the Satyam Number 6 building at the Kamikuishiki compound, where they believed the sect leader was hiding out. In reality there were few other places to which Asahara could flee. By now his picture was well known to everyone in the country. The heightened police watch at the nation's airports and sea terminals made escape via those routes highly doubtful. The one place he might have gone was to Russia, but after the Tokyo subway attack, President Boris Yeltsin ordered government investigative agencies to crack down hard on the Aum organization there. Soon the sect's official religious status in Russia was taken away, it was forbidden use of radio and television facilities, and Russian courts began to hear complaints against the sect. All this proved to be a prelude to closing Aum Shinri Kyo's operations in Russia.

With no place to run, it was logical that Asahara would seek refuge in his home, the one place left in Japan where he could feel truly safe. Satyam Number 6 was known to house the Asahara family living quarters on the first floor, and the police believed the guru's wife and children had been living there since the gassing in March. In recent weeks Aum spokesman Fumihiro Joyu, chief lawyer Yoshinobu Aoyama, and other high-ranking Aum executives were seen entering and leaving the building. Another indicator that suggested Asahara was hiding in Satyam Number 6 was the melons. The sect leader had an insatiable fondness for expensive melons, and in recent weeks commune members were frequently seen buying the sweet melons in local fruit shops near the compound. Considering the bland, cheap diet that was strictly followed by the commune, the police surmised the melons were intended for only one plate.

While the authorities were now convinced that Asahara was holed up in Satyam Number 6, moving in to arrest him required a very delicate sense of timing. Though more than one hundred fifty Aum members were now in jail, including a large number of middle-rank and senior officials, many of the top leaders remained at large. The police knew the whereabouts of some but not all of them, and it was feared that if they arrested Asahara the sect zealots might suddenly retaliate with another attack against the public or senior government officials. This was not a groundless concern; interrogation of those now in jail revealed the strong possibility there was still a quantity of sarin and other chemical poisons that had not been uncovered. The problem now was to coordinate the arrests so that police could net Shoko Asahara and as many of the top leaders as possible.

On May 15, the impasse came to a head when police on the outskirts of western Tokyo spotted Aum intelligence chief Yoshihiro Inoue in a car with three other sect members and arrested him. Inoue had dyed his hair brown and shaved off his beard. Inside the car police found more than eight hundred documents, notebooks, and computer disks. One notebook contained detailed information about the schedules of the subway lines in which the nerve-gas attacks took place. Inoue was a central figure in the Tokyo sarin attack and a leader in many of the sect's abductions. With one of Aum's main operational organizers now in jail, the police felt confidant they could arrest Asahara and the others. They obtained arrest warrants for Asahara and forty other sect members and the following day made their move.

At 5:30 A.M., on Tuesday, May 16, more than one thousand police officers entered the Kamikuishiki compound and proceeded to Satyam Number 6. The raid was no secret, and it could hardly have

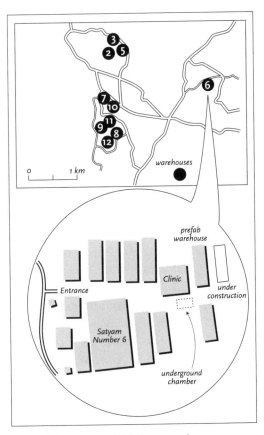

Map of the Kamikuishiki Compound (numbers refer to the Satyam buildings).

come as a surprise to the Aum members inside the compound. Tokyo newspapers were so certain Asahara would be arrested they had plastered the news across the front pages of their early morning editions. There were other, equally visible signs that "X-Day," the tag given the day of the guru's arrest by the press, had arrived. The streets of Tokyo were lined with more than eighty thousand extra police officers who were themselves augmented by Japanese Army chemical-defense teams, civilian medical units and fire-department personnel on special alert in the event of possible revenge attacks by the sect. Television camera crews in helicopters circled back and forth across the compound, which was covered in patches of fog and a light mist of rain. The force was part of a two-thousand-five-hundred-strong police raid on some eighty Aum Shinri Kyo facilities across the nation.

Police used a power saw to rip through the door of Satyam Number 6 and by 5:45 A.M. they were inside the building and beginning their search for Asahara. They met no resistance from commune members living in the building, although the interior lights had been turned off and police had to resort to flashlights in order to make their search. For the first few hours, the search of Satyam Number 6 yielded nothing. Outside, as the gray mist turned to light rain, speculation among the hundreds of news reporters shifted back and forth by the hour. Some believed the guru might not be in the building while others suggested he might be dead, a suicide. Then, four hours after the search began, one of the policemen tapping along a wall heard a hollow sound. A power saw quickly cut through the wall to reveal a dark coffin-like enclosure, some ten feet long and three feet high.

Inside, dressed in his favorite deep-purple silk robes and sitting in the lotus position, was Shoko Asahara. With him in the secret compartment were a small container of pills, a cassette tape recorder, and more than one hundred thousand dollars in cash. The brief exchange that followed his discovery was anticlimactic.

"Are you Shoko Asahara?" asked a police officer, shining a light upon the bearded figure.

"Yes, I am," Asahara said.

"What are you doing here?" the officer asked, probably at a loss for what to say.

"I've been here for two days, meditating and recuperating," replied Asahara.

At that point, the police decided they'd heard enough small talk and started to enter the dark chamber only to be warned off by the guru in an outburst of arrogance.

"I'll come out by myself," he told the startled police. "No one is allowed to touch the guru's body."

But the guru's days of giving orders and having them instantly obeyed were over. When he emerged from the secret chamber, the police not only touched him, they unceremoniously hauled him out to a waiting van that sped back to Tokyo flanked by a small convoy of protective vehicles. En route, a senior police official told Asahara that he was under arrest on charges of murdering eleven people in the Tokyo subway attack. Instinctively, Asahara reverted to the manipulative innocence he'd cultivated as a young student at the Kyushu school for the blind. "Could a blind man like me possibly do such a thing?" he asked the officers.

Asahara's parents would later appear before the press to publicly apologize for the "extraordinary trouble" their son had caused the people of Japan. But the day was not over.

The second attack in the legacy of violence dictated by Hideo Murai came only a few hours after the arrest of Asahara, when a book-shaped package bomb mailed to Tokyo Governor Yukio Aoshima five days earlier exploded in the hands of his secretary Masaaki Utsumi. The detonation occurred in the governor's outer office and although it blew off several fingers of the secretary's left hand, he survived the attack. The governor was in his office at the time of the explosion but uninjured. By early October, police had charged Intelligence Minister Inoue, Science and Technology Ministry member Toru Toyoda (also one of the five Tokyo subway attackers), top Asahara aide Tomomasa Nakagawa, and Masahiro Tominaga, a former doctor in the sect, with the crime. Toyoda confessed to police that he and Nakagawa made the package bomb under orders from Inoue and that Tominaga mailed it to the governor's office.

With the arrest of Asahara and most of his key followers, the people of Japan, and especially the frightened residents of Tokyo, breathed a collective sigh of relief. Ahead of the police was a serious mopping-up operation involving finding and arresting the remaining fanatical Aum leaders who were still at large. Also, not all of the chemicals produced by Aum Shinri Kyo had been accounted for and the threat remained that some of the devices might be used in attacks during the trials of the senior members, especially Asahara. In addition Aum Shinri Kyo still had substantial funds at its disposal. Only a portion of its estimated one billion dollars in assets had been seized or frozen by the government. As the trials of the sect leaders and others were about to get started, there was much police work still to be done. But with Asahara under lock and key, the public focus now turned to the courts.

Religion at the Bar:
The End of Aum Shinri Kyo?

From the arrest of Asahara in mid-May through the end of 1995, the Japanese police continued to mount a nationwide search for the senior Aum executives still at large. In interrogation cells they hammered away at the sect leaders they had arrested, extracting confessions and then laboriously comparing and confirming them against other confessions and the mountain of evidence they had seized during the raids. Criminal confessions are the key to Japan's unusually high arrest-conviction rate. Very few major cases move to court without them because prosecutors believe Japanese judges place more credence in confessions than other types of circumstantial evidence and testimony.

While American police agencies often chafe under the stringent laws and procedures designed to protect the rights of the accused, Japan's police have much more latitude. They are allowed to hold suspects up to twenty-three days for questioning, even on minor charges. Some Aum members, for example, were initially arrested for offenses such as riding an unregistered bicycle, traffic violations, and registering at a hotel under a false name. At the end of the twenty-three-day period police may extend the interrogation by rearresting suspects on other charges.

Police interrogation can be harsh by American legal standards and can go on for up to twelve hours daily, often without a lawyer present. In the past, civil-liberties groups have accused Japanese police of purposely demeaning suspects during questioning by subjecting them to loud noises, taking away their clothes, denying them food and water for several days, and using sleep-deprivation techniques and other tactics that stop just short of physical violence. Others say that the police often step over the line, coercing confessions by violence. A report prepared by the Tokyo Bar Association said police have been known to make detainees remain in one position for lengthy periods, often striking them if they are unable to maintain the position. Senior Japanese police officials deny that such conduct takes place, but in early June, Asahara complained his police interrogators were using intimidation in their sessions, calling him a "murder demon" and asserting that his partial blindness was caused by evil acts he had committed in a previous life.

Japan does not have a public defender system in which the state provides legal counsel to those detained as suspects. However, the bar associations in Tokyo and each prefecture operate a "duty-lawyer" system that provides temporary legal counsel to suspects before they are indicted. Before the duty-lawyer system was introduced, less than a third of suspects received legal help before indictment. The bar association duty lawyers have their names placed on a rotating roster and take whatever cases occur when their name is at the top of the list. They provided legal counsel to a number of Aum suspects in Tokyo and elsewhere in Japan.

As Shoko Asahara discovered a few days after his arrest, finding a good defense lawyer would be no easy task. Attorney Makoto Endo, Japan's most famous criminal defender and a devout Buddhist, met with Asahara in a cell in National Police headquarters to discuss his case. The highly eccentric Endo, known for his defense of left- and right-wing political figures as well as several groups of Japanese gangsters, later told a reporter that Asahara said the Buddha had appeared to him in a dream and told him to contact Endo. The attorney listened to the sect leader assert his innocence, and then turned him down cold, claiming he was too busy defending other Aum suspects to handle the guru's case.

After his meeting with Asahara, Endo met the news media and made statements about the sect leader that would have led to a disbarment procedure for breach of lawyer-client privilege had he been in America. He told reporters that "I, myself, have serious suspicions" about Asahara's involvement in the sarin attacks and that he could not take the case unless he was "one hundred fifty percent" convinced that Asahara was innocent. He said that when he told Asahara he could not defend him, the self-styled Worthy Master had cried out, "But what will become of me?"

It was a pertinent question, one that by late summer was beginning to worry senior officials in Japan's Federation of Bar Associations, a self-appointed monitoring group that was looking out for the rights of the sect and trying to assure that they were adequately represented in court. But unlike the defense attorneys and prosecutors in the O. J. Simpson trial, who became overnight celebrities, lawyers in Japan do not seek fame in cases that have aroused the public wrath, especially those involving religious sects. Thus, only a small number of lawyers stepped forward to defend the more than one hundred fifty Aum members then under arrest; most attorneys shied away from the cases because of the nature of the crimes and the extremely adverse public reaction they had generated. The Tokyo Bar Association had to promise attorneys their names would not be made public in order to get them even to assist with research in the Aum cases.

Under Japanese law, each person brought before the court must have a lawyer. If a defendant is unable to obtain an attorney by the trial date, then the court appoints one. In the Aum Shinri Kyo cases, most of the Japanese legal profession made it clear they felt it was better to be drafted than to volunteer. The number of lawyers required to handle the Aum cases is staggering. Asahara alone is said to need at least ten attorneys to provide a proper defense, though it remained doubtful he would be able to find more than one or two. The matter of attorney's fees was also a problem. Even though Aum's cash and other assets were thought to run into the hundreds of millions of dollars, the government had already frozen some of the sect's bank accounts and was planning to remove its official status as a religion. If that occurred, it would open the way for a large number of civil lawsuits that could quickly bankrupt the group and force the government to pay all the legal bills. Already legal experts were predicting the trial of Asahara alone could take ten years or longer, given the glacial speed of the Japanese court system and the time-consuming appeals that would follow a conviction.

Most major trials in Japan take several years to complete because court sessions are normally held one or two days each month rather than on a daily basis. In the more complex Aum cases, judges agreed to speed matters up somewhat by having a session each week. Japan does not have a jury system, and the verdict is decided by a panel of judges who also determine the sentence. Important cases are heard at the district court level and convicted defendants can appeal to one of eight higher courts, then finally to the supreme court. Except for a brief period before the defendant enters the courtroom, cameras are not allowed to film the proceedings and tape recorders are banned. Journalists and others may take notes. In handing down sentences, judges are often strongly influenced by confessions and contrite indications of remorse by defendants.

Capital punishment has broad public support in Japan, as it does in the United States, and is common in murder cases involving multiple victims. Hanging is the method of execution, and again as in America, the appeals process can create long intervals between sentencing and execution. Nearly six hundred prisoners have been hanged since the end of the second world war, and the government reports seven were executed in 1993, the most recent year for which it has given figures. In 1994 at least two people were hanged and three were put to death in 1995.

The execution procedure is straightforward. Once all appeals have been exhausted, the prisoner is confined to his cell and not allowed any visitors other than immediate family members. His execution may come any time during a six-month period after the final appeal is denied, but he is not told the date when it is finally set by officials. When his final day arrives, the prisoner is taken from his cell to a room where he is served his last meal and given time to prepare himself. He is then handcuffed, blindfolded, and taken to the execution chamber next door, where the noose is put in place and the trapdoor falls open. It may take ten to fifteen minutes for death to occur.

On June 6, prosecutors formally handed down their indictment of Asahara, still without a lawyer, on murder charges, along with six of his senior followers. Legal authorities said they expected to indict some two dozen other Aum members on murder and related charges within the next few days. Of the forty-one sect members formally charged with murder in the subway killings, only seven had not been arrested. In a rare move, police also freed five members who had previously been arrested on murder charges. According to some Japanese legal analysts the decision to release the five suggests they fully cooperated with the police by giving them highly helpful information. While the indictment did nothing to change Asahara's immediate legal situation, it was another formal step that would move him and his closest associates closer to the gallows.

The police, meanwhile, were uncovering new and more grisly evidence in their continuing search of the main Aum compound.

In early June some eighty police investigators, acting on the confession of sect doctor Tomomasa Nakagawa, searched the ground floor and basement of Satyam Number 2, where Nakagawa said the body of Kiyoshi Kariya was cremated after he died of a fatal injection. During the search police discovered makeshift incinerators, gas burners, fuel containers, and other incineration devices. In the basement they found soot on the walls and ceiling, indicating extensive burning had taken place there. Police collected samples of the soot, and in July announced that laboratory analysis had found what appeared to be human fat in the samples. Police officials said the sect began burning bodies in the basement two years earlier and that at least eight bodies were cremated there, including those of Kariya and Kotaro Ochida, an Aum member who was murdered in the compound. Police said some of the bodies may have been cremated by a modified microwave-oven device located in the building that several Aum members mentioned in their confessions.

Television networks vied with each other to be first to broadcast these gruesome details, along with every other twist and turn in the Aum Shinri Kyo case. In the process they were racking up some of the highest television ratings in Japan's history. The nation's print media, from the usually staid business publications to the colorful sports dailies, were devoting their front pages to the sect. The media's preoccupation with Aum cast most other important news into the inside pages or to the tail end of broadcasts, provoking criticism by some that more coverage was being provided than people wanted to see and read. But Japanese news executives, very much like their counterparts in America who received similar complaints during the O. J. Simpson trial, replied they were merely giving their readers and viewers what they wanted, and they cited polls and surveys to back up their claims.

Still others complained that some television networks were giving Aum spokesmen hours of broadcast time to defend the sect against police charges, and to extol the virtues of Shoko Asahara and his teachings. Much of that criticism was true; in the first months after the gas attack, television broadcasters discovered their ratings leaped when Aum members appeared on their shows. Soon some were agreeing to preconditions established by the sect for personal appearances of its members. Major networks bowed to Aum demands that certain well-informed and tough reporters be excluded from programs on which sect spokespeople appeared. Another demand routinely agreed to by the compliant broadcasters was to place certain sensitive areas of discussion off-limits during discussions with Aum representatives. Not all the networks went along with the sect's demands, however. Some realized that the prior censorship dictated by Aum's officials might result in short-term ratings gains, but those who refused the sect's conditions would later be lauded for their principled stands.

Still, the media exposure given the sect's spokesmen was powerful while it lasted, and it produced several unexpected trends. Fumihiro Joyu, Aum's boyish-looking spokesman and the man who would eventually take charge of the organization after Asahara and the other senior leaders were arrested, was a frequent guest on television talk shows along with Aum attorney Yoshinobu Aoyama. Both men, and especially Joyu, quickly found themselves instant celebrities. Young teenage girls who thought Joyu was "cute" formed ad-hoc fan clubs and followed them from one television station to another. They were frequently seen waiting with bouquets of flowers outside Aum's Tokyo headquarters in Minami-Aoyama, screaming and waving when the two emerged.

But even as Aum's popularity rose with the teenage set, its financial fortunes began to take a nose dive as the growing police evidence and leaked confessions from arrested senior members were made public.

Donations were the first to decline, then almost disappear, followed by a sharp drop in the sect's numerous business interests, such as the noodle shops and computer-sales outlets. Spokesman Joyu soon began to complain about "the hundreds of millions of yen" needed each month to pay for the sect's overhead. Further, Aum had more than one thousand members who had left their homes to live in the sect's communes, where they received free housing, food, clothing, and living expenses. The freezing of some the sect's bank accounts and other liquid assets only added to the problem. The sudden plunge in the group's cash flow pressed the surviving leadership to come up with new methods of fund raising to keep the slowly sinking organization afloat, if just barely. Under the guise of "religious training," sect members were ordered to seek part-time jobs and turn their salaries over to the group. Aum also opened a chain of member-staffed "Satyam Shops" in Tokyo, Yokohama, Osaka, and Fukuoka that sold Aum T-shirts emblazoned with Asahara's picture—much in demand by younger Japanese—and other sect paraphernalia such as books and magazines published by the group. Those working part-time took common laborer jobs as delivery men, construction workers, and security guards; some younger women found work in bars as hostesses. Despite all this, Aum Shinri Kyo was slowly spiraling downward in a sea of red ink and a number of members were beginning to leave the group, their faith badly shaken by each new revelation that appeared in the press. In jail, his communications to his followers cut off, Asahara was virtually powerless to assist his floundering sect.

By late summer the guru had finally managed to hire an attorney, Shoji Yokoyama, who told the media his client would plead not guilty to all the charges being brought against him. Police sources said the wily Asahara had made no confessions and maintained silence when questioned about the sect's crimes and his role in them. Of the one hundred four members indicted by the Tokyo District Court as of early October, fifty-five had hired lawyers and twenty-eight others had state-appointed attorneys. Five of the lawyers were hired by Aum and were assigned to defend more than ten sect members each. An overall legal defense strategy apparently was not considered, as none of the sect's lawyers was conferring with the others.

In late September, the police began closing another loophole in the Aum case when they arrested twenty-eight-year-old Mitsuo Sunaoshi, a senior member of the sect's Construction Ministry, in connection with the shooting of Takaji Kunimatsu, director-general of the Japan National Police Agency. Sunaoshi, the first person to be arrested in the shooting, was charged with suspicion of making threatening telephone calls to news organizations immediately after Kunimatsu was shot on March 30. Police sources said Sunaoshi called a Tokyo television station some ninety minutes after the shooting and said, "Stop the investigations into Aum . . . otherwise, Omori and Inoue will be next." The threat was apparently aimed at Yoshio Omori, who is chief of the Cabinet Information Research Office, a high-level government intelligence function, and Yukihiko Inoue, head of the Metropolitan Police Department. The call was tape recorded by the television station and turned over to police, who identified the voice of the caller with the help of jailed Aum members. Voiceprint analysis confirmed the voice of the caller was that of Sunaoshi and police believe he has important information about the shooting.

A few days after the arrest of Sunaoshi, the *Mainichi Daily News*, quoting police investigators, reported that at a meeting in January 1995, Shoko Asahara asked his senior executives if any of them would volunteer to attack the superintendent-general of the Metropolitan Police Department. According to *Mainichi* the discussion was recorded on a tape cassette that was later confiscated by police during a search of a sect facility. The tape reportedly reveals Asahara asking at one point, "Is there anybody who can hit the MPD superintendent-general on the hip?" A senior member present replied, "That's beyond my imagination, but I'll do so if the Sonshi orders me to do so." The shooting of head cop Kunimatsu, however, was a relatively minor matter compared to the murder charges piling up against the sect and its leadership.

The police were now vigorously pushing their investigations into the sect's activities across a wide front, and Aum's criminal past was unraveling before the public like a daily soap opera. On the legal front, Aum's numerous cases were heading to court at a fast clip. Already the trials of three minor sect figures had started in July, and forty-three others, including Asahara's, were set to start in September, October, and November. Trial dates for some fifty-eight others were to be set successively and the Tokyo District Court would use all of its fourteen criminal case departments to hear the cases. Typical of the nine trials that started in early September was that of an Aum member charged with harboring a sect member wanted in the abduction and murder of Tokyo notary public office manager Kiyoshi Kariya.

Kumi Nebuka, a thirty-one-year-old Aum hospital worker, was charged with helping the wanted man, Takeshi Matsumoto, evade capture from March through April. During the first day, Nebuka admitted most of the charges in the prosecution's opening statement. Her lawyer, however, contended she only abetted in the crime. The indictment alleges Nebuka helped hide Matsumoto in hotels and rental cottages in Tokyo and elsewhere and that she was accompanied by Ikuo Hayashi, the chief of Aum's medical ministry. She was also charged with carrying an escape fund of more than ten million yen and medical equipment to be used for plastic surgery on Matsumoto, including the erasure of his fingerprints. Nebuka said she was involved in only part of the plan and did not know whether the surgery on Matsumoto was performed.

More informative was the trial of one of Asahara's drivers and bodyguards, Satoshi Tamura. The body guard was charged with illegally installing a two-way radio in one of the sect cars. In testimony before the Tokyo District Court, Tamura called Aum a "devilish group" and asked the court to "Please put Asahara to death." He said that despite the strict dietary measures Asahara imposed on his followers, the guru was something of a glutton who often frequented restaurants where he ordered numerous dishes and full-course meals. "Asahara even ate ice cream," he testified, "which he prohibited us from eating."

Shopping, according to Tamura, was another favorite pastime for Asahara and his family. At toy shops he allowed his children to buy anything they wanted and when the car became too crowded with toys, Asahara ordered the driver to get out to make room for more. Tamura said Asahara then drove off, leaving him behind. In December 1994, a nail punctured the tire of the sect leader's Mercedes and Asahara promptly accused Tamura of being a spy and had him injected with truth serum. Both Tamura's and Nebuka's cases resumed hearings at a later date.

During the second week of October, the first of Aum's senior executives was sentenced to a year in jail after being found guilty of simple trespassing. Some legal experts interpreted this as a sign that the court intended to be unusually tough in trials of the sect's other leaders, since first-time trespass offenders do not normally receive prison terms. All other convicted Aum followers, most of them junior members convicted on very minor charges, had to that date received suspended sentences. The tough sentence passed on Tetsuya Kibe, the sect's Minister of Defense, made him the first to receive a prison sentence and was a strong hint that other Aum executives could look forward to equally harsh treatment. Kibe had trespassed into a private parking lot in Tokyo in order to pass gun parts from one car to another, thus avoiding their discovery in a police search. Although Kibe admitted he knew the sect was behind the Tokyo subway gassing and other criminal acts, police thus far had no evidence directly linking him to the gas attack or other crimes. Some observers said that if Kibe only serves one year in prison, he will be one of the luckiest members of Aum's top hierarchy.

On October 24, Tomomasa Nakagawa became the first Aum leader to stand trial for the Tokyo subway attack. Nakagawa freely admitted to the three-judge panel hearing his case that he made sarin at the express orders of Shoko Asahara, but he pleaded not guilty to murder and attempted murder filed against him in connection with the subway gassing. In addition to the subway-attack murder charges, Nakagawa faces a wide array of other murder charges including the strangulation death of Aum member Kotaro Ochida in 1994; the deaths of seven persons who died in the Matsumoto sarin attack in 1994; the kidnapping and murder of Kiyoshi Kariya; and the murder of the Sakamoto family in 1989. Trials for the Matsumoto gassing, the Kariya killing, and the Sakamoto murders will be held separately.

In the first day of a trial that is expected to take two years to complete, Nakagawa became the first top Aum official to publicly testify that Shoko Asahara ordered the production of sarin. Asahara's lawyer, Shoji Yokoyama, told newsmen a week earlier that the guru would plead not guilty to the charges against him and would contend that he knew nothing of the plans and actions of his top aides. But Nakagawa's testimony would undermine that defense when the guru's trial got under way. "Asahara ordered the production of sarin in mid-March," he told the three judges. He said he made the nerve gas as ordered, "But I was not aware of the conspiracy to release the gas, although I knew sarin was a dangerous chemical."

The crewcut doctor also admitted his involvement in the murder of Kotaro Ochida, but declared his part was only a "minor one." Ochida's murder took place after he was caught trying to help another Aum member's mother escape from the sect's hospital. Asahara ordered the murder, and several senior members of the sect bungled an attempt to strangle Ochida with a rope. Nakagawa testified that Ochida was writhing in agony and that he then helped kill him in order to relieve his suffering. Nakagawa's lawyer asked the court to change the charges against him to accessory to murder since he had not actually conspired with Asahara in either case. The request is not an unimportant one, since accessories to murder are not given capital punishment. Also during the trial, chief prosecutor Tadahiko Miyazaki corrected downward the tally of persons injured during the subway gas attack from the five thousand five hundred initially given by the police to three thousand seven hundred ninety-six. However, the Japanese media and others continued to use the higher figure, believing it was more accurate.

In the meantime, the news media continued to report more bizarre Aum stories. On October 22, the Japanese news agency Kyodo reported that in the summer of 1993, Shoko Asahara, along with Kiyohide Hayakawa and Fumihiro Joyu, circled the Imperial Palace in a car equipped with a special spraying device that was dispersing deadly botulism bacillus cultivated by the sect. Kyodo said the story was related to the Metropolitan Police Department by Hayakawa. He told police that in the middle of the operation Asahara fled the car fearing that his life was in danger from the bacillus, which kills through paralysis. Hayakawa was quoted as saying he cultivated the botulism bacillus at Aum's laboratory and that the group was puzzled by its failure to inflict casualties. Kyodo said the bacillus was ineffective because it loses its toxicity when released in large open spaces and mixes with the air. It was unclear whether the alleged attempt was intended as an attack on the Japanese imperial family or simply another Aum "field test" designed to create chaos in downtown Tokyo.

It was against this backdrop that the trial of Aum Shinri Kyo's Worthy Master was set to begin on October 26. The Japanese public was waiting for the opening with keen anticipation and all was ready as the court date approached for Japan's trial of the century. For the first time in Japanese legal history, metal detectors were put in place outside a courtroom, set up at the entrance to the austere Courtroom 104 of the Tokyo District Court to screen the lucky fifty persons chosen by lottery who were allowed inside to witness the first day's proceedings in the case of the Japanese People versus Shoko Asahara. No cameras were allowed in the courtroom, but television stations planned to provide commentary from the sidewalks outside. More than eight thousand police would be on extra duty around the courthouse, its surrounding neighborhood, and the city's central subway stations to guard against any actions that might be planned by the guru's followers, or by other violent elements of society that might want to harm the sect leader.

Inside the bare, gray-tiled courtroom, a four-judge panel headed by Chief Justice Fumihiro Abe prepared to ease into the black leather chairs on the podium to hear the case, decide its verdict, and then pass sentence. The ever-manipulative Asahara, however, had other ideas.

Four days before the trial was set to begin, Shoji Yokoyama, Asahara's attorney—his only attorney—was taken to a hospital following a minor auto accident in Tokyo. The accident occurred when Yokoyama was en route to police headquarters to confer with Asahara. He was riding in a car driven by an Aum member which made an illegal U-turn and was struck by two other cars. The only person hurt was passenger Yokoyama. On the evening after the accident, Yokoyama told court officials visiting him in the hospital that he would be well enough to attend court as scheduled on October 26. But medical officials said he might be suffering from whiplash and asked the sixty-seven-year-old lawyer to remain in the hospital for two weeks. It was not certain whether Yokoyama would be well enough to attend the trial, and in Japan a trial involving serious offenses cannot proceed without at least one lawyer for the defense present. Yokoyama's doctor said she would send the court an application for postponement based on his medical condition.

On October 25, the day before his trial was to commence, Shoko Asahara fired Yokoyama. It was a skillfully timed move; when the legal dust settled, it had delayed the trial for months, extending its start until April 1996. Stunned court officials told newsmen that Asahara gave no reason for the firing in the documents he sent to them just before the end of the day, but legal observers speculated that he was simply spinning out the legal process in order to put off his conviction and execution. The district court postponed the trial indefinitely and Chief Judge Abe ordered Asahara to report to him and explain why he fired his lawyer.

At the meeting, the judge brushed aside Asahara's arguments that he wanted to hire a new team of private defense lawyers. The following day the guru was formally notified that the court would appoint a lawyer to defend him. The court explained that while unusual, the swift appointment of a lawyer was necessary to keep the trial running smoothly. Asahara would be allowed to hire his new legal team, but he would also have in it the court-appointed lawyer, who could not be fired. The court coordinated its action with the bar associations, which quickly gave their approval. His delaying tactic met and countered, Asahara now realized he was boxed in; still, the gambit had bought him a few months to find his new defense team. The court was expected to set a new trial date sometime in early 1996 and by the end of the day, Asahara had reinstated Yokoyama, the man he'd fired just two days before.

Yokoyama appeared nonplussed by it all.

"Asahara apologized for having imprudently fired me," he told reporters after a meeting with the guru. "He asked me to defend him again."

October was also a fateful month for teen idol and acting Aum Shinri Kyo leader Fumihiro Joyu. As crowds of onlookers gawked outside, police arrested Joyu in the sect's Tokyo headquarters, charging him with inducing an Aum member to give false testimony during a criminal trial in 1992. Also arrested in the case were Yoshinobu Aoyama and a sect accountant, Toshiro Shibata. The arrest warrants charged Joyu and Aoyama with persuading Shibata to commit perjury in a court case involving an Aum land purchase in 1992. Persons convicted of perjury face up to ten years. By the end of the month, all three men had been indicted on the perjury charges.

In November and December, the trials set for other top Aum leaders began as scheduled, even as new murder charges and indictments for additional crimes continued to fall on Asahara and his key aides. Health and

Welfare Minister Seiichi Endo, one of the sect's leading chemists, told the judges hearing his case that he fully admitted his role in the Matsumoto and Tokyo gassings. In doing so he became the first senior leader to confirm in public that Aum released the deadly gas in Matsumoto. In a separate trial, Aum member Takeshi Matsumoto pleaded guilty to the abduction and confinement of notary public Kiyoshi Kariya.

In early December, police added a fresh murder charge to the string they'd already made against Asahara. The guru was charged with ordering the VX-gas murder of Osaka businessman Tadahito Hamaguchi in December 1994. Also charged in the crime, the first use of VX gas by terrorists, were Home Affairs Minister Tomomitsu Niimi; Intelligence Chief Yoshihiro Inoue; Tomomasa Nakagawa, head of the Household Agency; Masami Tsuchiya, Aum's chief chemist; and Akira Yamagata and Satoru Hirata, both of the Intelligence Agency. The police said Asahara ordered the group to kill Hamaguchi, who he feared was a police spy. Tsuchiya produced the VX gas and Yamagata along with others in the group sprayed it on Hamaguchi while he walked down an Osaka street. He died ten days later from the poisoning. As the new charges came down, Asahara decided once again to fire his attorney, Shoji Yokoyama. But this time Yokoyama's dismissal caused hardly a ruffle, as his lawyers appointed by the court continued to prepare his defense.

By early December, seven members of the Tokyo subway gassing attack team had been arrested and indicted, while three members remained at large, the focus of a nationwide police manhunt. In the first session of the trials of Toru Toyoda and Kenichi Hirose both admitted releasing sarin in the subway. Later in December, Ikuo Hayashi entered a plea of guilty to the same charge and apologized for the crime. Asahara's wife, Tomoko Matsumoto, had her first day in court in late December to plead not guilty to conspiracy to murder Kotaro Ochida, the young Aum member who had tried to help his friend's ailing mother escape from a sect hospital. According to the indictment handed down against her, Matsumoto sat by her husband and watched as Ochida was strangled by other sect leaders. She told the court that although she was in the room when Ochida was killed, she had felt "unbearable shame." But she denied taking part in the conspiracy. "I did not conspire with anybody," she said.

In addition to the trials of arrested Aum members, the government was moving ahead on other legal fronts to have the sect disbanded. By late October,

Tokyo District Court Judge Seishi Kanetsuki ruled that Aum Shinri Kyo had conspired to commit murder by producing sarin nerve gas and ordered the sect disbanded. Kanetsuki's order was made under the Religious Organizations Law, which permits courts to disband any religious group that commits illegal acts harming the public interest. The effect of the order was to strip Aum of its official religious status and take away its lucrative tax breaks and other financial advantages. The court was expected to appoint a financial executor to begin liquidating its assets. The sect can appeal the decision all the way to the supreme court, but legal experts were skeptical it would receive a favorable ruling in the higher courts.

Judge Kanetsuki's order made Aum Shinri Kyo the first religious group to be disbanded under the Religious Corporations Law for criminal activity. Aum lawyers immediately filed an appeal of the decision, which the High Court was expected to rule on in a month. In mid-December, Aum Shinri Kyo received another body blow to its continued existence as a religious entity. Japan's top security office, the Public Security Investigation Agency, recommended the government use the 1952 Subversive Activities Prevention Act —an unusually tough legal statute considered draconian by Japan's civil liberties groups—to begin breaking up the terrorist sect.

The law was promulgated during a period of extreme left-wing political agitation but was never used to suppress any group. The subversives law can be used against any organized group that engages in criminal activities and is considered likely to repeat such activities. If applied to Aum Shinri Kyo, it would bar the sect from meeting as a group, issuing its publications, or pursuing any of the normal functions of a religious organization. Under the religious freedoms guaranteed by the constitution, however, individual members of the sect would remain free to follow its tenets in private. Some Japanese political parties have long opposed use of the subversives law, comparing it to the prewar measures which gave police the authority to harshly repress anyone challenging the dictates of the military government. Even in the violent left-wing turbulence that often marked the 1970s and 1980s, the government was very reluctant to invoke it and did so only against a small number of individual extremists, not against groups.

One day after receiving the recommendation of the Public Security Investigation Agency to apply the subversives law to Aum Shinri Kyo and disband the sect, Prime Minister Tomiichi Murayama, an old-line Japanese socialist politician who had long opposed use of the law, gave his approval to apply it against Aum. In defending his decision, the prime minister said all of Aum's crimes were destructive and its political doctrine called for the overthrow of the government and the imposition of a dictatorship. He said the sect still posed a risk to society because there was danger that it would commit devastating crimes in the future. With Murayama's approval, the government set in motion the first step in the process by giving Aum an opportunity to defend itself in hearings, which were expected to get under way at least two weeks after the government's official notification of its intent to disband the sect.

After the hearings, the Public Security Investigation Agency must petition the Justice Ministry's Public Security Commission to determine whether Aum should be banned under the law. While Murayama was delivering his bad news, district court officials launched raids against eleven Aum Shinri Kyo facilities in the first move to freeze the sect's assets. The action came in response to a lawsuit filed by forty-five victims and their families seeking damages from the sect for injuries incurred during the subway attack. They charged that the sect's debts exceeded its assets, and they asked the court to declare it insolvent and seize its property to keep Aum members from transferring them before a ruling is made on their suit. The group was demanding more than seventeen million dollars in damages; it estimated that Aum had more than forty-five million dollars in debts and only twelve million dollars in assets. The court's action would prevent the sect from hiding its assets. Another legal shoe fell in mid-December when the Tokyo High Court upheld the district-court decision stripping Aum Shinri Kyo of its official religious status. The decision immediately put into motion procedures to liquidate the sect's assets, and when Aum is officially declared insolvent, the remaining commune members, now estimated to be down to seven to eight hundred persons, will have to vacate the sect's facilities.

By the end of December, Aum Shinri Kyo, the world's first ultraterrorist group, was being relentlessly ground into the dust of history by the combined weight of Japan's police, judiciary, and the government. The spectacle of the trials with their contrite apologies by senior Aum leaders, the court decisions to disband Aum and strip it of its official religious status, and even the government's decision to apply the dated, scary Cold War subversives law against the sect, were all good news to the Japanese people, who had weathered their worst year in the second half of the twentieth century. But beneath the nation's collective schadenfreude at seeing Aum Shinri Kyo finally brought to its knees, two vital questions lurked uneasily in the back of the mind of the Japanese public: How did this happen to us? And how can we prevent it from happening again?

Despite all the gallons of ink spilled and the hours of air time used on television and radio, these questions have never been answered satisfactorily. Perhaps that is because the answer to the first question is intertwined with the answer to the second, and both deal directly with a subject that makes many Japanese ill at ease—religion. Aum Shinri Kyo's rise to deadly prominence as an ultraterrorist group took place in the deep shadows of an outmoded Religious Corporations Law that sprang from the American-inspired constitution drafted under the U.S. occupation of Japan that began immediately after World War II. In the years that followed, successive waves of Japanese politicians, often for self-serving motives, amended, reinforced, and protected the law until it assumed the status of holy writ among the nation's bureaucrats and police. Politicians discovered early on that religion means money, and money is the oil that makes Japan's political machine work.

Aum Shinri Kyo, a small sect of some ten thousand members, never attached itself to the coattails of Japan's political parties; it might have fared better if it had, because that could have provided the power-hungry Asahara a small share of political influence, perhaps some leavening for his wilder schemes, and a high-profile outlet for his sect's wealth. But the dynamics all tilted in another direction. Asahara's sect was too insignificant to be taken seriously by anyone—not the politicians, who might have shown some interest had they known of Aum's large financial holdings; not the police, who largely regarded them as weird religious troublemakers best left alone if possible; and certainly not the Japanese and American intelligence agencies, on whose "radar screens" they never appeared until it was too late.

A number of Japanese commentators and politicians now believe the key to preventing the reccurrence of the Aum Shinri Kyo story lies in reforming the present Religious Corporations Law, a task Japanese politicians are now working on. Already the political fallout has been heavy, with one cabinet minister, Justice Minister Tomoharu Tazawa, resigning in the wake of reports that he had accepted some two million dollars in loans from another new religion, a Buddhist organization called Rissho Kosei Kai, and not reported them. The press speculated that Tazawa had agreed to oppose reform of the Religious Corporations Law in exchange for the loan. Tazawa denied the accusations, but his case made it clear that the religious reform law had become a political football.

Still others in Japan argue that the problems posed by Aum Shinri Kyo have nothing to do with the Religious Corporations Law or any other that concerns religious organizations. They assert that religious freedoms should not be curtailed—or "reformed"—simply because there are those who abuse the law and its privileges. They agree that police enforcement of criminal law is part of the issue, but disagree with the belief that the police tend to shrug off criminal activity by religious groups and cite a number of past instances in which the police have moved against Japan's new religions. The preservation of freedom involves risk-taking by the society at large, perhaps even the enormous risks posed by groups such as Aum Shinri Kyo.

But Japan's political machinery was already making an attempt to produce some reform in the nation's religious law. By the first week in December, the lower house of the parliament had passed a reform law that would give the government more supervisory and regulatory powers, require religions to submit annual financial reports, and enable police to question and require reports from religious groups in cases that could violate the group's status under the law. But the proposed law was expected to meet tough opposition when it goes before the upper house in 1996.

Epilogue

In Japan the first anniversary of the world's largest ultraterrorist attack came and went with only modest observance and emotion. In the Tokyo subway stations, where Aum Shinri Kyo's sarin killed eleven persons and injured five thousand five hundred others, makeshift altars with white flowers—the Japanese color of mourning—were placed on the platforms. Families of the deceased and transit officials held a small ceremony at Kasumigaseki Station, the main target of the attack, to honor the dead and unveil a memorial plaque. Later that afternoon Japan's recently elected prime minister, Ryutaro Hashimoto, visited the station to offer prayers.

Except for remembering the dead and injured, the subway gassing was an episode most Japanese would rather put behind them. But trial of Aum leader Shoko Asahara—dubbed by the media as "Japan's trial of the century" —and some fifty of his senior aides will make that impossible for several years at least. Asahara's trial, delayed for months by his own legal shenanigans, finally got under way on April 24 in the Tokyo district court. Handcuffed, wearing a dark blue jogging suit, the guru was attached by a rope around his waist to officers who brought him into the court room.

In a dramatic opening move, prosecutors began the trial with a roll call of the names of the eleven dead and thousands who were injured in the subway attack. During the reading, which went on for hours, Asahara appeared indifferent, fidgeting in his seat, rubbing his eyes, stretching. Although he faces seventeen formal indictments in fifteen separate cases that include multiple counts of murder, conspiracy to commit mass murder, attempted murder, and kidnapping, the first session dealt with the mass murder charges of the subway gassing, the murder of a rebellious young member, and illegal drug production. Speaking publicly for the first since his arrest, Asahara showed little inclination to be helpful in the proceedings. Asked his occupation, he said he was the "leader of Aum Shinri Kyo." He refused to acknowledge his real name, Chizu Matsumoto, saying "I threw away that name." He claimed to have forgotten his address and when asked to enter a plea to the murder charges, he told the Chief Judge Abe, "I won't speak." Under Japanese law, Asahara is not required to plead guilty or not guilty at this point and will be given another opportunity later in the trial.

Asahara's physical appearance surprised many Japanese, who are used to seeing photos depicting the Aum leader as an overweight man in flowing silk robes. In the courtroom he was much slimmer. Since being jailed in May 1995, Asahara reportedly has lost at least forty pounds, largely due to his habit of fasting every other day. Police say he faces daily interrogation, is amiable with his questioners, but still refuses to answer their questions. They are now said to be concerned about his health, mainly because of the weight loss and the fact that he spends most of his free time sleeping. But his stay in jail has not diminished the guru's belief in his supernatural powers. He recently informed police that soon he would "perform miracles." Legal experts believe a miracle is what he will need in order to escape the gallows.

As the curtain fell on the first day of a complex trial that is expected to last three to five years—and take ten years to appeal—Shoko Asahara could look back on his life and see the solid fulfillment of at least one of his old ambitions: national recognition. According to one news report, more people in Japan knew his name than that of either Emperor Akihito or Prime Minister Ryutaro Hashimoto.

Though Asahara's legal manuevers to delay his trial may have seemed cunning at the time, they ultimately worked against him because the extra time allowed prosecutors to accumulate more evidence to use against him in court.

The murder charges against Asahara and some of his top officials probably will increase in the weeks ahead as police press their investigation into the deaths of missing Aum members. Detectives said that at least thirty-three followers have died or were killed since 1988, and twenty others are listed as missing. Eighteen of the thirty-three dead were women and fifteen men. Some were killed in Aum's brutal "religious-training" sessions—practices that included total immersion in scalding hot water or being hung upside down for prolonged periods of time—while others were murdered in cold blood. Many were young, in their twenties and thirties, but some were much older. Typical of the elderly victims was an eighty-year-old Tokyo woman who donated a tract of expensive land to the sect and was then taken to an Aum-operated hospital where she was injected with drugs that killed her.

In addition to determining the fate of the missing members, police investigators also were concentrating on tracking down seven Aum follow-ers who remained at large in the wake of the Tokyo gassing. Large, full-color wanted posters of the fugitives dotted subway and train stations, airports, and other public venues across the nation as the manhunt got underway with renewed vigor. Of the one hundred seventy Aum members arrested by police, more than one hundred have been brought to trial. All were found guilty and received either prison terms or suspended sentences.

While the police were busy shifting into another phase of investigations, the news media continued to report grim new insights into the sect's activi-ties and the thinking of its leader. In one chilling instance police quoted eye-witnesses who said that on January 30, 1995, Aum chemical technicians dis-posed of a quantity of sarin nerve agent by releasing it in the main com-pound area at Kamikuishiki. The nerve agent gasified, then spread to the "children's-squad" dormitory, where some forty children inside and outside were stricken. The witnesses said the children screamed for help, and when they ran to the scene they found some with foamy blood bubbling from their mouths, others vomiting, and many writhing on the ground in convulsions. Also prone on the ground were a number of adults who tried to carry the chil-dren to safety. One man who tried to help told police he was knocked uncon-scious by the gas and woke later in the compound hospital surrounded by sick children. Medical technicians told him and the children that a U.S. mil-itary "C-130 cargo plane" had sprayed the compound with nerve gas. Though none of the children was believed killed by the gas, the full extent of their injuries was unknown. Ironically, many were grateful to their guru. One was quoted as saying, "Our master had predicted the gas attack and made us take the antidote. He saved us."

An equally macabre discovery was Asahara's request to his chemical team to add the scent of flowers to the sarin nerve agent they were producing. In testimony before the Tokyo district court, Kayoko Sasaki, a member of the sect's Household Agency who helped produce sarin, said that Asahara made the request in December 1993 to top Aum chemist Masami Tsuchiya. Puzzled, Tsuchiya asked why a floral odor was necessary and Asahara replied, "Because people will inhale the gas if it has a nice smell." Tsuchiya bought four types of floral reagents, but the idea was dropped before they could be added to the sarin formula.

Though reports like these will continue in the months and years ahead, Japanese society has now heard and absorbed the worst news about Aum Shinri Kyo and is closing ranks to relentlessly expunge the deadly group from its midst. Except for the initial outrage, and the unprecedented soul-searching of the national media, the public's reaction to the Matsumoto and Tokyo gassings has been deliberate and understandable, if not always temperate. Landlords throughout Japan are filing suits to evict Aum tenants from their buildings, telling courts that other tenants will not remain in their premises or lease space if an Aum office is in the building. In some regions local merchants refuse to sell Aum food and other supplies, while local officials are scrupulously reviewing the paperwork on all Aum buildings, looking for technical faults which will allow them order a closure. Fire inspection safety laws are being used to close others.

At higher governmental levels, the reaction is much the same. In January the Supreme Court rejected an appeal by Aum lawyers against an order by the lower district court dissolving the sect and stripping it of its status as an official religious corporation. The decision allows the government to seize Aum's property, including its expensive compound at Kamikuishiki near Mount Fuji, and other financial assets.

The government has moved ahead in other areas as well: Laws needed to correct abuses by religious groups are being studied; others outlawing the possession of sarin and dangerous chemicals have been passed; several thousand new policemen will be added to the national rolls; medical and other procedures for handling mass gassings have been updated; the subways have seven hundred new television cameras to watch the stations; fire department units now have special gas-analysis equipment; and gas-escape drills are being conducted. All of these steps, and others, reinforce an excellent emergency response system that was already in place—one that undoubtedly saved hundreds of lives on the morning of March 20, 1995.

The prospects for the Aum members who still cling to the faith are uniformly bleak. Their sect officially disbanded, their guru and top leaders in jail, and their property seized by the government, they have been all but cast adrift to face alone the horrible societal stigma that now attaches to the words "Aum Shinri Kyo." The diehard true believers, the estimated two to three hundred commune members still residing in sect buildings in the Kamikuishiki compound, at facilities in Fujinomiya, and in the general headquarters in Tokyo, faced forcible eviction by the police. Most had burned their bridges with their families, had nowhere to go, and little prospect for finding employment. Pariahs in their own land, they, along with the thousands of lay members, were innocent victims of Shoko Asahara. Misguided, sincere, and manipulated, they had no part in the sect's terrorist activities, but they now bear the heavy social taint of belonging to Aum Shinri Kyo for the rest of their lives.

The probability of another ultraterrorist-religious group emerging in Japan is extremely low, as is the possibility of anything other than low-order domestic terrorism. There were unconfirmed reports that Aum had managed to hide an unspecified quantity of sarin left over from earlier production, which might be used to create an incident when Asahara's trial began. But as the gassing of the children indicates, the sect tried to dispose of its incriminating nerve agents when it became apparent the police were closing in on them. Also militating against another sarin attack is the fact that most of the leaders who planned and executed the gassings are now safely under lock and key. The possibility of an attack from any outside quarter remains what it always was: virtually nil. For all its economic prominence on the world stage, Japan has no history of being attacked by outside terrorist groups.

Its house now back in order and its errant religious sect under firm control, Japan can once again lay honest claim to what it was before the advent of Aum: one of the safest nations in the world. But for the rest of the world, especially the urban centers of the West, the Japanese cultural aberration called Aum Shinri Kyo poses enormous new risks and grave challenges. Coping with the new threat of ultraterrorism will require large resources, strong political will, and education.

Given the history of terrorism, the odds are better than even that another ultraterrorist attack will be attempted somewhere in the world within the next decade. Terrorist groups tend to repeat operations that are successful, especially the hard-core groups whose blind hatred focuses only on hurting their enemies in the most dramatic and deadly manner possible. For them, ultraterrorism is the ultimate dream weapon, and because of Aum Shinri Kyo, it is no longer simply an untried, abstract ideal.

The target for the next attack could be any one of a number of Western cities or a densely populated site in the state of Israel. For some Middle Eastern terrorist groups the United States ranks high as a target because of its unstinting support of Israel, the American-led Gulf War against Iraq, and Washington's continuing opposition to states such as Libya and Iran. Libya, Iran, and Iraq are known to possess or be working on the development of chemical and biological weapons. They also have strong connections to terrorist groups in the Middle East. In targeting America, an ultraterrorist group in the Middle East would likely resort to "symbolic geography" to select its target, choosing a city that symbolizes America to most foreigners. An attack on New York, Chicago, Washington, Miami, Las Vegas, Los Angeles, or San Francisco would draw immediate international headlines. Other urban sites in the United States, while equally promising in terms of population and vulnerability, would probably be ignored because of their relative obscurity; only an American terrorist would seriously consider bombing a federal building in Oklahoma City. The weapon might be chemical or biological, but the odds are good that whatever is used in the next ultraterrorist attack probably will have a higher order of effectiveness than sarin.

The most pressing question facing vulnerable nations today is what can be done to prevent ultraterrorism. While the risk to open, democratic societies cannot be completely eliminated, a lot can be done to prevent an attack and to survive it if one occurs. For Americans, one of the most open of the vulnerable democracies, prevention and survival depends largely upon three factors, all of critical importance.

The first is education. The public, especially those who live in large cities, must be adequately informed about the nature of the threat and how to respond in event their city is attacked. Educated awareness of the new threat of ultraterrorism must also drive local and national political systems to allocate the needed resources for a trained emergency response force, and at the national level, for a comprehensive counterterrorist intelligence system which is the front—and last—line of defense in preventing an attack. Despite the horrible evidence produced by the Tokyo attack, only a few voices have been raised to alert the American public of the new danger it faces. One of the best informed has been that of Senator Sam Nunn, former chairman of the Senate Armed Services Committee and the Senate's leading expert on U.S. defense policy. Shortly after the Tokyo gassing, he dispatched a team of investigators from the Senate Permanent Subcommittee on Investigations to Japan, Russia, Ukraine, and Germany to obtain first-hand information concerning the activities of Aum Shinri Kyo. Their findings resulted in an exhaustively detailed report that constitutes one of the most informed documents on Aum Shinri Kyo's various criminal and terrorist activities. In addition to Senate hearings on Aum Shinri Kyo conducted in late 1995, Senator Nunn continued the vital education process by appearing on television programs such as CBS's *60 Minutes*, where he discussed the threat of germ warfare. He was candid in his comments.

"I'd be very surprised if a civilian population, even Washington, D.C. itself, were adequately protected [from a terrorist biological attack]. And I would doubt very seriously if that would be the case in other cities," stated the Senator. Asked about the possibility of an ultraterrorist attack on the United States, he replied, "I think we'd have to be very fortunate and we'd have to do a darn good job with intelligence and every other facet of law enforcement if we're going to avoid that kind of attack coming at some point in the years ahead."

As Nunn indicates, the second step is the establishment of a counterterrorist intelligence system that is second to none in the world. Sadly, there is nothing like that in existence today, although a Counterterrorism Center was put in place at CIA headquarters in Virginia more than ten years ago that combines CIA analysts, military intelligence officers, the State Department, and the FBI. This group, charged with monitoring worldwide terrorist activities, missed Aum Shinri Kyo altogether, even after the tell-tale Matsumoto nerve-gas attack. But in fairness, so did everyone else, including Japan's own intelligence services and its law enforcement agencies. Since the end of the Cold War a debate has roared in the American intelligence community and at the highest levels of government about what the new role of U.S. intelligence should be now that the Soviet Union has collapsed. A range of options were suggested including economic intelligence, international drug surveillance, environmental pollution monitoring, tracking the proliferation of nuclear weapons, and enhanced intelligence support for U.S. military interventions such as Grenada, Panama, Somalia, the Gulf War, and Bosnia.

Also on the list was counterterrorism. But as Aum Shinri Kyo has clearly shown, momentous events have a way of establishing their own threat priorities for intelligence. In recent testimony before a senate subcommittee, the CIA, Defense Intelligence Agency, and FBI all acknowledged they knew nothing about Aum Shinri Kyo before the Tokyo gassing. After hearing their negative replies, Sam Nunn made a telling observation: "I can see the next round being a whole set of congressional hearings after we've had some kind of chemical or biological disaster in this country, or, God forbid, even nuclear, asking 'Where were our law enforcement officials? Where was our intelligence community in all of this?'"

Conventional terrorism and ultraterrorism have now forged their way to higher prominence on the American intelligence agenda. President Clinton underscored this ascendancy in mid-March when he took Director of Central Intelligence John Deutsch with him to a high-level meeting in Egypt to discuss counterterrorism with other heads of state following the campaign of suicide bombings in Israel by the Hamas terrorist group—a series of attacks which nearly undermined the fragile Palestinian-Israeli peace accords. Deutsch's appearance at the meeting was most unusual. It is very rare for the Director of Central Intelligence to travel publicly outside the United States, and even rarer for him to accompany the President. Clinton's move in bringing along Deutsch was to emphasize the importance of intelligence in preventing terrorism and to allow the Director of Central Intelligence to begin laying the ground work among Middle Eastern nations that could ultimately lead to a joint, cooperative international intelligence effort, something on the order of a counterterrorism INTERPOL which could share critical intelligence.

The U.S. had another meeting on counterterrorism intelligence cooperation scheduled for late March in Washington, but veteran intelligence insiders are skeptical that anything workable will evolve from these initiatives. They point out that counterterrorism intelligence is almost entirely based on human sources—spies—and no intelligence service is willing to hand out information that will reveal those sources and the methods used to control them. An old intelligence principle, one that is believed around the world, holds there are friendly countries but no friendly intelligence services. The nature of intelligence—especially human-source intelligence, the only kind that is effective in the war against terrorism—is such that no intelligence service is going to share its real secrets with anyone.

While international intelligence cooperation is a worthy goal, and U.S. efforts will be made to pursue it, it should not become a substitute for an American counterterrorism intelligence system that vigilantly looks to its own fences. England, Germany, France, Italy, Israel, Jordan, The Palestinian Authority, Egypt, and Russia all have different perceptions of their national security as regards terrorism. Where those perceptions coincide with America's interests and cause no problems, there can be limited intelligence cooperation; but where they clash, as they have in the past, there will be silence, as there has been in the past. The plain truth is that the intelligence stakes involved in ultraterrorism are far too high for any nation to depend on anyone other than itself.

An essential corollary to good counterterrorism intelligence is the trained force necessary to act upon it preemptively. Of all the intelligence failures that have surfaced in the past years, one of the least noticed is the failure of national leaders to act decisively on the intelligence they receive. To learn that an ultraterrorist group possesses weapons of mass destruction and is planning to deploy them is useless if you cannot act, and act swiftly and decisively, to stop them. America's military counterterrorism forces are among the best trained and equipped in the world for handling conventional terrorist groups. But in meeting the ultraterrorist threat they will need to devise new tactics, acquire new equipment, react to much shorter time lines, and, like intelligence, personally come to grips with a new moral operational philosophy. In ultraterrorist attacks the potential casualties—the death rates—are so high that timing and the decisive application of force in preemptive military operations becomes everything. This is even more true if the ultraterrorist team is already on U.S. soil or still abroad, preparing to depart.

Finally, if all fails and an ultraterrorist attack does occur in a densely populated city, saving lives and minimizing injuries in the first critical hours will depend entirely on the ability of local emergency response teams to act swiftly and effectively. Again, timing is the critical factor. Once the casualty clock begins ticking, every minute that goes by will produce more victims and increase the suffering of those already stricken. The insidious nature of chemical and biological weapons is such that most people would not know they were under attack until the dead and injured start falling in the streets.

If properly produced, most such agents have no smell and can't be seen. On the high order end of the biological spectrum, there are studies which suggest that the spores of one disease—anthrax—can, when efficiently dispersed, produce two hundred thousand to four hundred thousand casualties in the first thirty-six hours. Casualty figures of this magnitude are normally associated with the use of nuclear weapons, and explain why anthrax is often referred to as "the poor man's atomic bomb."

Thus, before an attack occurs it is critical to have in place a well-trained, properly equipped, and coordinated medical, rescue, fire, and police response system that has conducted realistic exercises dealing with the various types of chemical and biological threats now posed by ultraterrorism. Medicines and other supplies such as decontamination units must be stockpiled in advance. The exercises also must take into account the high probability that many of the medics, police, and other emergency personnel will themselves be stricken in the first few hours. Doctors, nurses, firemen, transport personnel, policemen, and communications technicians will suffer the same casualty rates as the population at large, which means that any exercise which assumes a full staff will respond to the attack is unrealistic.

The list of variables involved in a chemical or biological attack on a major city reads like a nightmare. Uncontaminated hospitals and emergency shelters will be quickly overwhelmed; critical medical and other supplies may be located in highly contaminated areas which cannot be entered; large sections of the city may have to be evacuated, perhaps for weeks or months; panic may lead to breakdowns of law and order, further hampering medical and rescue operations—the list goes on and on.

At the moment, most U.S. cities are not adequately prepared to cope with the worst-case scenarios posed by ultraterrorism. Even isolated incidents such as subway or sports-stadium attacks might produce casualties so heavy that the best the local medical and rescue systems can do is hold the line until help arrives. Outside assistance, both from local communities and the federal government, will be essential in order to save lives and alleviate the suffering, whether the attack is full scale or more selective. The most capable federal agency for immediate intervention is the Department of Defense. The U.S. military is the best trained and equipped emergency-response force for any ultraterrorist attack on an American city. As always, timing is vital. Aircraft loaded with doctors, portable hospitals, medical supplies, chemical and biological warfare specialists, military police—the whole panoply of emergency response—must be moving to the site of the attack within hours. In order to achieve this, the military command bureaucracy must have "prior coordination" in order to allow commanders to move units instantly into the stricken areas. Any delay will be at the expense of human life.

America's ability to prevent ultraterrorism, and to cope with it if it occurs, depends then on three equally important components: education of the public and its political leaders about the new threat of ultraterrorism; allocation of resources to build an effective counterterrorism intelligence system along with a preemptive force trained to handle ultraterrorist threats; and a combination of local emergency response units that are trained and equipped to hold the line until federal assistance can reinforce them.

Today America is woefully deficient in all these areas.

Bibliography

Newspapers and News Services

Agence France Presse
Asiaweek
The Asian Wall Street Journal
The Associated Press
The Daily Yomiuri
The Far Eastern Economic Review

The Japan Times
Los Angeles Times
The Mainichi Daily News
The New York Times,
The Washington Post
Reuters

Television

"Germ Warfare." 60 *Minutes.* CBS, New York, February 18, 1996.

Books and Periodicals

Aera Henshubu. *Aum Maho o Toku.* Aera No. 23 (May 25, 1995). Tokyo: Asahi Shimbunsha.
Bungei Shunju. *"Aum Jiken" o Do Yomu ka.* Tokyo: Bungei Shunju, 1995.
Bessatsu Takarajima Henshubu. *Aum to Iu Akumu.* Bessatsu Takarajima 229 (August 1995). Tokyo: Takrajimasha.

Egawa, Shoko. *Kyuseishu no Yabo: Aum Shinri Kyo o Otte.* Tokyo: Kyoiku Shiryo Shuppansha, 1991.

————. *Aum Shinri Kyo—Tsuiseki 2200 Hi.* Tokyo: Bungei Shunju, 1995.

Fujita, Shoichi. *Aum Shinri Kyo Jiken.* Tokyo: Asahi News Shop, 1995.

Inoue, Nobutaka, Michio Takeda, and Kiyoyasu Kitabatake, eds. *Aum Shinri Kyo to wa Nani ka: Gendai Shakai ni Toikakeru Mono.* Tokyo: Asahi News Shop, 1995.

The Japan Times (Special Report). "Terror in the Heart of Japan: The Aum Shinri Kyo Doomsday Cult." Tokyo, July 1995.

Mainichi Shimbun Shakaibu. *Aum Jiken Shuzai Zenkodo.* Tokyo: Mainichi Shimbunsha, 1995.

Marshall, Andrew. "Death in the Air: The Attack of the Nazi Nerve Gas," *Tokyo Journal* (April 1995): 24.

Masuzoe, Yoichi. *Sengo Nihon no Gen'ei: Aum*

Reader, Ian. *A Poisonous Cocktail? Aum Shinrikyo's Path to Violence.* Copenhagen: NIAS Publications, 1996.

Shimazono, Susumu. *Aum Shinri Kyo no Kiseki.* Iwanami Booklet No. 379 (July 1995). Tokyo: Iwanami Shoten.

————"Tracing Aum Shinri Kyo's Tracks: The Formation and Transformation of Its Faith Universe." *Japanese Journal of Religious Studies,* 1995 22/3-4. Tokyo.

Shimizu, Masato, ed. *Shinshukyo Jidai.* Vol. 3. Tokyo: Okura Shuppan, 1995.

Takarajima 30 Henshubu. *Kaibunsho: Aum Shinri Kyo / Sarin Jiken.* Tokyo: Takarajimasha, 1995.

Tokyo Shimbun Shakaibu. *Aum: Soshiki Hanzai no Nazo.* Tokyo: Tokyo Shimbun Shuppankyoku, 1995.

Young, Richard F. "Lethal Achievements: Fragments of a Response to the Aum Shinri Kyo Affair." *Japanese Religions,* Volume 20 (2). NCC Center for the Study of Japanese Religions, Kyoto, Japan. July 1995.

U.S. Senate Permanent Subcommittee on Investigations (Minority Staff). Staff Statement. *Global Proliferation of Weapons of Mass Destruction: A Case Study on the Aum Shinri Kyo.* Washington, D.C. October 31, 1995.

Index

The "weathermark" identifies this book as a production of Weatherhill, Inc., publishers of fine books on Asia and the Pacific. Editorial supervision: Jeffrey Hunter. Book and jacket design: Mariana Canelo. Printing and binding: Quebecor, Kingsport. The typefaces used are Scala and Gill Sans.